T0376466

Educating Young Children in WPA Nursery Schools

Educating Young Children in WPA Nursery Schools, the first full-length national study of the WPA nursery school program, helps to explain why universal preschool remains an elusive goal. This book argues that program success in operating nursery schools throughout the United States during the Great Depression was an important New Deal achievement. By highlighting the program's strengths—its ideals, its curriculum, and its community outreach—the author offers a blueprint for creating a universal preschool program that benefits both children and their families. This volume uncovers the forgotten perspective of WPA nursery school leaders and highlights the program's innovative curriculum for young children by incorporating both extensive archival research and neglected sources.

Molly Quest Arboleda received a PhD in History from Claremont Graduate University, US.

Routledge Research in Education

This series aims to present the latest research from right across the field of education. It is not confined to any particular area or school of thought and seeks to provide coverage of a broad range of topics, theories and issues from around the world.

Recent titles in the series include:

Creativity and Learning in Later Life
An Ethnography of Museum Education
Shari Sabeti

Teachers and Teacher Unions in a Globalised World
International Perspectives on the Schooled Society
Edited by Julian Sefton-Green and Ola Erstad

Researching and Enacting Change in Postsecondary Education
Leveraging Instructors' Social Networks
Edited by Charles Henderson, Chris Rasmussen, Alexis V. Knaub, Naneh Apkarian, Kathleen Quardokus Fisher, and Alan J. Daly

Education and Muslim Identity During a Time of Tension
Inside an American Islamic School
Melanie C. Brooks

Moral Thought and Educational Practice
Hugh T. Sockett

Educating Young Children in WPA Nursery Schools
Federally Funded Early Childhood Education from 1933–1943
Molly Quest Arboleda

For a complete list of titles in this series, please visit www.routledge.com/Routledge-Research-in-Education/book-series/SE0393

Educating Young Children in WPA Nursery Schools
Federally Funded Early Childhood Education from 1933–1943

Molly Quest Arboleda

NEW YORK AND LONDON

First published 2019
by Routledge
711 Third Avenue, New York, NY 10017

and by Routledge
2 Park Square, Milton Park, Abingdon, Oxon, OX14 4RN

Routledge is an imprint of the Taylor & Francis Group, an informa business

© 2019 Taylor & Francis

The right of Molly Quest Arboleda to be identified as author of this work has been asserted by her in accordance with sections 77 and 78 of the Copyright, Designs and Patents Act 1988.

All rights reserved. No part of this book may be reprinted or reproduced or utilised in any form or by any electronic, mechanical, or other means, now known or hereafter invented, including photocopying and recording, or in any information storage or retrieval system, without permission in writing from the publishers.

Trademark notice: Product or corporate names may be trademarks or registered trademarks, and are used only for identification and explanation without intent to infringe.

Library of Congress Cataloguing-in-Publication Data
A catalog record for this book has been requested

ISBN: 978-0-815-38384-0 (hbk)
ISBN: 978-1-351-20535-1 (ebk)

Typeset in Sabon
by Apex CoVantage, LLC

Printed and bound in Great Britain by
TJ International Ltd, Padstow, Cornwall

To my children, Andrew and Katherine
To early childhood educators—past, present, and future

Contents

	List of Figures and Tables	viii
	Acknowledgments	ix
	Introduction	1
1	WPA Nursery Schools as Educational Reform	17
2	American Modernism and the WPA Nursery School Curriculum	45
3	The WPA Nursery School and the Community	79
4	In Time of War	105
5	Buried Treasure	133
	Index	161

Figures and Tables

Figures

0.1	Young Children Playing	10
1.1	Grace Langdon as National Director	26
1.2	Eleanor Roosevelt Visiting a WPA Nursery School	27
1.3	WPA Nursery School Teacher with Students	32
2.1	Before and After	49
2.2	The Built Environment	51
2.3	Health Inspections	52
2.4	Plenty of Rest	53
2.5	Nutritious Meals	55
2.6	Fresh Air and Sunshine	57
2.7–2.9	Opening the Door of the Arts	59
2.10	Homemade Toys	61
2.11–2.12	Raw Materials	62
2.13–2.14	Blocks, the Favorite Toy	64
2.15	Program Showcase at the 1939 New York World's Fair	66
3.1	Manzanar Nursery School	82
3.2	Arthurdale Nursery School	85
3.3	WPA Neighborhood Preschools	92
4.1	Langdon's Advisory Committee	117
4.2	Politicized Childcare	118
5.1	Smear Campaigns	145

Table

3.1	Nationwide Distribution of WPA Nursery Schools	80

Acknowledgments

Thank you to Janet Brodie, Hal Barron, and Julia Mickenberg for believing in me years ago. Thank you to Al Arboleda, Andrea Grasso, Sandy Hardie-Townsend, Jennifer Helgren, Charles Kerchner, Rebecca Kimitch, and Ben Quest for providing words of encouragement this past year as I wrote this manuscript. A very special thanks to Amy E. Davis, who beautifully line-edited. And finally, thank you to all of the archivists who created high-resolution images for me recently at the Claremont Colleges Library Special Collections, CSUN Oviatt Library Special Collections, FDR Presidential Library, The Herb Block Foundation, Library of Congress, National Archives, New Orleans Public Library, and the Walter P. Reuther Library, Wayne State University.

I am finishing this work of history seventy-five years after the demise of the WPA nursery school program. I hope its publication revitalizes discussion of why universal preschool is important. Thank you in advance for reading.

Molly Quest Arboleda
April 2018

Introduction

The Works Progress Administration (WPA) nursery school program transformed the lives of those it served and early childhood education itself. Not until Head Start in the 1960s would the nation again attempt to provide a similar program for children and families in need. The WPA's nursery schools, the first federally funded preschool education program in the United States, proved popular at the local level, and for nearly ten years, WPA nursery schools provided instruction for roughly 50,000 children annually in more than 1,500 schools nationwide.[1] Under the leadership of Grace Langdon, who held a doctorate from Columbia Teachers College, WPA nursery schools became models of early childhood education, and its administrators fully expected their program to lead to public preschools for all young children.[2]

WPA nursery schools revolutionized the care of young children with practices that often became the norm and remain in use today. Yet the program has been only briefly mentioned in histories of children, women, the New Deal, and progressive education. Never studied as the education reform it was, its innovative curriculum has not been analyzed, and its effort to cultivate community activism goes unrecognized.

This book examines the program's contributions to children, their families and communities, and progressive education. It also investigates the politicization of the program, which began with the Dies Committee investigation of the WPA in 1938, escalated into World War II–era attacks against government daycare for working mothers, and culminated with charges of communist leanings of its proponents during the Red Scare. WPA nursery school leaders helped create a supportive coalition comprising left-leaning men and women from the New Deal, the Congress of Industrial Organizations (CIO), and advocates for progressive education, civil rights, and the peace movement.[3] By exploring the overlapping networks of reformers often overlooked in New Deal scholarship, this book deepens our awareness of interwar progressive reform.

Scholars present a one-sided and often distorted account of the WPA nursery school program because they use the writings of groups that were, at best, lukewarm supporters. Those who do not ignore the program

2   Introduction

altogether shine their spotlights on the World War II childcare program, basing their interpretations on primary sources from the program's waning years, when political rivalries contributed to the program's demise. In the end, we neglect its rich history of progressive idealism, children's play, and community building. In addition, the viewpoints of social workers dominate scholarship on the WPA nursery school program. Studies generally make claims using information obtained from the Children's Bureau (CB) and archival holdings of the Federal Security Agency, the agency that tried to take control of the WPA's nursery school program during World War II.[4]

Explanations given for the program's failure to thrive show the use of tainted evidence.[5] Women's historians, in particular, appear to accept uncritically the notion that a group care ethos did not exist prior to World War II. Others focus on the WPA as a New Deal agency providing temporary work relief. This perspective suggests that because the WPA was constructed as an emergency measure, any expectations for permanence were foolish. Yet after World War II, Congress institutionalized other WPA projects, such as the school-lunch program. Some scholars claim that the WPA nursery school program failed because parents lacked interest in "socialistic group care" for children. I have found no evidence that the majority of Americans from 1933–1943 believed group care smacked of socialism, although certain kinds of anti-communism helped derail the program.[6]

This book uncovers the forgotten perspective of WPA nursery school leaders using both extensive archival research and neglected sources such as the journals *Childhood Education* and *Progressive Education*. Its corrections to previous works are based in part on the most complete survey yet of extant WPA nursery school literature.[7] The book's scope extends to perspectives besides those of WPA nursery school leaders and social welfare advocates. The analysis begins in 1920, when Patty Smith Hill ushered in the American nursery school movement. I identify which groups (like progressive educators) were early proponents of nursery schools and which (such as child welfare workers) were not. I use brief case studies to investigate the fate of the program in three states: California, Kentucky, and New York. To explore one of the least understood political battles of World War II—that over the 1943 hearings on the Thomas Bill addressing "Wartime Care and Protection of Children of Employed Mothers"—I turn to under-utilized congressional documents from hearings on federal aid to education and appropriations, WPA archival material, Grace Langdon's correspondence, and WPA literature by former bohemian radical Floyd Dell to delineate more clearly the issues that preoccupied those fighting over the program.

Background on psychology, anthropology, early childhood education, and folklore provides a deeper contextualization for investigating the lives of WPA nursery school children.[8] WPA nursery school toys, statistical data, photos, and archival film footage give important glimpses into the lives of children who were too young to leave records of their own.[9] Definitions

Introduction 3

of modern childhood by historians Paula Fass and Peter Stearns provide a framework for determining how WPA nursery schools helped children. This book is also influenced by those historians of childhood and progressive education who argue that children both shape and are shaped by their schools.[10] It covers forgotten WPA nursery school leaders like Langdon who, as members of the first significant cohort of American women with PhDs, struggled valiantly to achieve universal preschool for the entire nation.[11]

Since the early 1970s, a handful of scholars have painted positive pictures of the program and written of its demise, but their findings have been drowned out by the majority of scholars who disparage it. Some fail to analyze the program for reasons often tied to their chosen focus. Women's historians, both those of the 1980s, who focus more on working women, and those of the 1990s, who tend to emphasize American motherhood, follow the lead of those who wrote in the early 1970s and argued that World War II played a greater role than the New Deal in transforming American society and culture.[12] More recently, women's historians have shifted emphasis away from World War II to a re-examination of women in postwar America. Historians of progressive education focus largely on K-12 reform, and scholars of early childhood write about educational pioneers, often without historical context. New Deal historians continue to ignore the program, and most Cold War studies of progressive education fail to explore policy ties to the New Deal.[13] Historians of children, especially William Tuttle and Barbara Beatty, do call attention to the program's significance, however, and this book builds on their insights.

Head Start and President Nixon's veto of the 1971 Comprehensive Child Development Act (CCDA) awakened interest in the history of childcare.[14] Early childhood educators and psychologists, eager to retrieve their professions' pasts, were the first to re-examine the history of nursery schools. In 1971, James Hymes, one of the architects of Head Start, interviewed nursery school pioneers. The two histories that emerged reveal little awareness that the nursery school and child development professions shared a common history before World War II.[15]

Second-wave feminists also looked to the past to help explain why the federal government had not yet created a national program of childcare. Shirley Chisholm, the African American congresswoman who ran for president in 1972 and was a former New York City nursery school teacher, argued on the floor of the House of Representatives that "discrimination against women and indifference to the poor are at the center of this country's reluctance to expand its support for childcare programs."[16] Yet when scholars discuss WPA schools, they often show how little they know about the program, describing it as the antithesis of what it really was:

> The function of WPA nurseries, then, was not to educate the child, or to free the woman for work, or to bring social case work to the families, but simply to provide jobs to teachers and hot meals to poor

4 Introduction

children. As one would expect, turnover in both clients and staff was very high, facilities were inadequate (the basements of schools or public buildings), and the entire effort was really a minor venture in relief giving.[17]

A younger generation of women's historians has focused on women's employment during the Great Depression and World War II, but the WPA nursery school program largely escapes their attention. Alice Kessler-Harris takes issue with the argument that World War II was a turning point, but she dismisses the entire WPA in a sentence because "relief" women were paid lower salaries than men. She concentrates instead on painting a more complex picture for World War II–era childcare, which she concludes "never worked well."[18] Lynn Weiner dismisses the WPA nursery school program in similar fashion. She too describes it as what it was not:

> These nurseries were not geared towards the needs of mothers who worked or toward the educational and psychological needs of children. Rather, their avowed function was to provide employment for teachers, nurses, nutritionists, cooks, janitors, and clerical workers. With the end of the New Deal, the WPA nurseries lost their federal funding and began to close.[19]

Interdisciplinary scholarship on young children brings new life to the childcare discussion. The psychologist Emily Cahan asserts that the United States always had a two-tier system for educating young children: kindergartens and nursery schools for the wealthy, day nurseries for the poor. Her 1989 work argues that only wealthy children benefited from group care, and she consigns WPA nursery schools to an ambiguous status. They were neither day nurseries nor nursery schools, but *poverty-track institutions* of "narrow scope, uneven quality, and limited availability of health, nutrition, and childcare services."[20] William Tuttle renews interest in childcare politics; Hamilton Cravens provides important detail about George Stoddard's role in the WPA nursery school program; and Kriste Lindenmeyer's revisionist study touches on the animus of the CB toward the WPA.[21]

Barbara Beatty's 1995 book addresses why the United States does not have universal preschool.[22] Despite pointing to the uneven quality of WPA nursery schools at the local level, she resurrects the reputation of the WPA nursery school program in the roughly fifteen pages she devotes to it.[23] Making explicit her assumption that early childhood education benefits young children, she highlights the program's goal of achieving permanency within the public-school system. Most important, she argues that the World War II childcare program picked up the key threads of its WPA predecessor, noting that program director Grace Langdon had led the WPA nursery school program for nearly a decade before assuming control of the Lanham daycare program for working mothers in World War II.

Introduction 5

Sonya Michel focuses on the Washington battle over childcare during the war, trying to get a better sense of how rival agencies like the CB impeded the efforts of Grace Langdon and her boss, Florence Kerr, to provide group childcare to working mothers. Seeing the WPA's Langdon and Kerr as surrounded by hostile forces, including other women at the CB, Michel asserts that:

> the failure of child care policy should not be attributed solely to a "male conspiracy" to keep women out of the labor force but also to a politics of maternalism which accepted the notion that mothers properly belonged at home with their children.[24]

Focusing on how these schools met the childcare needs of working mothers, Michel explains their failure to take root in postwar society by their inability to serve enough women. Unlike earlier historians who dismiss the program to focus on Lanham, Judith Sealander highlights WPA nursery schools and relegates Lanham to a footnote.[25] In the end, Sealander minimizes the importance of the WPA nursery school program because it did not survive World War II. Her overall point is to show that New Deal reform has failed young children.

Others ignore the WPA program entirely. Susan Douglas and Meredith Michaels focus on the political battles fought over childcare in the early 1970s.[26] In their feisty chapter, "Dumb Men, Stupid Choices—or Why We Don't Have Childcare," they relate these battles to the wartime Lanham children's centers, which they depict in a favorable light, though they leave connections between the WPA nursery school program and Lanham unexplored. Natalie Fousekis argues that a coalition of early childhood educators, New Deal liberals, labor unions, African Americans, mainstream women's groups, Communist Party members, left feminists, and working mothers helped ensure that public preschools remained in California after the war.[27] In important ways, this discussion of a leftist coalition complements my own research. But she, too, leaves the WPA nursery school program unexamined, even though many of the California women she highlights began their early childhood education careers in WPA nursery schools.

Dismissal of the WPA nursery school program because of its relatively brief tenure helps explain the program's absence from the otherwise rich historiography on progressive education. It is a grievous omission. Although progressive educators were among the staunchest allies of the WPA nursery schools at both the national and local levels, they do not appear, and the program receives only the barest mention, in more than fifty works in this literature.[28] WPA educational programs and their administrators hardly make the history books.

A deeply ingrained gender bias is one reason for erasure. Early childhood educators have recognized this for some time, and the pioneering effort

6 Introduction

of James Hymes in the early 1970s began the reclamation of forgotten leaders.[29] Yet this fairly wide body of literature has been ignored by most historians of progressive education, who continue to emphasize continuity over change in educational practices. Some, like Larry Cuban and Arthur Zilversmit, argue that teachers tend to teach the way they themselves have been taught, and that for all the talk of reform, little real change has occurred in the classroom.[30] No wonder there is little inclination to look for innovation in the historical record when so many apparent examples of stasis abound.

Historians have long considered George Counts, professor of education at Columbia University, the quintessential radical progressive educator of the 1930s because he protested the evils of capitalism and continued to emphasize the potential of education to effect social reform.[31] Yet because they perceive progressive programs as devolving into "Life Skills Adjustment" after World War II, they discount the revolutionary import of his ideas. Noting, too, that George Counts became more conservative with age, historians have tended to view him and other 1930s radical educators as *men* filled with hot air who dared not act on their words.[32] Historians also emphasize that K-12 educators did not necessarily heed Counts' call to action, characterizing the great majority of teachers during the Depression as being mostly meek women fighting to hold onto their low-paying jobs and more interested in social control than in social revolution. Concluding that Counts personified the ivory tower intellectual who preached while teachers in the trenches concerned themselves with practical issues, historians often focus on whether progressive education ever really took root in the public schools and, if it did, if it ever really helped children.

Since Lawrence Cremin published his magisterial *Transformation of the School* in 1961, historians have tended to emphasize secondary education and exclude discussion of early childhood reform efforts like the WPA nursery school program.[33] Because of this emphasis on secondary school reform, Cremin's analysis of early childhood education as something apart from the public-school system goes unchallenged.[34] Cremin depicts Bank Street educator Caroline Pratt as his quintessential "Sentimentalist," the sort of interwar "child-centered" educator who let children do their own thing. What Cremin leaves out in his retelling is that socialist Bank Street educators like Pratt participated in a wide array of reform activities during the interwar period, including the WPA nursery school program.[35] Influenced by the increasingly conservative views of his former dissertation advisor, George Counts, Cremin focuses on private school education. In so doing, he renders invisible the efforts of Counts' own colleagues at Columbia University during the 1930s—especially WPA nursery school program leaders Grace Langdon, Patty Smith Hill, and Lois Meek Stolz.[36]

Chapter 1, "WPA Nursery Schools as Educational Reform," is an intellectual history of the WPA nursery school program and lays the foundation

Introduction 7

for the argument that the program was an important New Deal achievement. It demonstrates that WPA nursery school leaders were influential progressive educators, intent on expanding educational opportunity.[37] Program administrators devised a classroom curriculum devoted to the "whole child" and became pioneers in the scientific study of young children. They helped create two new interdisciplinary disciplines: child development and home economics. They (not John Watson, not Arnold Gesell, and not Benjamin Spock) ushered in the field of parent education. They encouraged cooperative play among preschoolers and offered education to all children, no matter what their background. Their response to the rise in totalitarianism abroad involved teaching the youngest of citizens to get along in a nonauthoritarian group setting. The chapter examines how program leaders developed their reform impulse within the context of the interwar progressive education movement and the ways they worked to make WPA nursery schools a permanent part of public schools. It concludes by exploring their belief that early childhood education strengthened democracy. Without calling for revolution, WPA nursery school leaders created a daring group care ideology that hoped to create a new social order.

Chapter 2, "American Modernism and the WPA Nursery School Curriculum," analyzes the WPA nursery school program's material culture. It moves beyond the thinking of leaders to focus on actual classroom practice and teacher training. The program aimed at enabling young children to flourish in the industrialized and urban world of the Great Depression, embracing modernism in this quest. Influenced by historian Robert Rydell's understanding that American modernism "was about the substance and meaning of modern life itself," I argue that sympathy for modern architectural forms, the modern mother working outside the home, and modern technology provided a framework for understanding the WPA's own research conclusions: young children learn *best* when they play with peers in large open spaces.[38] Emphasizing that program leaders designed a curriculum that incorporated cutting-edge ideas in child development, the chapter explores how leaders articulated the program's primary purpose—children's healthy development—and investigates how the schools promoted young children's physical as well as their emotional well-being. The program held that young children benefited because WPA nursery schools:

- assisted mothers without replacing them
- attended to children's emotional, physical, and social well-being
- celebrated freedom of choice with play materials
- promoted gender equality and cultural pluralism
- provided consistent, yet flexible, daily routines in spacious built environments.

Chapter 3, "The WPA Nursery School and the Community," highlights the program's popularity at the local level and shows the program's

8 Introduction

success in fostering healthy development in children and helping families survive hard times. The chapter argues that schools thrived at the local level because they enjoyed strong community support. The chapter examines the depth and breadth of the program as shown by statistical evidence. It also provides further contextualization for the famed Clark doll tests carried out in WPA nursery schools, the experiments that helped convince the Supreme Court that separate was inherently unequal as it reached its 1954 decision in *Brown v. Board of Education*. It then explores how the program cultivated community outreach through parent education and concludes by looking at how WPA nursery schools provided a space for community activism in both rural and urban areas.[39] Local communities, especially parents, were motivated by the desire to help small children and participated in letter-writing campaigns to save the schools, pushed for public kindergartens when federal appropriations for the WPA program were cut, and transformed some WPA nursery schools into parent cooperatives after federal funding ceased altogether.

Chapter 4, "In Time of War," explores the political tale of the program in its waning years, when its efforts to create a more inclusive society prompted several agencies in Washington to threaten its very existence. It offers a fresh interpretation of how rival federal agencies undermined the WPA nursery schools and obstructed the program's efforts to establish public nursery schools. When the federal government, preoccupied with war, turned away from New Deal reform, Grace Langdon remained confident that WPA nursery schools would become permanent because of the high level of support the program enjoyed at the local level. She fought off federal agency attempts to take over WPA nursery schools and succeeded in transforming many of the 1,500 WPA nursery schools into Lanham children's centers, which remained in operation under her leadership until the end of World War II. Even after the war, Langdon thought she could create a *new* interdisciplinary federal children's agency that would implement universal preschool. By contrast, the CB, long celebrated as the outstanding advocacy organization for children, did not always share the WPA's views of the needs and best interests of preschoolers. Despite the accomplishments of the WPA program, CB chief, Katherine Lenroot, remained ideologically opposed to group care for young children. From 1942 on, she tried to wrest control of the program away from Langdon, promoting counseling for working mothers and foster care for young children. She did not succeed in dismantling the WPA program, however, because Langdon enjoyed support from powerful New Deal women.[40] This chapter delineates how WPA nursery schools became identified with childcare for working mothers in defense industries. It then investigates how the CB and other rival agencies discredited the WPA nursery school program when they wanted control over childcare options for working mothers. It concludes by examining the role of WPA nursery

Introduction 9

school leaders in the most important childcare battle during wartime, the Thomas Bill hearings of 1943, which became part of the willful erasure of program accomplishments by political rivals.[41]

Chapter 5, "Buried Treasure," examines the program's legacy and develops further the book's contention that the program was willfully buried. It argues that erasure of program accomplishments increased dramatically after 1945. Group care for young children became ever more suspect, and prominent supporters fell victim to red-baiting. Other program leaders proved unwilling (and/or unable) to capitalize on their New Deal accomplishments, retreating largely into the private sector. Grace Langdon moved away from Washington, DC, for instance, to begin her postwar career as a toy consultant. George Stoddard, a fierce proponent of the program, gave up writing about early childhood education altogether, although he stayed active in higher education despite brushes with McCarthyism. Remnants of the program's achievements remained in wealthy private schools like Bank Street, in university nursery schools, in middle-class parent cooperative preschools, and in California's children's centers.[42] Although relatively few former WPA nursery school leaders worked directly with Head Start, some of the program's ideals inspired the 1971 CCDA. The chapter concludes with a brief remembrance of Langdon who, in the final years of her life, worked to bring early childhood education to First Nations in Arizona. In 1970, Langdon's death brought no recognition from the larger nursery school community. A year later, President Nixon, in vetoing the CCDA, made clear that his administration would not support "communal approaches to child rearing."[43] Both Langdon's lack of recognition and Nixon's anti-communist fear of group care were rooted in the Red Scare's contribution to the demise of the WPA nursery school program.

As Grace Langdon scrambled to finish her final report of the program midway through 1943, she lamented:

> It is unfortunate that figures are not available to show accurately the scope of the nursery school program throughout the entire period of its operation. Such figures would be of historical interest. They would also be of significance in planning any future program on a nationwide basis.[44]

Aware of the pitfalls faced because the program was part of the WPA, which she called a "national social experiment over which controversy raged" and frustrated by her own inability to control "procedures governing program operation," Langdon concluded her report with the words, "the true evaluation of the results of the program must therefore wait until time has thrown them into clearer relief." Seventy-five years in the waiting, here is one attempt to get the facts and the chronology straight. A reckoning with this country's first attempt at universal preschool is long overdue.

10 Introduction

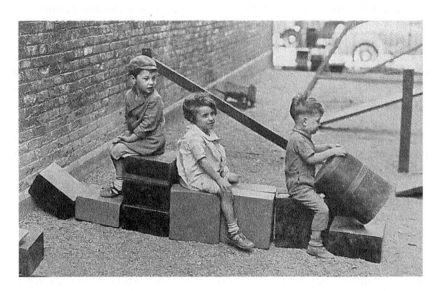

Figure 0.1 Young Children Playing[45]

Notes

1. The WPA nursery school program underwent several name changes from 1933–1943. It was officially called the Emergency Nursery School program during its earliest years. Then it became known as the WPA nursery school and parent education program (1937–1938), the WPA family life program (1938–42), and finally the WPA Child Protection program (1942–1943). After the Federal Emergency Relief Agency (FERA) became part of the WPA in late spring to early summer 1935, the use of the term WPA nursery school was commonly used.
2. Langdon safeguarded the high quality of WPA nursery schools during her tenure as national director from 1934–1943. As she wryly commented, "It has been assumed that the continuous charge leveled at the program that it did not serve all the children who needed it was a tacit tribute to the worth of the services." See Grace Langdon and Isabel Robinson, *The Nursery School Program, 1933–1943: Record of Program Operation and Accomplishment: Division of Service Projects: WPA, Federal Works Agency* (Washington, DC, 1943) 40. This book is also the first to provide sustained analysis of the interwar nursery school movement since 1950. See William Jordan, "The History, Scope and Prospects for the Future of the Nursery School Movement" (PhD dissertation, Harvard University, 1950). Local studies of WPA nursery schools include: Annette Moser Hodess, *A Study of the History of the WPA Nursery Schools of Boston* (PhD dissertation, Boston University, 1983); George Otey, "New Deal for Oklahoma's Children: Federal Day Care Centers, 1933–1946" *Chronicles of Oklahoma* 62 (1984) 296–311; and Lynn Burlbaw, "An Early Start: WPA Emergency Nursery Schools in Texas, 1934–1943" *American Educational History Journal* 36 (2009) 269–298.
3. A wide range of women reformers supported WPA nursery schools, including New Dealer Eleanor Roosevelt, Women's International League for Peace and Freedom (WILPF) and CIO leader Eleanor Fowler, National Youth Administration (NYA)

Introduction 11

and CIO women's auxiliary leader Susan B. Anthony II, anthropologist Margaret Mead, African American civil rights activist Mary Mcleod Bethune, and journalist Eunice Fuller Barnard. In addition, the program elicited strong support from men, including progressive educator Goodwin Watson, New Dealer Aubrey William, journalist and United Electrical labor leader Cedric Fowler, parent educator Ralph Bridgman, African American civil rights activist and educator A. W. Dent, and United Automobile Workers (UAW) labor leader Victor Reuther. They were all targeted by anti-communists after World War II.

4. In her widely cited work, historian Kriste Lindenmeyer concludes:

> During the Great Depression, Congress had funded the (WPA) Lanham Act, which provided federal funds to establish day nurseries. But the Lanham Act was primarily a welfare measure designed to furnish jobs for unemployed teachers and other child welfare workers. The program's benefits for working mothers and their children were secondary or even nonexistent in the minds of many. The placement of the first federal day care program with the WPA, and not the Children's Bureau, is one indication of the general attitude concerning such programs.

See her *"A Right to Childhood": The US Children's Bureau and Child Welfare, 1912–1946"* (1997) 217. However, Title II of Lanham (the Community Facilities Act) was not enacted until 1941, its funds for nursery schools did not become available until 1942, and only for a brief moment (in 1943) would it have been accurate to use the same term for both the WPA nursery school program and the Lanham children's centers that followed. Moreover, as educational institutions, WPA nursery schools were not day nurseries, a form of custodial daycare for children of working-class mothers. WPA Director Harry Hopkins stated that the program served multiple purposes: to help children, their families, and the unemployed. To assume, therefore, that children and working mothers could not possibly have been a high priority simply because the WPA was in charge illustrates the anti-WPA bias of nearly all CB evidence.

5. That the use of tainted evidence can yield widely disparate accounts occurred again in 2015. To provide a context for President Obama's mention of universal childcare during World War II, Lily Rothman at *Time* magazine used CB sources in her portrayal of both the WPA and Lanham programs. By contrast, Jennifer Ludden at NPR used WPA/Federal Works Agency evidence. Compare/contrast http://time.com/3676272/sotu-child-care-wwii/ and www.npr.org/2015/01/24/379530251/u-s-once-had-universal-child-care-but-rebuilding-it-wouldnt-be-easy.

6. Works that guide my analyses include: Howard Dratch, "Politics of Child Care in the 1940s" *Science and Society* 38 (Summer 1974) 167–204; Ellen Schrecker, *No Ivory Tower: McCarthyism and the Universities* (1986); Beatrix Hoffman, *The Wages of Sickness: The Politics of Health Insurance in Progressive America* (2001); Michael Ybarra, *Washington Gone Crazy: Senator Pat McCarran and the Great American Communist Hunt* (2004); Landon Storrs, *The Second Red Scare and the Unmaking of the New Deal Left* (2013); and David Price, *Cold War Anthropology: The CIA, the Pentagon, and the Growth of Dual Use Anthropology* (2016).

7. I rely heavily on collections in more than fifteen different archives around the country with holdings on the WPA nursery school program, and have obtained additional primary material online and through interlibrary loan. Archives include: National Archives, RG-69 (NARA) in College Park, MD; ACEI archives at the University of Maryland, College Park, MD; Pacific Oaks archives in Pasadena, CA; Barbara Greenwood Collection in Pomona, CA; Long Beach Public Library, Special Collections in Long Beach, CA; Rosalie Blau Collection (RB,

12   Introduction

CSUN), 1921–1987, California State University, Northridge: Urban Archives; Filson Club in Louisville, Kentucky; Teachers College Archives at Columbia University, New York City; Helen Gahagan Douglas papers at the University of Oklahoma, and Merrill-Palmer Institute: Edna Noble White Records (ENW), Walter P. Reuther Library of Labor and Urban Affairs, Wayne State University, Detroit. Documents also obtained from the Alice Keliher papers, NYU archives; Progressive Education Association Papers, University of Illinois; Lois Meek Stolz papers, National Library of Medicine archives; Florence Kerr collection, Grinnell College; NAEYC special collections, Indiana State University; Rose Haas Alschuler Papers at University of Illinois at Chicago; FWA scrapbooks at the Library of Congress; New York World's Fair Records, New York Public Library Archives and Manuscripts; Floyd Dell Papers, Newberry Library, Chicago; and Church League of America Collection at the Robert F. Wagner Labor Archive, New York University. Important online sources include congressional hearings, small-town newspapers, and the oral histories of Florence Kerr and the Society for the Research in Child Development.

8. Interdisciplinary studies of children that inform my research include Karin Calvert, *Children in the House: The Material Culture of Early Childhood, 1600–1900* (1992); William Tuttle, *Daddy's Gone to War: The Second World War in the Lives of America's Children* (1993); Gary Cross, *Kids' Stuff: Toys and the Changing World of American Childhood* (1997); Norman Brosterman, *Inventing Kindergarten* (2002); and Howard Chudacoff, *Children at Play: An American History* (2007).

9. Thomas Schlereth has argued that objects used by children are among the best sources for describing the subjective experience of childhood. See "The Material Culture of Childhood: Problems and Potential in Historical Explanation" *Material History Bulletin* 21 (1985) 1–14. I hope that the reproduced images help reclaim the voices of young children, whom historian Barbara Beatty has called among "the most silent and silenced of historical actors."

10. According to Paula Fass, a modern child was "a separate being whose nature was not pre-adult, but non-adult, and for whom play rather than work was the defining environment." See also N. Ray Hiner and Joseph M. Hawes, eds., *Growing Up in America: Children in Historical Perspective* (1985); Mary B. Lane, *Our Schools—Frontline for the 21st Century: What Schools Must Become* (1998); and Peter Stearns, "The Dilemma of Children's Happiness" *Childhood in World History* (2017, 3rd ed.) 166–172. Psychological theories for why young children's healthy development depends upon early childhood education inform my research as well. Philosophical influences include John Dewey's *Democracy and Education* (1916). Dewey argues that public education is a requisite for a more just and equitable society, and he influenced many of those described below.

11. For forgotten New Deal women, see especially Robyn Muncy, *Relentless Reformer: Josephine Roche and Progressivism in 20th Century America* (2015); Ida Jones, *Mary McLeod Bethune in Washington, D.C: Activism and Education in Logan Circle* (2013); Kirstin Downey, *The Woman Behind the New Deal: The Life and Legacy of Frances Perkin* (2009); and Martha Swain, *Ellen S. Woodward: New Deal Advocate for Women* (1995). Eleanor Roosevelt biographers rarely mention her support of WPA nursery schools. See, for example, Doris K. Goodwin, *No Ordinary Time* (1994); Robert Cohen, *Dear Mrs. Roosevelt: Letters from the Children of the Great Depression* (2002); and Blanche Wiesen Cook, *Eleanor Roosevelt: Volume 2, 1933–1938* (1999) and *Volume 3, 1939–1962* (2016). In *Defenseless Under the Night: The Roosevelt Years and the Origins of Homeland Security* (2016), Matthew Dallek details Eleanor Roosevelt's efforts in creating the Office of Civilian Defense. In *Feminism Unfinished* (2014), Dorothy Sue Cobble uses the term *social justice feminism* to describe leftist

Introduction 13

women like Eleanor Roosevelt who wanted to keep protective legislation for women in place and so did not support the Equal Rights amendment after World War I. In *The Second Red Scare and the Unmaking of the New Deal Left* (2013), Landon Storrs uses *left feminists* to describe women and men who pursued a vision of women's emancipation that also insisted on class and racial justice. Both terms apply to WPA nursery school program leaders and their supporters.

12. See especially, Richard Polenberg, *War and Society: The United States, 1941–1945* (1972); and William Chafe, *American Woman: Her Changing Social, Economic, and Political Roles, 1920–1970* (1972).

13. In *Freedom from Fear: The American People in Depression and War, 1929–1945* (1999), David Kennedy argues that "achieving security was the leitmotif of virtually everything the New Deal attempted." Like many New Deal scholars, Kennedy does not mention the WPA nursery school program. Instead, he focuses solely on World War II child care, perpetuating the myth that World War II women were simply not interested in group care. To his credit, Kennedy integrates both time periods (depression and war) into his overall narrative and eschews the ongoing debate as to which had a greater influence on postwar society. In a groundbreaking reassessment of the WPA, *Bring Back the WPA: Work, Relief, and the Origins of American Social Policy in Welfare Reform* (Spring 1998), Edwin Amenta argues that too much emphasis has been placed on the 1935 Social Security Act and not enough on other reform measures FDR put in place to achieve security. Recent overviews on the WPA's anti-communist critics include Nick Taylor, *American-Made: Enduring Legacy of the WPA—When FDR Put the Nation to Work* (2009); and Sandra Opdycke, *The WPA: Creating Jobs and Hope in the Great Depression* (2016).

14. See Barbara Harned, "Relationships Among the Federally Sponsored Nursery Schools of the 1930s, the Federally Sponsored Day Care Program of the 1940s and Project Head Start" (PhD dissertation, Rutgers University, 1968). For evidence of renewed interest in the built environment of the nursery school, see Jonathan Hale, "Child Care Centers" *Architectural Record* 151 (April 1972) 127–142.

15. D. Keith Osborn, *Early Childhood Education in Historical Perspective* (1975) and Robert Sears, "Your Ancients Revisited: A History of Child Development" *Review of Child Development Research* 5 (1975). Hymes also self-published his interviews as *Living History Interviews: Books 1–3* (1979).

16. Pamela Roby, ed., *Child Care—Who Cares? Foreign and Domestic Infant and Early Childhood Development Policies* (1973) xii.

17. Sheila Rothman, "Other People's Children: The Day Care Experience in America" *Public Interest* 30 (Winter 1973) 11–27 [quote is from page 20]. See also Margaret Steinfels, *Who's Minding the Children: History and Politics of Day Care in America* (1973) 68.

18. Alice Kessler-Harris, *Out to Work: A History of Wage-Earning Women in the US* (1982) 284–285.

19. Lynn Weiner, *From Working Girl to Working Mother* (1985) 134.

20. Emily Cahan, *Past Caring: A History of U.S. Preschool Care and Education for the Poor, 1820–1965* (1989) 27. Cahan cited both Chafe 1972 and Robert Tank, "Young Children, Families and Society in America since the 1820s: The Evolution of Health, Education, and Child Care Programs for Preschool Children" (PhD dissertation, University of Michigan, 1980). Although Cahan clearly felt herself in debt to Tank (he coined the term *poverty-track institution*, for instance), his work has been supplanted by Cahan and the other scholars who followed in her wake.

21. Tuttle's close analysis in *Daddy's Gone to War* (1993) and his follow-up 1995 article, "Rosie the Riveter and Her Latchkey Children," yields the following

14   Introduction

claim: "The United States was probably closer to having a national child day care policy in 1945 than it is today." Referencing Louis Covotsos's 1976 dissertation on the CB in "*A Right to Childhood": The US Children's Bureau and Child Welfare, 1912–46* (1997), Kriste Lindenmeyer asserts "He criticizes the female administrators and supporters of the bureau for being more interested in maintaining control and power for themselves than in developing an effective comprehensive child welfare policy. This judgment seems somewhat harsh." I am not convinced it was harsh. Hamilton Cravens' *Before Head Start* (1993) builds on the work of Steven Schlossman and Alice Smuts. See also Rose Kundanis, "Rosie the Riveter and the Eight-Hour Orphan: The Image of Child Day Care during WWII" in M. Paul Holsinger and Mary Anne Schofield, eds., *Visions of War: WWII in Popular Literature and Culture* (1992) and Geraldine Youcha, *Minding the Children: Child Care in America from Colonial Times to the Present* (1995).

22. Barbara Beatty, *Preschool Education in America: The Culture of Young Children from the Colonial Era to the Present* (1995).

23. Like Beatty, Elizabeth Rose argues for the uneven quality of WPA nursery schools in *A Mother's Job: The History of Day Care, 1890–1960* (1999). I think Beatty and Rose have overplayed this notion about the uneven quality of the schools. The evidence they used can also support an assessment of the schools as generally having been quite good. Langdon was a perfectionist; she tended to point out weaknesses in her field reports before she mentioned strengths. Primary evidence from a wide variety of sources generally suggests overall high quality. Rose builds on and supplants Linda Goldmintz, "The Growth of Day Care, 1890–1946" (PhD dissertation, Yeshiva University, 1987).

24. Sonya Michel, *Children's Interests/Mothers' Rights: The Shaping of America's Child Care Policy* (1999) 3. See also her online history https://socialwelfare. library.vcu.edu/programs/child-care-the-american-history/.

25. Judith Sealander, *The Failed Century of the Child: Governing America's Young in the 20th Century* (2003).

26. Susan Douglas and Meredith Michaels, *The Mommy Myth: The Idealization of Motherhood and How It Has Undermined Women* (2004).

27. Natalie Fousekis, *Demanding Child Care: Women's Activism and the Politics of Welfare, 1940–1971* (2011). See also Emile Stoltzfus, *Citizen, Mother, Worker: Debating Public Responsibility for Child Care after the Second World War* (2003) and Charles Dorn, *American Education, Democracy, and the Second World War* (2007).

28. One exception: David Tyack, Robert Lowe, and Elisabeth Hansot give a positive one-paragraph portrayal in *Public Schools in Hard Times* (1984), in part because they rely upon two sources that use WPA evidence: Doak Campbell, Frederick Bair, and Oswald Harvey, *Educational Activities of the Works Progress Administration* (Washington, DC: US Government Printing Office, 1939); and Harry Zeitlin, "Federal Relations in American Education, 1933–1943: A Study of New Deal Efforts and Innovations" (PhD dissertation, Columbia University, 1958).

29. Recent works include: Ruby Takanisihi, "Federal Involvement in Early Education (1933–1973): The Need for Historical Perspectives" in Lilian Katz, ed., *Current Issues in Early Childhood Education* (1977); Carolyn Burns, "A Comparative Study of the History of Day Care Centers and Nursery Schools in the United States" (Bank Street master's thesis, 1979); Millie Almy, ed., *Profiles in Childhood Education, 1931–1960* (1992); Maxine Seller, ed., *Women Educators in the United States, 1820–1993* (1994); Kathleen Tebb, ed., *Thoughtful Reflections for Future Directions: Los Angeles County Child Care Oral History* (1996); Barbara Ruth Peltzman, *Pioneers of Early Childhood Education: A Bio-Bibliographical Guide* (1998); Dorothy Hewes, "*It's the Camaraderie*":

Introduction 15

A History of Parent Cooperative Preschools (1998); Jennifer Wolfe, *Learning from the Past: Historical Voices in Early Childhood Education* (2000); V. Celia Lascarides and Blythe Hinitz, *A History of Early Childhood Education* (2000), *NAEYC at 75: Reflections on the Past, Challenges for the Future* (2001); Jane Fowler Morse, "Ignored but Not Forgotten: The Work of Helen Bradford Thompson Woolley" *NWSA Journal* 14 (Summer 2002) 121–147; Ann Taylor Allen, "Gender, Professionalization, and the Child in the Progressive Era: Patty Smith Hill, 1868–1946" *Journal of Women's History* 23 (Summer 2011) 112–136; Susan Adler and Jeanne Iorio, "Progressive Teachers of Young Children: Creating Contemporary Agents of Change" *International Journal of Progressive Education* 9 (November 2013); Blythe Hinitz, ed., *Hidden History of Early Childhood Education* (2013); Patricia Giardiello, *Pioneers in Early Childhood Education: The Roots and Legacies of Rachel and Margaret McMillan, Maria Montessori and Susan Isaacs* (2014); NAEYC, *Young Children—Our Proud Heritage* series. Examples include: "Abigail Eliot and Margaret McMillan—Bringing the Nursery School to the United States" (May 2016).

30. Larry Cuban, *How Teachers Taught: Constancy and Change in American Classrooms, 1890–1990* (1993); and Arthur Zilversmit, *Changing Schools: Progressive Education Theory and Practice, 1930–1960* (1993). See also Jonathan Zimmerman, "Why Is American Teaching So Bad" (December 4, 2014) in *The New York Review of Books*; and Dana Goldstein, *Teaching Wars: A History of America's Most Embattled Profession* (2014).

31. See, for example, Lawrence Cremin, *The Transformation of the School: Progressivism in American Education, 1876–1957* (1962); C.A. Bowers, *The Progressive Educator and the Depression: The Radical Years* (1969); and Helen Horowitz, "The Progressive Education Movement After WWI" *History of Education Quarterly* 11 (Spring 1971) 79–84.

32. See Marjorie Murphy, *Blackboard Unions: The AFT and the NEA, 1900–1980* (1990). Many women, including WPA teachers, were involved in the American Federation of Teachers (AFT). When it was red-baited, George Counts was brought in to try to purge the communists, 1939–1941.

33. See, for example, John Rury, "Transformation in Perspective: Lawrence Cremin's Transformation of the School" *History of Education Quarterly* 31 (Spring 1991) 66–76; and Diane Ravitch, *Left Back: A Century of Failed School Reform* (2001).

34. One notable exception remains Kathleen Weiler. See especially her *Democracy and Schooling in California: The Legacy of Helen Heffernan and Corinne Seeds* (2011).

35. See Joyce Antler, *Lucy Sprague Mitchell: The Making of a Modern Woman* (1987). In addition to Pratt, Bank Street Educators involved in WPA nursery schools included Harriet Johnson, Agnes Snyder, and Jessie Stanton.

36. Hill gets referenced as a kindergarten (but not nursery school) reformer in two sentences (173, 176). Langdon and Stolz are not cited at all. Cremin mentions James (Jimmy) Hymes and George Stoddard in passing, but he does not tell of their involvement in the WPA nursery school program.

37. The nursery school movement itself may be a little-known tale of American socialism. According to Ilse Forest in *Preschool Education: A Historical and Critical Study* (1927), educator Grace Owen was Robert Owen's granddaughter. Because she helped introduced the nursery school concept to American women, the American and British nursery school movement might well be characterized as literal descendants of Robert Owen's utopian vision. My assessment is based also on correspondence with Jane Fowler Morse, Helen T. Woolley's granddaughter and Eleanor Fowler's daughter.

16 Introduction

38. See Robert Rydell, *Designing Tomorrow: America's World Fairs of the 1930s* (2010) 7–8. Daniel Singal, "Towards a Definition of American Modernism" *American Quarterly* 39 (Spring 1987) 7–26, also highlights how modernism influenced progressive education.

39. I believe WPA nursery school evidence calls into serious question Anthony Badger's assertion in *The New Deal: The Depression Years, 1933–1940* (1989) that "New Deal relief and welfare programs made no attempt to draw on the tradition of urban community organization that came from the settlement houses. . . . It would be the 1960s before urban welfare policy with Community Action Programs took up that approach again" (307–308).

40. In addition to Eleanor Roosevelt, staunch supporters included anthropologist Margaret Mead, Representatives Mary Norton (D-NJ) and Helen Gahagan Douglas (D-CA), and CIO labor leaders Eleanor Fowler and Susan B. Anthony II, grandniece of the suffragist. All were red-baited.

41. Susan B. Anthony II called the Thomas Bill hearings "The Battle of the Child" in *Out of the Kitchen and into the War: Women's Winning Role in the Nation's Drama* (1943).

42. See especially, Joyce Antler, *Lucy Sprague Mitchell: The Making of a Modern Woman* (1987); Mary B. Lane, *Our Schools—Frontline for the 21st Century: What Schools Must Become* (1998); Robyn Muncy, "Cooperative Motherhood and Democratic Civic Culture in Postwar Suburbia, 1940–1965" *Journal of Social History* 38 (Winter 2004) 285–310; and Natalie Fousekis, *Demanding Child Care: Women's Activism and the Politics of Welfare, 1940–1971* (2013).

43. See Kimberly Morgan, "A Child of the Sixties: The Great Society, the New Right, and the Politics of Federal Child Care" *The Journal of Policy History* 13 (2) (2001) 215–250. For a pithy overview, which relates the CCDA to Obama's call for universal preschool in 2013, see the *New York Times* editorial by Gail Collins, "The State of the 4-Year-Olds" (February 14, 2013). For more detailed discussion, see Elizabeth Palley and Corey Shdaimah, *In Our Hands: The Struggle for US Child Care Policy* (2014). See also an excellent NPR article by Jennifer Ludden, www.npr.org/2016/10/13/497850292/how-politics-killed-universal-childcare-in-the-1970s.

44. Grace Langdon and Isabel Robinson, *The Nursery School Program, 1933–1943: Record of Program Operation and Accomplishment: Division of Service Projects: WPA, Federal Works Agency* (Washington, DC, 1943) 38. This manuscript of over two-hundred pages is un-paginated.

45. Helen Post, *An Auto Ride: In Curriculum Guides for Teachers of Children from Two to Six Years of Age* (New York: John Day, 1936) 148. See also the Helen Post Papers—Amon Carter Museum of American Art.

1 WPA Nursery Schools as Educational Reform

In the 1930s, WPA nursery school leaders positioned themselves as cutting-edge educational reformers who could change the lives of small children and even the course of society as a whole.[1] Minnie Bean, a Washington state elementary supervisor, told one group:

> You really are pioneering in every sense of the word. You are going to be very, very, proud twenty or thirty years from now when you read that every school has a nursery school. You can say: "I was one of the first teachers in that movement."[2]

Willard Givens, Secretary of the National Educational Association (NEA), saw a stark choice before the nation:

> A new age has come. Its trend no man can forecast, but the spirit of America, our love for our children and our faith in the validity of education and the equality of education opportunity lies at the center. Any people losing hold of its traditions and its ideals cannot long survive. We are at the parting of the ways—one path leads to national decay—the other to renewed life and strength for our county. Let us accept the challenge of the day by protecting and developing our children.[3]

Givens made nursery schools for all a key issue for the NEA. British nursery school pioneer Grace Owen framed the program's social significance in an international context. Voicing optimism that all countries would eventually have government-funded preschool programs, she placed great faith in the transformative power of the nursery school:

> The nursery school . . . may serve as a bond of true sympathy and understanding between citizens of all classes and conditions. Still happier is the thought of the nursery school movement as one which has its place in *all nations amongst all races, and which must therefore become a bond between all*. . . . As each nation comes, as it must come, to exalt the significance of a perfect childhood for its own people, so each must

18 WPA Nursery Schools as Educational Reform

come to respect the childhood of other nations, and the world movement towards the deeper study of care of the pre-school years will play no mean part in bringing about between all nations *the sympathy that comes from realizing together a great common purpose: full development for all*, of the *promise of childhood*.[4]

Believing early childhood education strengthened democracy, WPA nursery school leaders wanted to transform society through nursery schools. Developing their ideas in the context of the interwar progressive education movement, they hoped to bring universal preschool to American public schools. Creating a group care model that encouraged young children to cooperate with one another, WPA nursery school leaders hoped to build a new social order.[5]

Nursery School Pioneers

WPA nursery school leaders were important progressive educators. They promoted both a classroom curriculum devoted to the "whole child" and the scientific study of young children. They argued that nursery schools should act as agents for social reform in the belief that educating young children into new ways of thinking and behaving would ultimately transform society.[6] With John Dewey as their intellectual godfather, they advocated the growth of nursery schools, and the WPA provided their most important opportunity:

> The Emergency Nursery Schools were a powerful statement to the country—a very dramatic statement—that the early years in a child's life are important educationally. Their very existence made it clear that it matters, in the ultimate development of the human, what children learn in their earliest years, and how they learn it.[7]

As nursery school pioneers, WPA nursery school leaders epitomized the progressive "who was dissatisfied with things as they are, who had a philosophy of what should be, and who was doing something about it."[8] Some, like Lois Meek Stolz, maintained close ties to John Dewey and William Heard Kilpatrick, the founders of progressive education.[9] Others drew upon their experiences in the pre–World War I kindergarten reform movement, which had encouraged home visits as one way to help children and their families.[10] The Great Depression led many of those involved with early childhood education to reflect on its implications for society at large:

> This enhanced interest in early childhood has resulted in part from the discovery that many of the adults who are involved today in serious social difficulties were the neglected, dependent, poorly nurtured, or otherwise maladjusted children of yesterday.[11]

WPA Nursery Schools as Educational Reform 19

The WPA nursery school program took off as quickly as it did "only because there already existed a well-established and functioning program of nursery school education."[12] Yet few schools for very young children predated World War I. The handful that existed were so experimental they either faded away or did not encourage emulation. "Infant schools" developed in Boston in the late 1820s and early 1830s and in Robert Owen's antebellum utopian community of New Harmony, Indiana, did not take root.[13] From the 1870s on, kindergartens sometimes included preschool-age children in addition to those on the verge of entering first grade.[14]

Sidonie Gruenberg, Maria Montessori, and Harriet Johnson helped renew interest in preschool education in the years immediately preceding American involvement in World War I. In 1912, the same year that Montessori published *The Montessori Method*, Gruenberg published *Your Child Today and Tomorrow*.[15] Accessible to a lay audience, it emphasizes parent participation in young children's education. Soon after, University of Chicago faculty mothers banded together to form a play school for their young children, as did faculty mothers at the California Institute of Technology.[16] Montessori, the first female doctor in Italy, drew mixed reactions from American educators when she toured the United States in 1913, but schools inspired by her model sprung up, especially in the Northeast and California.[17] Harriet Johnson's interest in preschool education began after meeting progressive educators Caroline Pratt and Lucy Sprague Mitchell in New York City.[18] In 1917, Johnson opened a school near Pratt's City and Country School in Greenwich Village that catered to the needs of children from fifteen months to three years old.[19] It became the first "genuine nursery school in America."[20] In 1919, Johnson and Mitchell organized the Bureau of Educational Experiments, which eventually developed into the Bank Street College of Education. They continued to collaborate with Pratt and created learning environments focused on children's development.[21] In the process, these three women provided researchers with rich opportunities to analyze young children's physical, social, and emotional growth, a distinguishing feature of Bank Street to this day.[22]

Bank Street leaders like Harriet Johnson, parent educators like Sidonie Gruenberg, and, to a lesser extent, leaders of parent cooperatives and Montessori schools continued to influence early childhood education in the two decades following World War I.[23] From 1919 to 1923, others created additional "pioneer nursery schools."[24] Harriet Johnson herself played a formative role in helping organize the WPA program during its first school year, 1933–1934, and was especially admired for her teaching, as "perhaps the most sensitive and creative of all of the workers with young children that this country has ever known."[25]

Patty Smith Hill, a Columbia University professor of education with an activist past, initiated the American nursery school movement.[26] An influential leader in the push for kindergartens before World War I, Hill earned the title "young radical from the South" because her kindergartens did not

20 *WPA Nursery Schools as Educational Reform*

rigidly adhere to the curriculum of German kindergarten founder Friedrich Froebel. Whereas traditional kindergartens used only play materials he advocated, Hill rebelled to create toys, books, and music based on children's actual interests. She designed, for example, large floor blocks and wrote the popular tune "Happy Birthday to You."[27] Refusing to think in terms of a single perfect curriculum, she criticized Maria Montessori, whom she believed a genius, for underestimating children's desire to work in groups.[28] Others admired this experimentation with new ideas and practices.[29] John Dewey thought Hill was an outstanding educator.[30]

Hill capitalized on her reputation among educators to fashion the American nursery school into a quintessentially progressive institution.[31] Hill had worked with children as young as a year in the 1890s, and the dismal test results of World War I military recruits prompted her to begin working again with children who were too young for kindergarten. Accounts by British pioneers Margaret McMillan and Grace Owen led Hill to invite Owen (a former student) to New York in the spring of 1921 to train Hill's staff and students.[32] A year later, Owen's protégé, Kathleen Edwards, arrived from England to establish a nursery school for Hill, the Manhattanville Day Nursery School.[33] Writing in 1921, Patty Smith Hill asked:

> When will America awaken to the fact that . . . if we wait until the child is three years old, it may be too late to form those habits of physical, mental and moral health, which are the foundation of character and citizenship?[34]

Other nursery school pioneers soon mirrored Hill's efforts, including home economist Edna Noble White, social worker Abigail Eliot, kindergarten reformers Barbara Greenwood and Amy Hostler, doctor (MD/PhD) Arnold Gesell, and psychologists Helen T. Woolley, George Stoddard, and Lois Meek Stolz.[35]

Unlike Britain, where the focus was on saving children living in slums, the first American nursery schools before the WPA program generally catered to the wealthy. They also differed from the American day nursery, a charity institution that began around 1900 to provide custodial care for young children of working-class mothers.[36] About three-quarters of the nursery schools established after 1925 were in thirty-five states, the District of Columbia, and Hawaii and were largely an urban phenomenon. Located in 121 cities around the country, more than half were in cities of 100,000 or more. New York City's thirty-five schools made up the largest group.[37] By the time the WPA nursery school program began, some 300 nursery schools existed in the United States.[38]

Worried about quality, Patty Smith Hill brought together a select group of early nursery school leaders to create the National Association of

WPA Nursery Schools as Educational Reform 21

Nursery Educators (NANE) in February 1926.[39] Convinced that she would wield more power by working behind the scenes, she nominated Stolz to be the first president.[40] Hill celebrated the diversity of peoples involved in preschool education, and NANE attracted men and women from a wide variety of professional and non-professional backgrounds—mothers and fathers, parent educators, kindergartners, doctors, nurses, sociologists, psychologists, psychiatrists, nutritionists, home economists, and social workers.

The diverse leaders of the organization shared the belief that early childhood education fostered healthy social, emotional, and physical development in young children. Citing scientific research in biology, psychology, and sociology, Edna Noble White described how, between ages two and five, "the child gains control of his body; develops the beginnings of response to tone, rhythm, color and form, forms his speech habits and acquires a vocabulary" and also asserted:

> that the physical habits of sleeping, feeding, elimination and exercise, the mental habits of concentration, self-control and self-reliance, or their opposites, and social attitudes toward authority, reality and affection, whether good or bad, are developed in this period and are likely to be little changed in future years.[41]

Arnold Gesell argued that the preschool years were vitally important in terms of overall human development, "for the simple but sufficient reason that it comes first."[42] Lois Meek Stolz stressed the nursery school's education of parents, and George Stoddard championed the right of young children everywhere to attend nursery school:

> If we believe that there are essential and permanent values in the nursery school idea, we should attempt accordingly to alter the course of the stream of wealth. The banker goes out to get what he wants and so does the veteran, the farmer, the manufacturer, the corporation lawyer. Only educators hesitate. We have before us the hard task of welding, once and for all, the needs of the five million pre-school children to the great body of public education. What are we waiting for?[43]

Working with the Association for Childhood Education (ACE), NANE leaders proved instrumental in securing Article Eight of the Children's Charter, a bill of rights drafted at the 1930 White House Conference on Child Health and Protection:

> For every child a school which is safe from hazards, sanitary, properly equipped, lighted, and ventilated. For younger children nursery schools and kindergartens to supplement home care. . . . For EVERY child these

22   WPA Nursery Schools as Educational Reform

rights, regardless of race, or color, or situation, wherever he may live under the protection of the American flag.[44]

Many NANE leaders participated in ACE, but significant differences existed between the two organizations. The intellectual underpinnings of NANE came from John Dewey, whereas ACE was more in line with the thinking of Friedrich Froebel. NANE initially voiced enthusiasm for privatization, but ACE strongly endorsed public education. In the mid-1920s, Patty Smith Hill and Barbara Greenwood wanted not to rush into establishing public nursery schools because they believed that kindergartens' potential to bring reform had been hurt when they became civic institutions.[45] Then, too, NANE leaders emphasized the scientific study of young children.[46] Whereas kindergarten pioneers a generation earlier implemented a curriculum centered on young children's love of play, NANE leaders considered the physical and emotional needs of children as well as their social and cognitive needs.

NANE leaders gained more research opportunities after the Laura Spelman Rockefeller Memorial fund (LSRM) provided universities with generous grants to develop nursery schools as child development laboratories.[47] Early LSRM beneficiaries included Columbia University, The University of Iowa, Case Western University, and Yale.[48] Studies took place nationwide. At Iowa Station, Stoddard investigated whether children's IQs rose if they attended nursery school, and Barbara Greenwood did the same at UCLA.[49] At the Child Development Institute at Columbia Teachers College, Stolz focused on children's emotional development in group settings. Edna Noble White at Merrill-Palmer investigated children's nutritional needs and food habits. Patty Smith Hill and her many graduate students, including Grace Langdon, studied how children from ages two to eight responded to an integrated curriculum designed especially for them. Arnold Gesell at Yale devoted much of his distinguished career to measuring the various development patterns of preschool-age children.[50]

NANE leaders also completed two major statistical surveys of nursery schools prior to 1930. Stolz wrote one under the sponsorship of Lawrence Frank's LSRM fund.[51] John Anderson, Director of the Child Welfare Institute at the University of Minnesota, wrote the second, comparing nursery schools with kindergartens and day nurseries.[52] Studying the 300 nursery schools in existence in the late 1920s, Anderson and Stolz independently noted that all combined a child-centered curriculum with the scientific study of children, which they defined as including health inspections, records of developmental patterns, and the inclusion of psychologists, nurses, and doctors on staff. Both determined that nursery schools included more of these elements than the two other types of institutions combined. Defining a child-centered curriculum as one growing out of the children's interests, both concluded that nursery schools offered greater

WPA Nursery Schools as Educational Reform   23

opportunity for free play and more choice of toys than did kindergartens or day nurseries. Stolz and Anderson proudly announced the arrival of a new institution on the American educational landscape.

Early childhood education was viewed as an especially promising branch of educational reform, one reason that nursery, kindergarten, and primary teachers dominated the constituency of the Progressive Education Association (PEA) during the interwar years.[53] NANE leaders generally identified themselves, and were identified by others, as outstanding progressive educators, a status they maintained once they became WPA nursery school administrators.[54] Grace Langdon, the director of the WPA nursery school program from 1934 to 1943, worked with prominent progressive educators and organizations.[55] She regularly contributed articles to *Progressive Education*, the primary publication of the PEA, whose mission statement embodied principles WPA nursery school leaders themselves practiced:

> Education should use more and more laboratory methods which entail a greater physical and mental freedom; that in the training of teachers the study of human nature and child reaction should have equal emphasis with methods of presenting facts.[56]

Program Foundations

The Great Depression provided the catalyst for promoting the expansion of nursery schools. Without it, "movement might have been indefinitely limited largely to institutions of higher learning."[57] The creation of WPA nursery schools was remarkable given that it occurred despite the massive slashing of public-school funding. Many in government understood the value of and demand for the program. When US Commissioner of Education George Zook spoke of "The Child in Our Educational Crisis" in November 1934, he referred to the WPA nursery school initiative as "one of the most interesting and stimulating things that I have ever had anything to do with . . . all want them, and what is more, it looks as if in the future they are going to have them."[58]

Shortly after President Roosevelt (FDR) took office in March 1933, Patty Smith Hill issued a call to arms in response to the elimination of kindergartens from school budgets. Concerned that the Children's Charter was becoming a "scrap of paper," she suggested that parents protest the closings. According to Hill, school officials listened to parents even if they did not listen to teachers. She called for budget cuts to be distributed across all grade levels and urged teachers to accept pay cuts rather than allow entire programs to disappear. Most provocatively, Hill proposed that kindergartens be kept open for "children of misfortune" and asked "are communistic

24　WPA Nursery Schools as Educational Reform

and socialistic governments the only ones stirred with compassion for the most helpless?"[59]

Hill's message resonated with many inside the new administration. After Harry Hopkins became the director of the Federal Emergency Relief Agency (FERA, as the WPA was called before July 1935), two of his New York staff members, Rebecca Reyher, the former editor of *Equal Rights* (the weekly newspaper of the National Women's Party, published from 1923 until 1954), and Jacob Baker, the former literary editor of Vanguard Press, began to structure the program, which Hopkins insisted be based on dispensing work and not putting the unemployed on the dole.[60] Reyher suggested nursery schools as a way to benefit both "working mothers and needy children."[61] Baker then visited Stolz, who was especially enthusiastic about emergency nursery schools as a step toward public nursery schools for all.[62] While she and Baker watched young children play, they created a list of all the people who could take part—teachers, nurses, doctors, psychologists, custodians, cooks, laundresses, carpenters, seamstresses, and of course, children. Baker then went back to Washington and sold Harry Hopkins and Ellen Woodward (Chief of Women's Projects at the WPA) on the idea.[63] In early October 1933, Woodward met formally with Mary Dabney Davis, Nursery-Kindergarten Specialist at the Office of Education (OE), to create a program that would be jointly sponsored by the OE and the WPA. Davis, who had close ties to Patty Smith Hill, agreed to take a six-month leave to start the emergency nursery school program.[64] Although not always successful at reinstating public kindergartens during the 1930s, she nonetheless made young "children of misfortune" a national priority.

NANE leaders immediately took charge. Flexing their collective muscle, they created a National Advisory Committee of specialists who contributed complementary professional expertise.[65] Upon electing home economist Edna Noble White as chair, the committee met in Washington, D.C. twice in November 1933. At their first meeting, the group formulated tentative plans for organizing nursery schools on a statewide basis and based on initial experiments in Michigan, Pennsylvania, Ohio, and Iowa.[66] In late May 1934, WPA director Harry Hopkins acceded to the committee's request that state nursery school supervisors and teachers be paid through WPA funds. He also agreed that supervisors need not be chosen from relief rolls, ensuring that professionals would administer the program through each state's Emergency Relief and Education office.[67] Program leaders also secured additional financing from the LSRM to employ Grace Langdon (a colleague of Hill and Stolz at Columbia University) as the program's salaried director.[68]

Nearly all important interwar nursery school leaders participated in the program.[69] Once Congress appropriated $2 million a month for WPA education projects (including also adult education programs in literacy and vocational and rehabilitative training), the advisory committee met again to develop a budget. Because the WPA designated its funds for salaries of teachers and other staff, the National Advisory Committee capitalized on its support from the broader nursery school movement to secure a seed grant from the LSRM to pay for supervisors and consultants.[70] That enabled the committee to call on state superintendents and others for assistance, including printing and distributing literature offering help in equipping and conducting nursery schools. Most WPA supervisors had doctorates, and many had a connection to Columbia University.[71] Christine Heinig's experience was typical. Released from her responsibilities as head nursery school teacher at the Child Development Institute at Columbia Teachers College, she traveled to eleven western states from January through May 1934. Consulting with state superintendents of education, she helped find qualified local people to help in the schools. When the LSRM grant expired a month later, she and others continued to assist the WPA program as "[top] people gladly gave many extra hours of work so children could benefit out of this emergency situation."[72]

From the beginning, program leaders resisted class and racial segregation, even when such segregation (de jure and de facto) dominated the American educational landscape.[73] This task was easier than it might have been because harsh economic realities guaranteed classroom diversity. As one WPA leader put it, "the Great Depression didn't respect socioeconomic level."[74] Reflecting 1930s population distributions, 85% of WPA nursery school children were white, 11% African American, and 4% other.[75] Most were three and four years old, with roughly equal numbers of boys and girls.[76] Grace Langdon championed the idea that public housing children should go to WPA nursery schools rather than having new classrooms and play areas created just for them.[77]

Although widespread integration, especially along racial lines, proved elusive in many parts of the country, Langdon and other program leaders took pride in knowing that their program (along with that of the National Youth Administration, NYA) marked the return to the South of federal funds for educating African American children for the first time since the end of Reconstruction. In South Carolina and Georgia, WPA nursery schools may even have helped lay the groundwork for the post–World War II Civil Rights movement.[78] At the Mary Bethune Academy in Lynchburg, Virginia, discussions have continued into the 21st century about how much its WPA nursery school program helped local people. It frames its status as a once-segregated school by proclaiming:

> Bethune's success during the Depression years and later during World War II can be largely attributed to the efforts of both black and white women in Lynchburg, working side by side. These dedicated women saw the need, even in those early days for quality care for children of all races.[79]

Figure 1.1 Grace Langdon as National Director[80]

Trying to Make the Program Permanent

One reason movement leaders supported this New Deal project was their expectation the nursery schools would become a permanent fixture of public education.[81] When Davis left Washington in late spring 1934 to study federally sponsored early childhood programs in Europe, George Stoddard became interim director of the WPA nursery school program.[82] He had been among the first to argue for universal preschool education and asked consistently throughout the 1930s and early 1940s, "why not make [WPA nursery schools] legitimate, sound and universal?"[83]

WPA nursery leaders assumed strong support for their program would lead to strong support for public nursery schools. They made sure Harry Hopkins located the majority of WPA nursery classrooms (75%) inside public-school buildings to maximize their chances for subsidies and perhaps lead them to be adopted by local school districts. They also believed molding public opinion on behalf of their program would help bring about universal preschool.[84] They did receive favorable publicity, and the program proved popular among other reformers. George Counts led the American Federation of Teachers (AFT) to adopt the position of "nursery schools for all."[85] Moreover, the program elicited the enthusiastic support of First Lady Eleanor Roosevelt:

WPA Nursery Schools as Educational Reform 27

Fifty years from now, when the history of these years of depression is written, I hope they will say that out of the depression there came the beginning of the nursery schools which are a permanent part of public education.[86]

When, however, it became increasingly clear that public approval of the WPA nursery schools did not necessarily translate into support for public nursery schools, staff turned to legislative channels. Upon returning to the

Figure 1.2 Eleanor Roosevelt Visiting a WPA Nursery School[87]

28 WPA Nursery Schools as Educational Reform

US Office of Education as its Nursery-Kindergarten specialist, Mary Dabney Davis spearheaded this effort, asserting, "Public opinion expressing the desires of parents or citizens is a deciding factor, but this opinion needs to be expressed in legal form."[88] Building on the successful campaigns of turn-of-the-century kindergarten reformers, Davis outlined her strategy. First, interested citizens needed to "remove legal obstructions which prevent the distribution of state and local general funds for the benefit of the children under six years of age." Second, citizens needed to secure legislation that would give "a reasonable number of parents or citizens who desire kindergartens or nursery schools for young children the right to require school boards generally to establish and maintain appropriate facilities."[89] But legislative efforts at the state and local levels met with limited success during the economically depressed 1930s.[90]

Public-school personnel strongly desired the program's permanence, but no local district proved capable of fully funding WPA nursery schools.[91] Because operational costs remained high, Grace Langdon began to wonder aloud whether any local WPA nursery school could achieve permanence without some form of continued federal aid. In 1939, as WPA nursery school director and NANE president, she convinced proponents of the WPA nursery school program to begin supporting legislation to increase federal aid to education.[92]

As both director of the federal initiative and leading citizen-advocate, Langdon also focused on increasing access to the schools.[93] Traveling extensively throughout the country, she administered a program a colleague called "epoch-making in the history of early childhood education," one that adhered to national standards of excellence.[94] Because Langdon dealt swiftly with local problems around the country, WPA nursery schools became models of early childhood education, lending credence to the idea that education benefits children under five.[95]

Once FDR declared a federal state of emergency on the eve of World War II, Langdon maintained program continuity by retaining the services of the national advisory committee, providing ongoing teacher training for returning staff as well as new hires, and making regular field visits to WPA nursery schools around the country.[96] She continued to support low-income families—her original focus—by placing additional classrooms in urban housing projects and migrant camps and expanding the program to include children of working mothers and fathers in defense industries.[97] In doing so, she met 90% of the childcare needs of low-income African American women in war-related industry and agriculture at the time.[98]

Langdon's efforts on behalf of low-income families, the young children of defense workers, and African American working mothers, earned her the support of the CIO Women's Auxiliaries and the African American Alpha Kappa Alpha Sorority. She continued to receive endorsements from progressive educators and women's organizations, including the League of Women Voters and the American Association of University Women (AAUW). But despite widening her base of support, Langdon found her ability to maintain a high-quality early childhood education program stymied by congressional politics. Budget cuts hit as she was trying to move toward universal preschool.[99]

WPA Nursery Schools as Educational Reform   29

In 1939, a more conservative Congress not only reduced appropriations but also limited WPA employment in the field to eighteen months and enacted a regulation that forced WPA teachers and other staff to accept offers of private employment.[100] At least one WPA nursery school teacher openly resisted the eighteen-month employment regulation. In March 1941, Langdon discovered that a teacher had been fired when she refused a job at a childcare institute to stay at her WPA nursery school. "This is very serious. Child caring institutes pay notoriously low wages and demand long hours of work."[101] Days later, Langdon obtained permission to use volunteers as one means to keep highly trained staff in the classrooms.[102] In the face of congressional intransigence, she developed a training program for volunteers under the auspices of NANE. Florence Kerr designed a similar program for the newly created Office of Civilian Defense.[103] By early summer 1941, NANE and the Office of Civilian Defense worked in concert to train volunteers for WPA nursery schools.[104]

In sparsely populated areas where there were fewer volunteers, the eighteen-month employment regulation wreaked havoc. It forced nearly every WPA nursery school in Kentucky to lay off teachers and other staff, both of whose numbers plummeted.[105] In Danville, a school for African American children did the best it could in the face of staff losses:

The cook has been dropped because of the eighteen-month regulation, but the high school home economics classes have taken over the planning, preparation, serving and cleaning of the kitchen. This assignment becomes part of the regular course and they are graded for their accomplishments. The principal and home economics instructor are very enthusiastic about the plan and would like to make it permanent.

At the Cabbage Patch Settlement House nursery school for white children in Louisville:

The nursery school wing was added by an interested physician who spent about $2000 to make the project possible in this neighborhood. Outstanding work has been done in the health of these children. A recent dental clinic showed that not one child in the nursery school had a single cavity. The examining dentist was so surprised that he asked for the menus. The head teacher who has been largely responsible for the development of the project was off because of the eighteen-month regulation. . . . It is hoped that she may return to carry on the fine program which she has developed.

And for an unnamed "nursery school in Catholic Youth Organization" in Louisville:

There was only one person left on the staff as all of the others were off because of the eighteen-month regulations. Mothers are volunteering

30 WPA Nursery Schools as Educational Reform

to do washing, cleaning and cooking, but one teacher is insufficient for the 20 children enrolled. It was recommended that the enrollment be reduced and that no new children be entered until the regular staff can be increased.[106]

Grace Langdon continued to champion the adoption of WPA nursery schools by public-school systems.[107] Emphasizing that they benefited all children, she made Patty Smith Hill's mantra, "Life, Liberty and Happiness for Children Now," the theme of the October 1941 NANE conference.[108] Langdon followed in Hill's footsteps by promoting the program as strengthening democracy.[109]

In calling for the program's permanence, WPA leaders repeated the early argument that cooperative group play was essential for children's healthy social development in a democracy: "Only as each child feels that he belongs to the group . . . can he gain the emotional poise and social identification which are the bulwarks of democratic living."[110] Cooperation with adults and family members was not the point.[111] Healthy social development meant that children needed to get along with their peers.[112] Corinne Seeds, active with WPA nursery schools in Southern California, asserted:

> In brief, it is the principle of each for all and all for each. This would mean that teachers should make provision for large group activities to which each individual makes his contribution in the light of what he can do best to promote the common good, and for guidance, so that *democratic social ideals* develop.[113]

By helping young children develop a peer culture celebrating cultural pluralism and tolerance, program leaders emphasized that cooperative group play fostered social awareness—the ability to have concern for other people's welfare:

> A good nursery school at two can do far more for [a child] than any amount of preaching concerning the beauties of unselfishness. There the child can have many experiences of give and take early enough in life to make a deep and lasting impression.[114]

In this respect, they carried on the legacy of social democracy that Jane Addams had earlier promoted at Hull House. As Hill put it:

> Let us picture the child in a warless world, one where the present apparently futile efforts of the League of Nations are respected, and where old-age pensions, compulsory education laws, social hygiene, and slum clearance, together with decent minimum-wage laws and unemployment insurance, promise life, liberty, and the pursuit of happiness to even the youngest and most helpless.[115]

WPA Nursery Schools as Educational Reform   31

Despite admiration for the Soviet Union's federally sponsored nursery school system, leaders remained firmly committed to achieving democracy and did not see such cooperation as distinctive of communism.[116] Educating young children in a cooperative group setting did not mean WPA nursery school leaders adopted communist ideals. As one staff member put it, "The American way of life . . . is a cooperative way, emphasizing service to the common good; it is a democratic way, based on human brotherhood and the Golden Rule."[117] If they endorsed collectivism, they did so because they were convinced that young children and their families would be better off if society could:

> develop some form of economic system in which production will not be as chaotic as at present, but where machines, men, and natural resources can be combined to produce for human need irrespective of whether or not adequate profit margins appear.[118]

Indeed, the rise of totalitarianism abroad did not dampen WPA nursery school leaders' efforts to link their cooperative ideals to democracy.[119] Nearly all continued to insist that group cooperation was an integral part of maintaining a healthy democracy.[120] Like other progressive educators, they also began to think long and hard about what distinguished a democratic form of education, determining that their collaborative approach to learning and emphasis on the balanced development of each child within a group setting had much to contribute to the larger discussion of how to reduce the authoritarian structure of the learning environment.[121] Other prominent educators agreed. As reiterated by Carl Friedrich, professor of government at Harvard:

> The foundation for democratic citizenship is laid by those who guide and direct children between two and six. If I were to name a single character trait which is of all-inclusive significance for such democratic citizenship, I would say the firm belief in and the capacity for cooperation. For what is democracy but the cooperative pattern of society, as contrasted with the authoritarian?[122]

This commitment to democracy also explains why WPA nursery schools attracted the attention of the Children's Bureau (CB), arguably the most important children's advocacy organization in Washington, D.C.[123] In preparing talking points for the 1940 White House Conference on Children in a Democracy, CB staff member Philip Klein made preschools his *top* means for improving public education. Despite his own agency's ambivalence about group care for young children, he believed that as a way to spread democracy through education, "the greatest advance has come through the establishment by the WPA of more than 1500 nursery schools." Klein also envisioned that access to early childhood education would create "the most nearly perfect form of school education yet devised."[124]

Intent upon creating a permanent program of public nursery schools, WPA nursery school leaders believed that the social democracy manifested in their

32 WPA Nursery Schools as Educational Reform

classrooms could powerfully transform society. In early 1942, a WPA nursery school teacher reflected on the group care of her own toddler students:

> Sometimes I think if I'd had Hitler in nursery school at the age of two, I could have done a job on him. I mean, you know, there wouldn't have been any war and all that sort of thing. Shucks! . . . I don't think. I *know* I could![125]

Figure 1.3 WPA Nursery School Teacher with Students[126]

As progressive educators, program staff created a standard for group care that provided the model for the first federally funded early childhood education program in American history. As New Dealers, they leveled the playing field so that all young children, not just the privileged few, had the right to attend nursery school. As movement leaders, they dreamed that universal preschool would create a more just and peaceful society. Confident in the redemptive power of group cooperation, WPA nursery school leaders believed that by helping young children get along, they could bring about a new social order.

Notes

1. George Stoddard refers to the nursery school as the final educational frontier in "Shackling Concepts in Nursery Education" *School and Society* 50 (December 9, 1939) 737–740. Barbara Biber uses the expression 'Educational Buck Rogers' in "Is This the Time to Dream a Dream?" *Progressive Education* 19 (May 1942) 242–250.
2. Washington State Superintendent of Public Instruction, Report of State conferences for Emergency Nursery School Teachers in Seattle, Washington, January 19, 1935 and Centralia, Washington January 26, 1935, (Olympia, Washington, DC, 1935) 2.
3. Willard Givens, "In Support of Nursery Schools" *Childhood Education* 11 (April 1935) 294.
4. Grace Owen, "The Social Significance of the Nursery School" *Childhood Education* 10 (June 1934) 459.
5. See George Counts, *Dare the School Build a New Social Order?* (1932); George Stoddard, "Shall Early Childhood Education Be Modified to Respond to the Changing Social Order?" *Childhood Education* (1934) 397–399; and Patty Smith Hill, "Hilltop—A Community Experiment" *Childhood Education* (January 1937) 205.
6. Cedric Fowler, "They Train the Young" *New Outlook* 165 (February 1935) 34.
7. Christine Heinig, "The Emergency Nursery Schools and The Wartime Child Care Centers 1933–1946" in James Hymes, Jr., ed., *Living History Interviews: Book 3* (1979) 21.
8. Paul Dietrich, "What Kind of Society Do We Want?" *Progressive Education* (November 1936) 534.
9. This book refers to Lois Meek Stolz as "Stolz" even though she didn't marry Herbert Stolz until 1938. Lois Hayden Meek is the maiden name Stolz wrote under professionally until 1940.
10. Barbara Greenwood (1867–1960) was an early childhood specialist in both the kindergarten and nursery school movements in Southern California.
11. Mary Dabney Davis, "Legislative Action for Young Children" *School Life* 21 (March 1936) 170.
12. Over 1700 schools were created during the first year of the program. See Grace Langdon, "The Facts About Emergency Nursery Schools" *Childhood Education* 11 (March 1935) 255–258.
13. See especially, Barbara Beatty, *Preschool Education in America: The Culture of Young Children from the Colonial Era to the Present* (1995), Chapter 2.
14. See, for example, Michael Shapiro, *Child's Garden: The Kindergarten Movement from Froebel to Dewey* (1983); and Norman Brosterman, *Inventing Kindergarten* (2002).

34 WPA Nursery Schools as Educational Reform

15. Roberta Wollons' entry in Notable American Women provides a useful starting point for studying Sidonie Matsner Gruenberg (1881–1974).
16. Another early parent cooperative was the Cambridge Nursery School organized in 1923. See Ilse Forest, *Preschool Education: A Historical and Critical Study* (1927); Lois Meek Stolz, *28th Yearbook, National Society for the Study of Education: Preschool and Parental Education* (1929) and Dorothy Hewes, *"It's the Camaraderie": A History of Parent Cooperative Preschools* (1998).
17. Montessori describes how she had achieved dramatic results in educating both children with disabilities and three- to six-year-olds from Rome's slums. Dorothy Canfield Fisher introduces Montessori to an American audience through works like *The Montessori Mother* (1912). William H. Kilpatrick's panning of Montessori's work in *The Montessori System Examined* (1914) may be why the number of Montessori schools dropped off. Very few existed by the late 1920s. See Mary Dabney Davis, "Nursery Schools in the United States, 1929–1930" US Dept. of the Interior, Office of Education, Circular No. 1. January 1930, 17 pages.
18. Johnson met Pratt and Mitchell while working for the Public Education Association of New York City. For detail on their collaboration, see Joyce Antler, *Lucy Sprague Mitchell: The Making of a Modern Woman* (1987).
19. For other accounts of Caroline Pratt, see John and Evelyn Dewey, *Schools of Tomorrow* (1915); Caroline Pratt, *I Learn from Children: An Adventure in Progressive Education* (1948); and Lawrence Cremin, *The Transformation of the School: Progressivism in American Education, 1876–1957* (1962).
20. Lucy Sprague Mitchell, "Harriet M. Johnson: Pioneer, 1867–1934" *Progressive Education* 11 (November 1934) 427. See also Barbara Biber, "Harriet M. Johnson: The Scientific Attitude in Education" *Childhood Education* (1934) 483–486.
21. Published accounts of their work include Caroline Pratt and Jessie Stanton, *Before Books* (1926); and Harriet Johnson, *Children in the Nursery School* (1928).
22. Overviews of Bank Street include Edith Gordon, "Educating the Whole Child: Progressive Education and Bank Street College of Education, 1916–1966" (PhD Dissertation, SUNY Stony Brook, 1988); and Joan Cenedella, *The Bureau of Educational Experiments: A Study in Progressive Education* (Columbia University, Teachers College, 1996). See also Joyce Antler, *Lucy Sprague Mitchell: The Making of a Modern Woman* (1987).
23. Katherine Whiteside Taylor was one post–World War I parent cooperative leader who became a WPA nursery school and family life leader in Berkeley, Long Beach, California and Seattle. Anna McLin, the Montessori director of Bowling Green Nursery School, was an early leader in NANE as well.
24. Lois Meek Stolz, *Preschool and Parental Education* (1929) 29.
25. Harriet Johnson died six years before Rose Alschuler stated this in *Children's Centers* (1942) 6.
26. Historian Dorothy Hewes writes, "Hill so dominated the early nursery school movement that it still retains a remarkable resemblance to the educational philosophy which characterized her professional and personal life." See Dorothy Hewes, *NAEYC's First Half Century: 1926–1976* (1976) 297.
27. Hill wrote song with her sister, Mildred, in 1893. See "Miss Patty" *The New Yorker* (March 8, 1941) 12.
28. See Hill's introduction to Charlotte Garrison, *Permanent Play Materials for Young Children* (1926).
29. Caroline Pratt modeled her unit block on Hill's floor block. Edward Thorndike admired her attempts to measure accurately the play habits of young children.

WPA Nursery Schools as Educational Reform   35

30. See especially Dewey's description of Hill's kindergarten in his *Schools of Tomorrow* (1915), Chapter V, "Play."
31. See, for example, Benjamin Fine, "Patty Smith Hill and Progressive Education" *American Childhood* (June 1936) and "Patty Smith Hill: A Great Educator" *American Childhood* (May 1936) 17–18.
32. See Margaret Mcmillan, *The Nursery School* (1919) and Grace Owen, *Nursery School Education* (1920). Owen was Hill's student at Columbia in the early 1900s. According to Ilse Forest in *Preschool Education: A Historical and Critical Study* (1927), Owen was both the granddaughter of utopian socialist Robert Owen and the sister-in-law of Dr. James McKeen Cattell, a psychology professor at Columbia University. In ~1909, Grace Owen began nursery schools in Manchester, while Margaret McMillan (working with her sister Rachel) began nursery schools in London. In 1918, Owen and McMillan helped get the Fisher Act passed, which mandated nursery schools for all young children in Great Britain. In 1921, Abigail Eliot studied with both Owen and McMillan, and Edna Noble White studied with McMillan before beginning their nursery schools in Boston and Detroit, respectively. Secondary works consulted include: Kevin Brehony, "English Revisionist Froebelians and the Schooling of the Urban Poor" in Mary Hilton and Pam Hirsch, eds., *Practical Visionaries: Women, Education and Social Progress, 1790–1930* (2000); Carolyn Steedman, *Childhood, Culture and Class in Britain: Margaret McMillan, 1860–1931* (1990); and Patricia Giardiello, *Pioneers in Early Childhood Education: The Roots and Legacies of Rachel and Margaret McMillan, Maria Montessori and Susan Isaacs* (2014).
33. See Helen Christianson, "An All-Day Nursery School Set-Up" *Childhood Education* (early 1930s) 356–360. Christianson, another student of Hill, eventually become a WPA nursery school leader in California.
34. The first edition of McMillan's *The Nursery School* was published in London in 1919. The American edition with Hill's preface was published in 1921; quote is from page xi.
35. Dates based on Lois Meek Stolz's assessments in *Preschool and Parental Education* (1929) and Edna Noble White's "The Nursery School Movement: Yesterday and Today" (1941). Nursery school pioneers included:

> Patty Smith Hill (Kindergartner)—Manhattanville in New York, NY (1922)
> Helen T. Woolley (Psychologist) and Edna Noble White (Home Economist)—Merrill-Palmer in Detroit, MI (1922)
> Abigail Eliot (Social Worker)—Ruggles Street in Boston, MA (1922)
> Barbara Greenwood (Kindergartner)—UCLA in Los Angeles, CA (1923)
> Lois Meek Stolz (Psychologist) and Christine Heinig (Kindergartner)—Teachers College, Columbia in New York, NY (1924)
> Bird Baldwin and George Stoddard (Psychologists)—Iowa Child Welfare Station in Des Moines, IA (1925)
> Rose Alschuler (Progressive Educator)—Franklin Public School in Chicago, IL (1925)
> Arnold Gesell (Psychologist and Medical Doctor)—Yale Child Study Center in New Haven, CT (1926)

36. An important exception to this was Abigail Eliot's nursery school in Boston, which followed the English model and focused on "poor" children. For histories of day nurseries, see especially Elizabeth Rose, *A Mother's Job: The History of Day Care, 1890–1960* (1999).
37. A rapid increase took place from 1926–1928, and a big drop-off in new schools occurred after 1929. Before the WPA nursery school program, only seven states had ten or more nursery schools.
38. The 1930 White House Conference on children listed 343 nursery schools with a total enrollment of 6,500 children. The overall number of schools may have

36 WPA Nursery Schools as Educational Reform

declined slightly in the next two years. In September 1932, *School Life* (page 17) reported on only 203 nursery schools in the United States.

39. Of those involved in experimental schools for young children before 1920, only Harriet Johnson of Bank Street and Anna McLin of the Montessori-inspired Bowling Green Nursery School in NYC were invited to join by Hill. NANE is now known as the National Association for the Education of Young Children (NAEYC).

40. Dorothy Hewes, *NAEYC's First Half Century: 1926–1976* (1976). See also Abigail Eliot, "How the NANE Began" and Helen Christianson and Barbara Greenwood, "The Western Share in NANE Beginnings, 1925–1935" *Journal of Nursery Education* 14 (Fall 1958) 26–29.

41. Edna Noble White, "Nursery Schools: Great Britain and the United States" in *Encyclopedia Britannica* 16 (1929/1945 edition) 642–643.

42. Barbara Beatty, *Preschool Education in America: The Culture of Young Children from the Colonial Era to the Present* (1995)146. See also Arnold Gesell, "The Significance of the Nursery School" *Childhood Education* 1 (1926) 11–20.

43. George Stoddard, "Emergency Nursery Schools on Trial" *Childhood Education* (March 1935) 261. Stoddard's speech promoting universal preschool at the 1931 NANE convention marked a turn away from NANE's earlier emphasis on privatization. See also his "What of the Nursery School" *Progressive Education* (October 1937) 441–451, and "For the Sake of the Youngest" *Parents Magazine* 16 (April 1941) 21.

44. The ACE was known as the International Kindergarten Union before 1930 and today is called the Association for Childhood Education International (ACEI).

45. Hill, for instance, lamented the following cost-cutting measure: public school kindergarten teachers no longer made home visits during the afternoon but instead taught two sets of children each day. See NANE Biannual Conference Proceedings 2–6 (April 1927—October 1935), Lois Meek Stolz (chair), *Minimum Essentials for Nursery School Education* (1929) foreword, and Ilse Forest, *Patty Smith Hill: Pioneer in Early Childhood Education* (Unpublished manuscript, Filson Club, 1949). Rose Alschuler bucked this trend. From 1925 on, she used her own money to subsidize public nursery schools in Chicago and Winnetka, Illinois. See Sandra Bornstein, "Rose Haas Alschuler: A Chicago Jewish Woman's Life of Service 1887–1979" (Master's thesis, Spertus Institute of Jewish Studies, Chicago, 1999).

46. Dorothy Hewes argues, "Probably no educational movement in history has had the scientific base of those early nursery schools." See her *NAEYC's First Half Century: 1926–1976* (1976) 302 and Ilse Forest, *Preschool Education: A Historical and Critical Study* (1927).

47. LSRM funding began in 1924. For overviews, see Robert Sears, "Your Ancients Revisited: A History of Child Development" *Review of Child Development Research* 5 (1975) 1–74, Alice Smuts and John Hagen, eds., "History and Research in Child Development" *Monographs of the Society for Research in Child Development* 50 (1985); and Alice Smuts, *Science in the Service of Children, 1893–1935* (2008).

48. LSRM beneficiaries in the late 1920s included: UC Berkeley, Cornell, the University of Minnesota, and the University of Toronto. Recent histories on these child development institutes include: Julia Grant, *Raising Baby by the Book: The Education of American Mothers* (1998) [Cornell's program]; Hamilton Cravens, *Before Head Start: The Iowa Station and America's Children* (1993); and Jocelyn Raymond, *The Nursery World of Dr. Blatz* (1991) [about the University of Toronto's center].

49. Stoddard (along with his assistant Beth Wellman) argues that they did. Greenwood's findings are less conclusive. See Barbara Greenwood and Charles

WPA Nursery Schools as Educational Reform   37

Waddell, *A Six-Year Experiment with a Nursery School* (1931) and George Stoddard, *The Meaning of Intelligence* (1943).

50. Florence Goodenough, "New Evidence on the Value of Preschool Education" *Elementary School Journal* 39 (April 1939) 571–574; Lois Barclay Murphy, *Social Behavior and Child Personality: An Exploratory Study of Some Roots of Sympathy* (1937); Arthur Jersild and Mary Fite, *The Influence of Nursery School Experience on Children's Social Adjustments* (1939); Mary Sweeny and Marian Breckenridge, *How to Feed Children in Nursery Schools* (1944); Dorothy Van Alstyne, *Play Behavior and Choice of Play Materials of Preschool Children* (1932); and Arnold Gesell, *The First Five Years of Life* (1940). See also Hamilton Cravens, *Before Head Start: The Iowa Station and America's Children* (1993).

51. Lois Meek Stolz (chair), *28th Yearbook, National Society for the Study of Education: Preschool and Parental Education* (1929). See also Lois Meek Stolz (chair), *Minimum Essentials for Nursery School Education* (1929).

52. John Anderson (chair), *Nursery Education: A Survey of Day Nurseries, Nursery Schools, Private Kindergartens in the US* (The White House Conference on Child Health and Protection, 1931).

53. According to C. A. Bowers. "Followers [of the PEA] were drawn almost exclusively from the ranks of elementary school teachers, of whom approximately 30% were in the public schools and 70% in private schools." See his *The Progressive Educator and the Depression: The Radical Years* (1969) 11.

54. According to Robert Tank, "for the first time a body of psychological and medical science knowledge, derived by specialists largely through the use of the scientific method, underpinned and legitimated the transfer of the guidance of behavioral and physical development in very young children from the home to an extra-familial agency." See his "Young Children, Families, and Society in American Since the 1820s: The Evolution of Health, Education, and Child Care Programs for Preschool Children" (PhD. dissertation, University of Michigan, 1980) 262.

55. Like John Dewey, Langdon believed "all of education should be a very fundamental part of everyday life." See her message dated 9/23/39 to the president of St. John's College, NARA. Langdon regularly attended progressive education meetings in New York City, and succeeded in obtaining a discounted subscription rate to *Progressive Education* for WPA nursery school teachers around the country.

56. Quote on the back cover of Volume 1, No. 2 (1924) of *Progressive Education*. In addition to Langdon, other contributors included Lois Meek Stolz, Rose Alschuler, Ruth Andrus, and George Stoddard.

57. Edna Noble White, "The Nursery School Movement: Yesterday and Today" NANE conference publication, October 1941, Walter P. Reuther Labor Archives, Detroit. Ruth Andrus (another nursery school pioneer) echoes White in asserting that WPA nursery schools "put the [nursery] movement a quarter-century ahead in a few years" in Eunice Fuller Barnard, ed., "Definitely Woman's Work" *Independent Woman* 21 (April 1942) 108.

58. Zook gave this speech at George Stoddard's Iowa Child Welfare Research Station at the 8th Iowa Conference on Child Development and Parent Education. Reprinted in Child Welfare Research Station, Pamphlet #43, page 10.

59. She asks, "Must a truly democratic country such as our own is supposed to be, save money for older girls and boys—age levels far more able to protect themselves—by turning the youngest children in our public schools into the streets?" Leaflet distributed by *Parents Magazine* in spring 1933. Condensed version published as Patty Smith Hill, "Shall the Youngest Suffer Most?" *Parents Magazine* 8 (April 1933) 13. Full-text version printed in *Childhood*

38 WPA Nursery Schools as Educational Reform

Education (June 1933) and *California Journal of Elementary Education* 2 (November 1933) 62–65.

60. The WPA replaced the Federal Emergency Relief Agency (FERA) during spring—summer 1935. I use the term WPA throughout to avoid confusion since, in the case of the nursery school program, the same personnel are involved, 1933–1943.

61. Letter from Reyher to Dr. Lewis Alderman (April 1938). Reyher juggled her editorial job at Equal Rights with raising a child in the early 1920s. See her oral history, "Rebecca Hourwich Reyher (1897–1987): Search and Struggle for Equality and Independence" Interview conducted by Amelia Fry and Fern Ingersoll. Regents of the University of California, 1977. Suffragists Oral History Project.

62. See Stolz's oral history conducted by Ruby Takanishi, *An American Child Development Pioneer: Lois Hayden Meek Stolz* (Stanford University, 1977/78). See also "Wide Study Program for Nurseries Urged: Dr. L.H. Meek of Columbia Seeks to Develop Teaching of Pre-School Children" *New York Times* (April 10, 1936).

63. As assistant WPA administrator, Baker also succeeded in getting surplus commodity items delivered to schools. See *Emergency Nursery Schools During the Second Year, 1934–1935*, page 19.

64. Days after Hopkins issued his press release on the new WPA nursery school program, Davis flew to Toronto to meet with fellow nursery school leaders at the fifth Biennial NANE conference. Years later, Abigail Eliot recalled the furor (the tone but not the content) of this meeting in *American's First Nursery Schools Living History Interviews: Books 1–3*, ed. James Hymes, Jr. (1979). NANE leaders subsequently decided that official sponsorship of the WPA nursery school program should come from the three professional organizations (NANE, ACE, and the National Council of Parent Education) they regarded as most successful at promoting early childhood education.

65. When Davis left during the second year of the program, Ruth Andrus (WPA supervisor in New York State and then NANE president) and Bess Goodykoontz, Assistant Commissioner of Education, US Office of Education, joined. Both George Stoddard and Lois Meek Stolz resigned in 1938. From 1938–1943, members included: Edna Noble White, Edna Dean Baker, Dr. William G. Carr, Bess Goodykoontz, Amy Hostler, William Kletzer, Dr. C.S. Marsh, Dr. Kathryn McHale, Mary Murphy, and Dr. Louise Stanley. Director Grace Langdon attended all meetings and White remained the chair for the entire time.

66. According to *Emergency Nursery Schools During the First Year, 1933–1934*, seventeen schools opened in late 1933. By the end of January 1934, thirty states were organizing or had plans to organize emergency nursery schools, including one that Patty Smith Hill contemplated for a Harlem neighborhood near Columbia University.

67. Hopkins' Document E-26 (May 24, 1934) reads: "These specialists need not be eligible for relief, and may be paid at the prevailing stipend for such work in the respective states. An allowance for essential travel in supervisory work may also be assigned to them. Reprinted in *Emergency Nursery Schools During the Second Year, 1934–1935*, page 19.

68. Davis was the first director of the WPA nursery school program, Winter 1933–Spring 1934; Stoddard was the second director, Spring–Summer 1934, and Langdon was the third and final director, Fall 1934–Spring 1943.

69. The one important NANE leader who did not participate in the WPA nursery school program was Helen T. Woolley. See the wonderful article written about her by her granddaughter, Jane Fowler Morse, "Ignored but Not Forgotten:

WPA Nursery Schools as Educational Reform 39

The Work of Helen Bradford Thompson Woolley" *NWSA Journal* 14 (Summer 2002) 121–147.

70. Ralph Bridgman, with the tacit consent of the committee, approached Lawrence Frank, chair of the General Education Board (a Laura Spelman Rockefeller fund) in late 1933. For more information on Lawrence Frank, see Alice Smuts, *Science in the Service of Children, 1893–1935* (2008).

71. Leaders with links to Columbia and Hill included Ruth Andrus, Winifred Bain, Mary Dabney Davis, Grace Langdon, Agnes Snyder, and Lois Meek Stolz.

72. Christine Heinig, "The Emergency Nursery Schools and The Wartime Child Care Centers 1933–1946" in James Hymes, ed., *Living History Interviews: Books 3* (1978–79) 14. Heinig co-wrote WPA nursery school *Bulletin #2 and Play: The Child's Response to Life* (1936) with fellow WPA nursery school leader, Rose Alschuler. She then moved to Australia to start up a government-funded preschool program in the late 1930s.

73. In "Report of Field Trip to Missouri" (April 29–May 3, 1940), NARA. Grace Langdon, for instance, characterized the program as one that benefited and included *all* children. Private nursery schools, by contrast, regularly practiced both racial and religious segregation.

74. *Emergency Nursery Schools During the Second Year, 1934–1935* (1936) 29–31and Edna Kelley, "Uncle Sam's Nursery Schools" *Parents Magazine* (March 1936) 25–26; 48–49.

75. Other included Native Americans (especially in Southwest and Minnesota), Mexican Americans (Southwest and Chicago), Chinese Americans (California), Japanese Americans (Internment camps), and Puerto Ricans (New York City and Puerto Rico). Indicative of the changing standards for relief, here is the following demographic breakdown for the month of June 1940: 39,853 nursery school children: 31,464 white (79%); 7,403 "negro" (19%); and 986 other (2%). Grace Langdon files, NARA.

76. In Massachusetts, Payson Smith, Commissioner of Education, respected the wish of WPA nursery school state supervisor, Abigail Eliot (sister of Dr. Martha Eliot, assistant CB chief) to not admit children under the age of three to WPA nursery schools.

77. After Pearl Harbor, when families on relief no longer took center stage, she continued to draw attention to the plight of young children living in poverty. See Grace Langdon, "The Young Ones Need Defense" *Progressive Education* 19 (February 1942) 118–119. See also Eva Evans, "Uncle Sam's Migrant Children" *Childhood Education* 18 (April 1942) 362–366; Susan Fleisher, "Preschool Education for Migrants" *Childhood Education* (December 1943) 181–183; and Mebane Martensen, "Care for Migrants' Children" *Survey Midmonthly* 80 (May 1944) 152–154.

78. See especially Edwin Hoffman, "The Genesis of the Modern Movement for Equal Rights in South Carolina, 1930–1939" *Journal of Negro Education* 44 (October 1959) 346–369 and Sarah Wilkerson-Freeman, "The Creation of a Subversive Feminist Dominion: Interracialist Social Workers and the Georgia New Deal" *Journal of Women's History* 13 (Winter 2002) 132–154. After 1937, program leaders refused to hold national meetings in the South as a means to protest segregation. See Dorothy Hewes, *NAEYC's First Half Century: 1926–1976* (1976) 297.

79. http://marybethuneacademy.org/our-history/. This overview concludes, "Mary McLeod Bethune [WPA & NYA] "devoted her life to ensuring the right to education and freedom from discrimination for black Americans." Mary McLeod Bethune was red-baited as an NYA leader, beginning in 1941. See Landon Storrs, *The Second Red Scare and the Unmaking of the New Deal Left* (2013) 269. For a brief introduction to Bethune, see Audrey McCluskey and

40 WPA Nursery Schools as Educational Reform

Elaine Smith, eds., *Mary McLeod Bethune: Building a Better World* (2001); Ida Jones, *Mary McLeod Bethune in Washington, D.C.: Activism and Education in Logan Circle* (2013); and Ashley Robertson, *Mary McLeod Bethune in Florida: Bringing Social Justice to the Sunshine State* (2015).

80. Dr. Grace Langdon of Washington, national WPA specialist in family life education, visits the Wisner Playground nursery school. January 1942. Children of the WPA, Louisiana Division/City Archives, New Orleans Public Library.

81. *WPA Bulletin #1* (1933) 7 and "Emergency Nursery Schools" *Childhood Education* 10 (January 1934) 201–207.

82. Stoddard was also a member of the national WPA advisory committee member, 1933–1938 and NANE president 1931–1933. For a detailed description of his work at Iowa Station, see Hamilton Cravens, *Before Head Start: The Iowa Station and America's Children* (1993); and Steve McNutt, "A Dangerous Man: Lewis Terman and George Stoddard, their Debates on Intelligence Testing, and the Legacy of the Iowa Child Welfare Research Station" *The Annals of Iowa* 72 (2013) 1–30.

83. George Stoddard, "For the Sake of the Youngest" *Parents Magazine* 16 (April 1941) 21.

84. This approach worked well in California. See especially, Dorothy Baruch, Evangeline Burgess, and Dorothy Jones, "How to Start Publicity for Nursery Education in Your Community" *NANE* (1940).

85. The AFT promoted WPA nursery schools at their August 1941 meeting in Detroit, Michigan. They mailed their official support to FDR in November to ensure that "nursery schools may be established in every center in our country." See Marjorie Murphy, *Blackboard Unions: The AFT and the NEA, 1900–1980* (1990).

86. Eleanor Roosevelt quoted in a letter dated 6/2/37 from Grace Langdon to Edna Noble White. Edna Noble White Collection: Merrill-Palmer Institute, Boxes 4–8, archived at the Walter P. Reuther Library of Labor and Urban History, Detroit, MI.

87. Eleanor Roosevelt visiting WPA Negro [sic] Nursery School in Des Moines, Iowa. June 8, 1936. FDR Library Photograph Collection, NPx #64–141.

88. Mary Dabney Davis, "Legislative Action for Young Children" *School Life* (March 1936) 170.

89. Ibid: 176, 190.

90. Two consistently successful public nursery schools were Rose Alschuler's schools in Chicago and Winnetka, Illinois. During the 1930s, both charged a fee to stay afloat. Some private schools in existence prior to the WPA accepted funds to stay afloat. Examples include Katharine Whiteside Taylor's' cooperative in Berkeley, CA and Mrs. Fred Bixby's day nursery in Long Beach, CA.

91. See Willard Goslin's strong endorsement of the program in Missouri in Grace Langdon, "Development in Field of Emergency Nursery Schools: How these Developments Are Becoming a Part of Permanent Programs" *School Life* (March 1938) 242–246.

92. As both NANE president and WPA director, Langdon called for local support of HR 3517 and SB1305, which authorized federal funds for public nursery schools: "40 Million for Fiscal Year 1940, up to 140 Million in 1945 for Specially-Designated Education Purposes, Including Nursery Schools and Kindergartens" *Langdon to Edna Noble White* (October 1939) letter. See also Federal Aid to Education Act of 1939, SB 1305, 76th Congress. (March 1939) and Educational Finance Act of 1941, SB 1311: 77th Congress (April 28–30, 1941). For overview, see Martha Swain, "The Harrison Education Bills, 1936–1941" *Mississippi Quarterly* 31 (1) (1977–78) 119–132.

WPA Nursery Schools as Educational Reform 41

93. NANE meeting minutes, 1939–1947, are missing from the NAEYC Archives at Indiana State University. For announcements of Langdon's presidency, see *School and Society* 50 (October 21, 1939) 525; *School Life* 25 (January 1940) 119–120 by Mary Dabney Davis, *Progressive Education* 16 (December 1939) 534. Shortly after Langdon became NANE president, George Stoddard argued that only war could destroy the WPA nursery school program; see his "Shackling Concepts in Nursery Education" *School and Society* 50 (December 9, 1939) 737–740.

94. Edna Noble White, chair, National Advisory Committee, 2nd year report: preface. In the early 1970s, Abigail Eliot (former WPA nursery school leader in Massachusetts) recalled that "At the beginning some people were sure the WPA schools would ruin the nursery school movement because standards would be low." Her final take: "The movement was not killed. It fact, it was broadened and enhanced." See Abigail Eliot, "American's First Nursery Schools" in James Hymes, ed., *Living History Interviews* 1 (1979) 21.

95. Langdon also succeeded in holding onto highly competent personnel. WPA nursery school state supervisors as well as head teachers, *professionals* with advanced degrees, made among the highest salaries paid any WPA worker. Salaries given for WPA nursery school teachers in first- and second-year reports can be compared with those given by Donald Howard for all WPA workers in *The WPA and Federal Relief Policy* (1943/1973). Harriet O'Shea, a prominent nursery school leader in the Midwest, was initially skeptical about whether or not the program could maintain high-quality nursery schools through the hiring of "relief" personnel. By 1941, she was completely won over. See Grace Langdon and Harriet O'Shea correspondence, July 1941, NARA.

96. FDR declared a limited state of emergency in September 1939, and a full-scale one in May 1941. According to Donald Howard,

> That the WPA should continue to be the federal agency through which special needs of defense communities might be met was the hope of many friends of that agency. However, the WPA was never able to develop its defense activities sufficiently to overcome the increasing congressional insistence on limiting these jobs to needy workers. . . . The WPA was gradually squeezed out of the defense picture because the communities in which the rearmament program created the greatest need for expanded facilities and services were those in which employment was booming and needy unemployed workers eligible for WPA employment scarce.

See his "The Lanham Act in Operation" *Survey Midmonthly* 79 (February 1943) 38.

97. For the theoretical basis of Langdon's preference, see her article with Patty Smith Hill, "Continuity in Curricula" *Childhood Education* 7 (June 1931) 530–541+, in which they make the case for an integrated curriculum for all young children, ages 2–8.

98. As reported by the National Council of Negro Women and cited by Geraldine Youcha, *Minding the Children: Child Care in America from Colonial Times to the Present* (1995) 310.

99. Edwin Amenta and Drew Halfmann, "Who Voted with Hopkins? Institutional Politics and the WPA" *Journal of Policy History* 13 (2) (2001) 251–277.

100. As FDR had foreseen when he signed the bill in protest, the clause created hardships for WPA nursery school workers and their families. Workers were also required to take a loyalty oath, and Congress prohibited the WPA from hiring workers from the Workers' Alliance. See FDR Statement on Signing a Work Relief Bill, June 30, 1939, www.presidency.ucsb.edu. See also discussion

42   WPA Nursery Schools as Educational Reform

in Nick Taylor, *American-Made: The Enduring Legacy of the WPA* (2008) 473–478. On June 13, 1941, the House eliminated the eighteen-month time limit for the WPA.

101. Langdon Report on Ohio visit, March 10–13, 1941, NARA. Local institution also tried to circumvent this ruling: The University in Knoxville, TN, asked Langdon in July 1940 if they could open up a WPA nursery school without having to go through local WPA channels. In her 1943 history of the program, she responds, "Many workers who had been with the program for a period of time and were genuinely interested in the well-being of the children left the program for other employment with great reluctance" (123).

102. On March 11, 1941, Kerr telegrammed Langdon, "ok to use volunteers—no legal liability." Langdon also wrote letters of recommendation to place her trained staff in more lucrative positions and encouraged men to get in the classroom as well. Well-qualified teachers (e.g., Rosalie Blau in Los Angeles) were moved into "new" supervisory positions so that they could continue to work in the program. In addition to facing mandatory layoffs, women may also have left on their own recognizance for better-paying defense jobs.

103. Florence Kerr was Langdon's boss at the WPA, 1939–1943. Kerr, a former English professor at Grinnell College, appreciated Langdon's devotion to early childhood education. Kerr was also longtime friend of Harry Hopkins (she took care of his daughter, Diana, when his wife died) and had been a regional WPA director in the Midwest before she moved to Washington and took over Ellen Woodward's job at the national WPA headquarters. Kerr still awaits a full-length biography. On May 20, 1941, FDR established by executive order the Office of Civilian Defense. Its purpose: protect the civilian population, maintain morale, and promote volunteer involvement in defense.

104. By April 1942, volunteers worked in NY (state as well as city), Baltimore, DC, Denver, and Chicago. Mary E. Murphy, director of the Elizabeth McCormick Memorial Fund and member of Langdon's Advisory Committee, for instance, was put in charge of the agency's childcare in Chicago; see its 1942–1945 records at the Chicago Public Library.

105. Although Kentucky maintained an average of sixty nursery schools over the course of the program, by 1941, only thirty-seven remained in operation.

106. Isabel Robinson field report: Kentucky (May 1941), 10 pages, NARA. Robinson was Langdon's assistant.

107. To April 1940 staff in Wisconsin, Langdon asserted, "It has been the policy from the beginning of the program to continue carrying on the program as if it were going on indefinitely," NARA.

108. Mary Dabney Davis, "NANE 1941 Conference" *School Life* 27 (January 1942) 113. See also *American Journal of Public Health* 32 (January 1942) 91–92, *School and Society* 54 (September 13, 1941) 186–187 and *Childhood Education* (December 1941).

109. Hill herself offered a particularly convincing rationale for why early childhood education fostered democracy in *Permanent Play Materials for Young Children*, a widely distributed text in WPA nursery schools. Hill's rationale held that children learned the arts of sharing, compromise, and taking turns when they played together, thus reducing competition and increasing their ability to get along with others, cooperative skills needed for democracy itself. Due in large measure to her influence, group play with blocks became a distinguishing feature of the WPA program. In *Emergency Nursery Schools During the Second Year, 1934–1935*, 95% of the schools (1,780 out of 1,818) had blocks.

110. Lois Meek Stolz, "Editorial Comment" *Childhood Education* (January 1942) 196. Teacher-training sessions at nearby universities encouraged new teachers

WPA Nursery Schools as Educational Reform   43

to relinquish absolute control and focus instead on a student-directed learning. Carefully observing children's actual behavior, leaders determined a wide variety of toys in spacious settings fostered cooperation while minimizing quarreling among young children.

111. Katherine McKinnon, "Margeurite: Coming of Age in America" *Progressive Education* (April 1941) 217–219.
112. See LaBerta Hattwick, "The Young Child Needs Companionship" *Parents Magazine* 16 (September 1941) 24–25. Hattwick, a psychologist, worked in Rose Alschuler's nursery schools in the Chicago area.
113. Corinne Seeds, "Dramatic Play as a Means to Democratic Social Living" *Childhood Education* 19 (January 1943) 218–222. See also Kathleen Weiler, "The Struggle for Democratic Public Schools in California: Helen Heffernan and Corinne Seeds" in *Pedagogies of Resistance: Women Educator Activists, 1880–1960* (1999) and Kathleen Weiler, *Democracy and Schooling in California: The Legacy of Helen Heffernan and Corinne Seeds* (2011).
114. Dorothy Baruch, *You, Your Children, and War* (1942) 107. See also Baruch's "Intolerance by Any Other Name" *Progressive Education* 18 (November 1941) 374–382, "Sleep Comes Hard" *The Nation* 160 (January 27, 1945) 95–96 and *Glass House of Prejudice* (1946), her pioneering work on mid-century race relations.
115. Patty Smith Hill, "Right of the Young Child to Security in an Insecure World" *NEA* 76 (June 26–30, 1938) 467. For a rich discussion of the ideals of social democracy Jane Addams promoted, see especially Jean Bethke Elshtain, *Jane Addams and the Dream of American Democracy* (2002).
116. Four women who became WPA nursery school leaders—Patty Smith Hill, Mary Dabney Davis, Lois Meek Stolz, and Rose Alschuler—traveled together in 1929 to investigate the USSR's fledgling early childhood education program. They met with Lenin's widow (a strong advocate for nursery schools because she believed they helped emancipate women) and maintained their ties to Vera Fediaevsky, a Russian early childhood specialist, upon their return to the United States. In 1936, Patty Smith Hill collaborated with Fediaevsky to write Nursery School and Parent Education in Soviet Russia, a book the NYA later used in training young workers for WPA nursery schools. For instance, Annette Lang's *A Suggestive Plan for Inservice Training of NYA Girls Assisting on the WPA Nursery School and Parent Education Program* (Oregon Superintendent of Public Instruction, May 1937) mentions Hill/Fediaevsky book by name. See also Edith Osswald papers, ACEI archives; N.S. Timasheff, "The Soviet School Experiment" *Russian Review* 4 (Spring 1945) 72–87; and Lewis Feuer, "American Travelers to the Soviet Union, 1917–1932: The Formation of a Component of New Deal Ideology" *American Quarterly* 14 (Summer 1962) 119–149. For overviews of the Soviet system, see Lisa Kirschenbaum, *Small Comrades: Revolutionizing Childhood in Soviet Russia, 1917–1932* (2001) and Yordanka Valkanova, "The Passion for Educating the 'New Man': Debates about Preschooling in Soviet Russia, 1917–1925" *History of Education Quarterly* 49 (May 2009) 211–221.
117. WPA, Mississippi. *Homes for Democracy: Curriculum Produced in Conference for the Education of Teachers of Adults and Nursery Schools* (August 5–23, 1940) 41.
118. Paul Douglas, "The Impact of Recent Social and Economic Changes upon the Family" *Child Welfare Pamphlet* 38 (October 1934). Paul Douglas became a civil rights activist and US Senator (D-IL) following World War II.
119. When asked the question, "What are you doing in your nursery school to preserve democracy?" national nursery school leaders (i.e., WPA program leaders)

44 WPA Nursery Schools as Educational Reform

responded, "Giving children opportunities to practice cooperation." Survey results reported in *Childhood Education* (December 1941) 188. Under Grace Langdon's stewardship, NANE also argued:

> For our national defense, the future is as crucial as the present. We must bring children up to live in the Democratic way: The early years are the most important ones. Roots of democracy must be planted then. An agency taking vital cognizance of this fact is the modern nursery school.

See *The Roots of Democracy* (Los Angeles: Angelus Press, 1941) 1.

120. See Agnes Snyder, "Keeping Faith with Democracy" *Childhood Education* 19 (November 1942) 106–110. See also Winifred Bain et al., *Democracy in Education* (Washington, DC: ACE, 1949), William H. Kilpatrick, *Group Education for a Democracy* (1940) and W.E. Blatz, *Hostages to Peace: Parents and the Children of Democracy* (1940).

121. See Grace Langdon, "Home as the Place for Learning Democratic Living" *Progressive Education* 17 (April 1940) 247–250. See also "Education's Present Responsibility for Interpreting Democracy" *Progressive Education* (2/39—entire issue), *Child Study* (May 1939—entire issue), "The Challenge of Democracy to Education" *Survey Graphic* 28 (October 1939—entire issue), and George Counts, *The Schools Can Teach Democracy* (1939).

122. Friedrich's speech at the October 1943 NANE conference (Langdon was the keynote speaker) was reprinted as "Childhood Education and World Citizenship" *Childhood Education* (May 1944) 394. Author of *New Belief in the Common Man*, Friedrich would take part in congressional hearings on *Creating Palestine* (1945) and *Nuclear Disarmament Talks* (1955).

123. Kriste Lindenmeyer makes this argument in *"A Right to Childhood": The US Children's Bureau and Child Welfare, 1912–46* (1997).

124. Philip Klein to Mary Leeper, *The White House Conference on Children in a Democracy: Memo on Education: Prepared by Hutchins* (October 1939). ACEI archives. The conference took place in Washington, DC, January 18–20, 1940.

125. Eunice Fuller Barnard, "Definitely Woman's Work" *Independent Woman* 21 (April 1942) 106–108.

126. WPA Queens Nursery School, near a bridge that feeds traffic into New York, is in one of the most crowded districts in the world. These two [sic] little friends on their way to the playground are being taught the necessity of walking carefully and looking often. [no date]. National Archives photo no. 69-N-11-18445-D.

2 American Modernism and the WPA Nursery School Curriculum

Program leaders paid great attention to the spaces in which children play.[1] More than half of WPA nursery schools were concentrated in big cities where, Lois Meek Stolz pointed out, "play space is most inadequate."[2] Moreover, WPA nursery school children typically lived in especially cramped living quarters. Whether residing in city, town, or country, nearly half were in homes with four rooms or less, and 93% slept in rooms with others.[3] As early childhood specialists, leaders understood such living conditions limited young children's opportunities to play and so made it difficult for them to develop normally:

> taut muscles, avid appetites, and joyous emotional release through skilled play can be no part of the lives of these children unless the school provides the opportunity which modern conditions of living have taken away.[4]

At the same time, leaders emphasized that their program helped young children cope with smaller family size, another facet of modern life. As the University of Chicago economist (and later US Senator) Paul Douglas noted in late 1934, fewer children under the age of five lived in the United States in 1934 than in 1920.[5] This marked decline in nuclear family size (along with the demise of extended families) meant that preschoolers did not always get to play with children of their own age, one basis for arguing that nursery schools provided a better environment for play.[6]

Adopting the rhetoric of machine-age modernism, program leaders also championed the right of mothers to work outside of the home.[7] Here, they took inspiration from the influential American journalist and literary modernist, Floyd Dell, who argued that American industrial growth would soon liberate humans from property-based capitalism and that companionate marriage and a new family structure based on sexual equality and democracy would soon free women and children from patriarchal rule.[8] Dell spoke at length about the revolutionary potential of working mothers in a speech

46 American Modernism and the WPA

to WPA nursery school leaders shortly before becoming a WPA publicist and speech-writer:

> Now with factories a half-hour's ride from the home, the woman has her work and also her duties as a wife and mother. . . . That is one way in which young people can get married—by permitting the young wife to continue working. . . . This is one thing which young people are doing as a way of getting away from the old patriarchal scheme. We are at every turn influencing our children in regard to these things. A boy who is brought up to feel that he would not be a man unless he could support his wife and children and that it would be unmanly if his wife worked after marriage is just so much at a disadvantage in his own love live and his chances for happiness.[9]

Or as George Stoddard put it in 1937:

> The modern mother realizes that to do well by her children she must do well by herself; that the old-style, self-sacrificing type of mother, subservient to masculine discipline, out of circulation vocationally and professionally, and devoted to social activities only by way of anesthesia, should be a thing of the past. Mothers are persons and personalities. To the extent that they realize this in their own growth and development we have a concept which will serve to strengthen and enrich home life. The nursery school can do its part here.[10]

Complementing their enthusiasm for modern architecture and the machine-age mother, program leaders used new technology to promote their work. On December 24, 1939, Director Grace Langdon introduced WPA nursery school toys and play equipment to the listeners of the "General Electric Hour," an NBC radio show.[11] She created at least two film series about WPA nursery schools in 1940.[12] Langdon also publicized the program using the work of documentary photographers for the WPA and Farm Security Administration. Lewis Hine, Dorothea Lange, and others captured images of hundreds of WPA nursery school children and teachers from around the country, images that provide dramatic evidence of a program that celebrated modern childhood—young children at play.[13]

Educating Young Children

The WPA nursery school program put children's education at the top of its agenda, ahead of its other purposes "of employing women and of relieving the distress of mothers and young children in homes suffering from current economic and social difficulties."[14] WPA Director Harry Hopkins emphasized the program's benefits for children, arguing that nursery schools "can aid as nothing else in combating the physical and mental handicaps being

American Modernism and the WPA 47

imposed upon these young children."[15] As the newly appointed program director, Mary Dabney Davis explained in October 1933:[16]

The purpose of the federal project is to give education for children for whom the school system is not now responsible, that is, children under five years of age, and particularly to provide an environment for them so normal and happy that they shall be relieved of the tensions of worry and despair which are found in many homes suffering financial insecurity or overcrowding, due to the Depression.

In pursuit of this "normal and happy" environment, George Stoddard and Edna Noble White spent the next two months writing *Bulletin #1: Administration and Program*, the first of five widely distributed curriculum manuals:

The emergency nursery school has as its primary purpose the physical welfare and wholesome mental development of the young children entrusted to its care. It carries out this purpose by providing physical examinations and health care, by providing nutritious and well balanced meals and by setting up an environment favorable to growth and a schedule of activities suited to the needs of the young children.[17]

Quick to suggest that any program of activities must adapt to the individual children and their varied stages of development, leaders focused on what could be addressed well at school: sense experience, motor skills, vocal expression, social experience, and creativity. Yet they also stressed that cooperation between home and school was necessary to assure young children's well-being and that the program assisted "the mother without taking her place."[18] This would be a quintessentially modern education, one that complemented, but did not replace, home authority.[19] To ensure children's healthy development in this context, program leaders offered teacher training for those receiving work relief from the WPA.[20] They wanted to prepare the progressive educators they believed young children deserved.

Most of the new teachers were women, which created controversy. Impoverished mothers, of whom there were so many during the Great Depression, often preferred working in nursery schools to staying at home and receiving mother's pensions (welfare).[21] The program's success in training them created consternation at the CB, which welcomed mother's pensions to allow poor women to stay at home with their offspring:

To give work relief outside their own homes to mothers of young children was a mistake. WPA paid women to take care of other women's children; it would have been much more useful to pay them to take care of their own.[22]

48 *American Modernism and the WPA*

Chase Woodhouse, a longtime advocate of women in the workplace, disagreed, celebrating the WPA nursery school program precisely because it helped working mothers.[23]

Although Harry Hopkins downplayed the idea of creating jobs for women, the WPA nursery school transformed its teachers into professionals able to handle all aspects of a difficult job:

> A mother is just asking for advice about Bobby's thumb-sucking or about her husband's drinking, while Jimmie incessantly repeats in a penetrating voice: "Teacher! Look what I do!" Mary and Betty fight and scream; little Barbara sucks a burnt match stick which she picked up, goodness knows where; and while Dicky needs right at this moment some suggestions about how not to handle books and while Mrs. Smith has to be convinced that Gloria better stay out of school until her cold is over, little Johnny sits, happily and proudly smiling, in a fresh puddle—the third this morning.
>
> The person who masters that situation, who remains calm and friendly and yet manages to get it all straightened out,—that is the FNST [Federal Nursery School Teacher].
>
> Cooking and Nursery, Nutrition and Hygiene, Singing and Dancing, Washing and Sewing, Painting and Modeling, Child Psychology and Mental Hygiene, the Raising of Chickens and Rats, of Flowers and Vegetables, Parent Education and Family Relations, Scrubbing Floors and Washing Windows, Bookkeeping and Budgeting, writing Reports and filling out lengthy Rating Scales—these are just a few of the skills and fields of knowledge of the FNST.
>
> To watch her at work is an inspiration. Children and mothers alike admire her. Friends of the Nursery School idea recognize her to-day as the back bone of the whole movement. Let us sing her praise! I think the world ought to know about her.[24]

The program's top administrators managed to have their program included in the professional projects division of the WPA, which meant that federal nursery school teachers were better educated and paid than many others employed by New Deal programs.[25] A substantial number of these WPA teachers stayed active in early childhood education for the rest of their lives.[26]

WPA nursery school teachers also learned from one another. Teachers studied the latest research in parent education, child psychology, and children's literature, art, and music. They observed one another teaching and met regularly to talk over ideas for lessons.[27] That they team taught (two teachers plus assistants were assigned to every group of twenty-five children) also brought innovation.[28] Many of the program's practices are still considered among the most effective means of teacher training.[29] Asked to

Figure 2.1 Before and After[30]

50   American Modernism and the WPA

comment on the founding of California's children centers (established during World War II), one teacher said:

> In many school districts there was no kind of catching up with the times, and with the new understandings and knowledge of child development. They just did what had been done fifteen years before in the WPA program.[31]

Collaboration at all levels helps explain how WPA nursery schools provided a cutting-edge curriculum that moved beyond young children's bathing, dressing, eating, and toileting to spread the new idea of educating young children through healthy development.

Healthy Development

Annually educating 50,000 children from poor and unemployed families, leaders defined *need* loosely enough that children from a wide cross section of the general population attended the schools. A nationwide study revealed subtle differences between WPA students and other preschoolers. WPA enrollees tended to live in smaller homes with more mobile families.[32] They were less likely to have toys and books (nearly 70% of these children resided in homes with three books or fewer) and more likely to have health problems (over 40% were considered to be in poor or "frail" health). By developing a curriculum that addressed their physical welfare as well as emotional development, staff introduced modern education to WPA nursery school children.[33] As Ruth Andrus, WPA nursery school supervisor in New York, declared:

> The time has passed when one considers it possible to separate mind and body. It is now clear that a healthy body is part of a healthy mind, and the opposite is true. Physical growth is an integral part of total development, so physical growth and health needs are as much a part of curriculum guides as social needs or any other experience needs of children.[34]

As part of creating an integrated learning environment, program leaders began by preparing the physical plant of a school. Seventy-five percent were housed in public schools, although they could also be found in factories, settlement houses, and church basements.[35] Local communities helped the program reconfigure classrooms to create play space and to better address young children's physical and emotional development. In the meantime, newly hired teachers traveled to teacher training courses at nearby universities.

Embracing the modern architectural aesthetic of maximizing space and light, the WPA nursery school program succeeded in minimizing the institutional feel of existing schools to create child-friendly places. In 1938, the modernist architecture critic Douglas Haskell wrote that the ideal nursery school, a series of rooms adjacent to a large outdoor play area (free of clutter but with child-sized furniture and equipment), benefited young children because it brought light, air, space, and freedom to the classroom.[36] WPA nursery schools typically provided room for up to twenty-five young children in three classrooms with an outdoor playground. School leaders promoted the use of special equipment and facilities, including tile floors, movable tables and chairs, saddle seats for good posture, open wardrobes to allow the students to hang their clothes easily, floors heated from below so that "children may rest without danger of cold drafts," cots for naps, and low toilets, wash trays, and drinking fountains.[37] At one school, a teacher reported:

> We chose as our colors, a warm yellow and orange, with touches of green. These three colors are in our linoleum and furniture, and we have light cream gauze curtains, embroidered in colored wool. We have a dozen or so apple boxes arranged for our toys and blocks. The boxes serve a double purpose; they are used also as benches for the children.
> One room, the kitchen, is used as both office for the Nursery School and workroom. The bed-room is used as a playroom, with miniature furniture; a stove, sink, kitchen dish cabinet, chairs, table, carpet sweeper, mop, broom, etc., for the use of the Nursery children only. The largest room, with the boxes, has a piano, Victrola, round table and chairs for story-telling or other activities, and a large cabinet for our supplies. . . . We are planting flowers of all sorts in window boxes—also, we plan to have a vegetable patch very soon.[38]

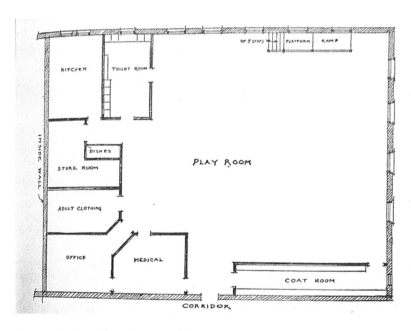

Figure 2.2 The Built Environment[39]

52 American Modernism and the WPA

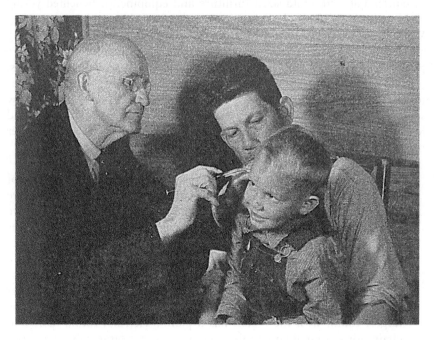

Figure 2.3 Health Inspections[40]

Daily schedules, like the built environment, integrated concern for children's physical well-being with their emotional and cognitive development. Monday through Friday, from 8:30 am to 3:00 pm, WPA nursery children spent their 6.5-hour school day tending to health and nutritional needs, resting, and, for the most part, playing. Cared for by at least two full-time teachers and additional support staff, children began each morning with a health inspection.[41] They then played, inside or out, depending on the weather. At approximately 10 am, fifteen minutes were given to a snack that included a dose of cod liver oil washed down with orange or tomato juice. Engaging in a variety of play activities for the rest of the morning, the children took a break at noon for lunch and a nap. When they woke, they had another snack (e.g., graham crackers and milk) and played with classmates until leaving for home.[42]

Physical Welfare

Emphasizing prevention and therapy, WPA nursery schools aimed to provide medical attention for all young children, which was especially important for those who did not have easy access to doctors, adequate rest facilities, or nutritious meals.[43] Keeping track of these requirements required extensive

American Modernism and the WPA   53

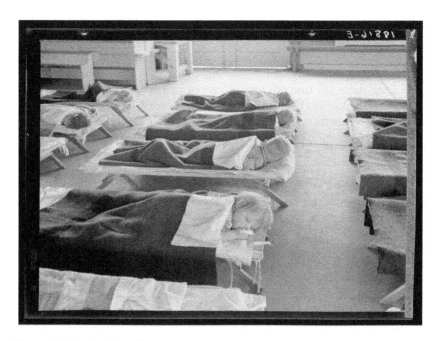

Figure 2.4 Plenty of Rest[44]

home-to-school cooperation. Before being accepted into the program, children needed a clean bill of health from a doctor, and their parents filled out brief questionnaires on their general health since infancy.[45] Then, with parents in attendance, medical staff treated children for rotten teeth and tuberculosis and also provided free immunizations for illnesses like smallpox and diphtheria.[46] Once children received medical clearance, school staff maintained individual files with family medical information, morning inspection reports, daily food intake, sleep and elimination records, and monthly height and weight measurements.[47]

The children rested and slept at scheduled times. Many WPA nursery schools included a quiet time before lunch to calm children who had been active. The program's two-hour naps derived from the view that children between ages two and five need from ten to thirteen hours of sleep daily.[48] One school director observed that students often lived "in such crowded quarters that early bedtime is [an] impossibility."[49] Local communities generally made the tiny-sized cots for young children.

Although the schools operated on extremely tight budgets, they tried to provide half the daily nutrients young children required, often using surplus commodities like canned beef.[50] One recommended noontime meal consisted of liver loaf, buttered peas and carrots, cabbage sandwiches, apple tapioca,

54   American Modernism and the WPA

and milk.[51] A recipe for Plain Cake indicates staff celebrated birthdays by making unfrosted cakes low in fat and sugar.[52] Staff helped students recover from malnourishment by emphasizing such foods as evaporated milk, whole wheat bread, and fresh fruits and vegetables.[53] In 1940, a supervisor in California defined a healthy diet for young children as including four cups of fresh milk daily (or one tall can of evaporated milk), three to four eggs a week, a daily portion of fruit and a second offering of either fresh or dried fruit, one daily portion of potato, rice, or macaroni (with a recommendation that evaporated milk be used in mashed potatoes).

Healthy food was not the only benefit of school lunches. Helen Salisbury in Los Angeles used mealtimes to foster intercultural awareness. In 1936, a student invited an entire WPA nursery school class of children whose parents were Chinese, Japanese, and Mexican immigrants to her home to celebrate the Chinese New Year:[54]

> At each place was a portion of rice, loaf shaped, containing shrimp and almonds. We were given beautiful ivory chop sticks with which we labored, until the mother gave us forks. In the center of the table were bowls filled with various edibles—potatoes, browned in deep fat and looking much like small twigs. . . . We were told the mother had been weeks preparing these food. . . . Throughout the meals our small tea bowls were constantly replenished with the finest tea we ever tasted—made from lichi nuts and tea leaves. . . . When we left, the Chinese mother, whose feet had been bound when she was a baby in Canton, China, smiled and we felt we had had a never-to-be-forgotten experience.

Later, Salisbury staged an Easter tea for her students' mothers. Japanese mothers provided refreshments, and:

> Easter cards were given to all present and a very friendly informal time was enjoyed while we drank tea and laughed over the fortunes found in the rice cakes. At two-thirty when the children were awake, the guest re-assembled in the Nursery School and listened with beaming faces while the children sang some of our Nursery School songs.[55]

Salisbury told the *Los Angeles Times*, "At the Amelia-street school nursery we have a little League of Nations, sans diplomats, of which we are very proud."[56] That the program succeeded in fostering an inclusive, diverse society by serving healthy, yet inexpensive food from around the world attracted the notice of many at the vanguard of modernist thought, including the anthropologist Margaret Mead, who joined Grace Landon's World War II–era advisory committee, a group committed to helping all young children reap the benefits, nutritional and otherwise, of WPA nursery schools.[57]

American Modernism and the WPA   55

Figure 2.5 Nutritious Meals[58]

Mental Health

Staff members monitored children's emotions to guide their charges' psychological development. Often, their close observation helped children with emotional issues and problematic behavior. When a shy four-year-old sat apart at the beginning of the school day and did not respond to invitations to join the group, the teacher allowed her to remain there the entire day. Five days later, she convinced the girl to take part in routines like washing hands, but the child always went back to her chair when the other children played. After home visits that led the teacher to realize that the girl had no playthings and spent all her time helping her mother with chores, she provided some toys for the household. At that point, the little girl began to interact with the other children:

> After two months, Julia feels secure, has overcome her shyness, and enjoys nursery school because she was allowed to learn by herself with the minimum of direct adult interference.[59]

The notion that play fostered children's sense of security signaled an important milestone in efforts to define healthy psychological development.[60]

56 American Modernism and the WPA

In the early years of the program, WPA nursery schools were influenced by behaviorism, and teachers cultivated a detached, almost clinical stance towards their young charges with a focus on negative aspects of mental health, defining and helping children with temper tantrums and fears of the dark, for example.[61] This emphasis on the negative grew from current definitions of sound mental health rather than from the teachers' observations.[62]

As the program evolved, its administrators placed greater emphasis on being sufficiently flexible to adapt routines to meet the emotional needs of young children, focusing on personality development rather than on "curricula for the development of control habits."[63] One key intellectual foundation for moving away from a preoccupation with problem behaviors came in 1937 at the Seventh Biennial NANE Conference. Lawrence Frank, a psychologist who funded pioneer nursery schools in the 1920s and was a staunch supporter of the WPA nursery school program, argued that young children needed love and affection at all stages of development. He called on WPA nursery school teachers to mother their young charges, to give them "a feeling of being liked and wanted, of belonging to someone who cares, and of being guided in the conduct of life with benevolent interest and confidence."[64] WPA nursery school teachers were asked to participate in studies, all of which concluded that the program contributed to healthy emotional development.[65] Destructively aggressive children became creative and original through the nursery school experience, and shyness turned to spontaneity through interaction with peers.[66]

By 1939, program leaders confidently asserted that to achieve happiness, children needed security, a sense of adequacy, and acknowledgement of their real feelings, even unpleasant ones like anger.[67] Dorothy Baruch's "Therapeutic Procedures as Part of the Educative Process" (1940) proved seminal in this regard because she advocated play therapy ("mishandling" clay, for instance), through which a child could act out and relieve aggression.[68] The emphasis on personality development helped usher in the permissive parenting style that took root following World War II.[69]

Learning through Play

The program stressed social growth, defined as the ability to get along with others, as critical to physical and emotional well-being. Arguing such maturation occurred in the context of play, administrators drew inspiration from the writings of Friedrich Froebel, G. Stanley Hall, and John Dewey and borrowed heavily from the rich tradition of play developed in the kindergarten movement a generation earlier. Relying also on the cognitive studies of contemporaries Jean Piaget and Lev Vygotsky, they emphasized that children learn through play.

Teachers regularly encouraged outdoor play and the use of jungle gyms, slides, and ladders for adequate exercise.[70] Rings and hollow blocks were held to promote healthy posture and motor development.[71] Schools even provided sun-suits (absorbent cotton clothing provided by local WPA

Figure 2.6 Fresh Air and Sunshine[72]

sewing circles) so that children would have attire appropriate for fresh air and sunshine.[73] Access to outdoor equipment was one of the most tangible benefits children received from WPA nursery schools.[74] As Harry Hopkins put it, "Nourishing food, sun and air, rest, and healthful playful opportunities are laying the foundation for the health and happiness of these future citizens."[75]

Believing music, art, and literature enhanced children's play, the WPA program gave teachers specialized training in storytelling, puppetry, crafts, and music appreciation.[76] Rather than engaging young children's attention through an emphasis on letters or numbers, WPA nursery schools opened "the door of the arts" in two ways.[77] During both their early and mid-morning play, children could choose musical instruments, painting materials, and picture books from among the wide variety of available toys. Teachers regularly pulled four to five children aside for fifteen to twenty minutes at a time to give more formal lessons. They tried to spark children's literary interest by choosing books that related to young children's everyday lives.[78] Leaders like Dorothy Baruch also encouraged teachers to recite the work of modern poets and craft poems based on children's speech patterns.[79] Her own "STOP-GO" (1935) introduced traffic signals and underscored her modernist conviction that "pre-school children need (and prefer, if they are given the chance) stories of their really-real everyday world."[80]

58 *American Modernism and the WPA*

Automobiles
In a row
Wait to go
While the signal says
STOP
Bells ring
Tingaling
Red light's gone
Green light's on
Horn's blow!
And the row
Starts
TO GO[81]

WPA nursery schools also introduced young children to music. In *Songs for the Nursery School* (1937), Laura Pendleton MacCarteney emphasized "the here and now." She lowered the pitches of classic nursery rhymes to encourage more children to participate and wrote songs that celebrated contemporary urban life.[82] The book's Foreword, written by Lois Meek Stolz, held that children:

> enjoy music more if they can dramatize in some way the rhythm or story of the song. They can be tugboats or elephants or sleeping babies with equal versatility. Mrs. MacCarteney has given some excellent suggestions for these dramatic plays. . . . But she has been careful not to suggest complicated or formal interpretations, rather has she indicated the informality and freedom that must be given.

Jazz, quintessential of modern sounds, introduced WPA nursery school children to freedom of movement and innovation in rhyme. Arthur Herzog, Jr., who wrote the jazz standard "God Bless the Child," also wrote the lovely ballad "Hush, My Baby" in *Songs for the Nursery School*.

Believing children learn more easily while doing the things they like, the program emphasized free play. It was a time for children to initiate activities with as little direction as possible.[83] The schools considered toys essential "tools of play."[84] In addition to outdoor apparatus for climbing, swinging, hanging, pulling and pushing, schools provided toys and equipment for playing house, boat, and train, and equipment for building, piling, digging, and painting. Many toys, including outdoor balls, wagons, and more were designed for greater action. Dolls, playhouses, and other toys were meant to give children a chance to use their imaginations, and clay, sand, paint, and other tools to spur creativity.

WPA nursery schools did not let the hard times of the Great Depression get in the way of providing children with a material-rich environment. With

Figures 2.7–2.9 Opening the Door of the Arts[85]

60 *American Modernism and the WPA*

Figures 2.7–2.9 (Continued)

very little money available, local communities did what they could to provide what the program saw as critical:

> Toys are as necessary for the young child as books; outdoor-play apparatus is as necessary as spinach and orange juice. In some form these facilities should be provided, even if for economic reasons they must be makeshift and homemade.[86]

Parents, WPA sewing circles, local carpenters, high school shop classes, and New Deal agencies like the Civilian Conservation Corps (CCC) and NYA all helped WPA nursery schools repair castoffs and fabricate toys. *WPA Bulletin #5, Suggestions, Drawings and Specifications for Nursery School Equipment* (1936), included explicit instructions and line drawings for making toys like outdoor ladders, sandboxes, pull wagons, and easels.[87]

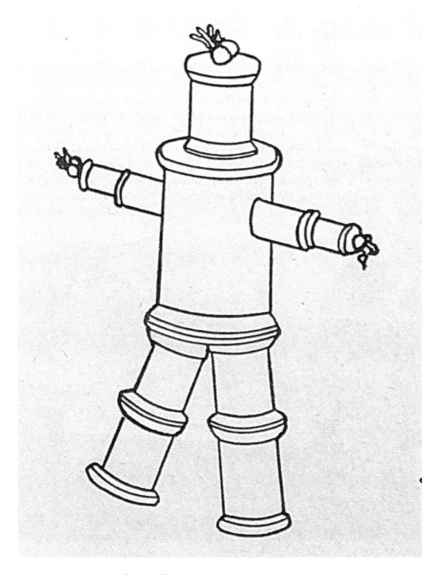

Figure 2.10 Homemade Toys[88]

Toys designed by parents included a doll made of spools, a swing made of a recycled prune box, and a tugboat and barge made from scraps of wood, a cigar box, and large-headed nails.[89] Program leaders also saw homemade toys as a superior alternative to the rising consumerism of the age.[90] At a time when the material culture of children was becoming inextricably linked to the marketplace, WPA nursery schools advocated an ethic that prized ingenuity and creativity in the use of recycled materials rather than purchased ones.[91] Making toys from scratch "affords far more fun than expensive toys."[92]

Given the variety of toys available, program leaders expressed keen interest in learning which children preferred. Around the country, staff and visitors routinely described children's activities during free play. They focused on the most popular play materials, how children stood up for their rights, and how gender and age affected the choice of toys.[93] They concluded that young children favored raw materials—paint, clay, water, paper, sand, wood, hammer and nails, blocks, dolls, and wagons—perhaps "because their use depends on the children's own efforts and ideas and provides unlimited possibilities."[94] These materials let the children take a literal hand in shaping curriculum.

Blocks were "the most popular and probably most valuable of all materials" for young children.[95] According to staff, two-year-old children preferred

Figures 2.11 and 2.12 Raw Materials[96]

American Modernism and the WPA 63

Figures 2.11 and 2.12 (Continued)

hollow blocks. Closed on all sides except for two grip-holes, hollow blocks were large enough and strong enough for children to sit or stand on. WPA nursery schools either made them at local carpentry shops (including those at local high schools) or from donations of cigar, cheese, and prune boxes from which they soaked off the labels and nailed the covers tightly shut. Weighing no more than four pounds and close to a foot square, toddlers derived "great joy in [their] simple manipulation."[97] Three- and four-year-olds preferred the classic building block, which Caroline Pratt of Bank Street, inspired by Patty Smith Hill, had designed before World War I. Pratt took a "simple geometric shape," the rectangle, and combined it with cylinders, triangles, curves, half units—all of which could be manipulated easily by tiny hands.[98] Children over four years old preferred Hill Floor Blocks, which Patty Smith Hill had designed in the early 1900s after observing four- to six-year-olds for more than a decade. Inspired by the wooden spheres, cylinders, cubes, and rectangles that Friedrich Froebel had designed in the 1840s, Hill made the last of these several times higher.[99] Her interlocking blocks allowed children to build playhouses and forts, an especially popular activity at many WPA nursery schools.[100] Groups played with blocks, added toys like stuffed animals, trains, and dolls, constructed imagined communities,

64 American Modernism and the WPA

and created works of block art. The role of these toys was understood to promote the cooperative ideal:

> Blocks, probably more than any other one kind of play material, lend themselves to the child's constructive interests and needs ... [affording] the greatest opportunity for the development of cooperative thinking and acting.[101]

WPA nursery school leaders also applauded block play as encouraging creativity:

> We have been led to the conclusion that blocks are essentially the most admirable plastic material for young children, because with blocks they seem able to arrange, to design, to compose.[102]

Carefully observing children's use of blocks, program leaders determined that "the most important factor in determining type of play is the age of the child."[103] Adopting the phrase *age-appropriate*, program staff detected clear developmental differences: two-year-olds stacked blocks independently, whereas four-year-olds cooperated with their newfound friends in building forts.[104] They did not detect gender differences in block play, which stands

Figures 2.13 and 2.14 Blocks, the Favorite Toy[105]

Figures 2.13 and 2.14 (Continued)

in contrast to the later fixation with labeling toys for children as being either for girls or boys.[106] WPA nursery school leaders subscribed to the modern theory of the nursery school instead:

> All the children should have the opportunity to become well acquainted with all the types of equipment and that groups should be set up on the basis of stage of development and of interest in material but never on the basis of sex.[107]

In 1937, the WPA celebrated its nursery schools in all forty-eight states through the modern medium of films explaining the program's benefits for both children and adults. These offered vivid images of children playing, eating, and resting. Although the activities depicted varied by state, the message, voiced by pleasant baritones, remained the same:

> Where the children of working or needy mothers are cared for during the day, given hot lunches and prepared by trained instructors for graduation into the public school system. . . . Part of a broad educational program in which WPA has helped millions of children and adults. Here is another case where an investment made today promises great dividends in a future of good citizenship.[108]

66 American Modernism and the WPA

The narration asserted that WPA nursery schools promised great dividends. Good citizens would develop from the provision of spacious schools, well-trained teachers, nourishing food, and a curriculum supportive of diversity, inclusiveness, sustainability, and gender equality. Working mothers would play a vital role in this modern landscape, as would the built environment designed for learning through play. Touting its own benefits, the program created a vision of American modernism by pointing to a better future for all young children who gained access to a modern education that celebrated the Machine Age, paid attention to both physical and mental health, and fostered children's ability to choose curricular materials.

The WPA earned a spot at the 1939 New York World's Fair because, as the fair's press release announced:

> The Fair will exhibit the most promising developments of ideas, products, services and social factors of the present day in such a fashion that the visitor may get a vision of what he could obtain for himself, and for his community, by intelligent, co-operative planning toward the better life of the future.[109]

Designed by modernist graphics designer Will Burtin in his first job in the United States after fleeing Nazi Germany, the exhibit displayed WPA accomplishments in recreation, education, and construction.[110] For the nursery school exhibit, Burtin placed a child-sized table with two chairs at the center.

Figure 2.15 Program Showcase at the 1939 New York World's Fair[111]

American Modernism and the WPA   67

American Modern dinnerware sat on the table surrounded by streamlined toys created by WPA Milwaukee toymakers. To the right of the table, Burtin hung large photos showing school lunches, doctor's visits, and parent education. To the left were photos of children at play and a showcase filled with dolls.[112] Program staff, accompanied by other WPA workers (like the makers of nursery school cot-blankets and toys) staged live demonstrations.[113]

The showcase in Figure 2.15 epitomized what the program hoped to accomplish. The multicultural hand-crafted dolls underscored the program's embrace of diversity. [114] The caption, "WPA helps children and parents to be happier" reflected the program's desire to ensure that families flourished in the Machine Age. If society could embrace the program's vision of modernism, children and adults would thrive in the industrialized World of Tomorrow.

Notes

1. Grace Langdon opened a business to advise "architects and manufactures in all matters appertaining to children's homes, buildings and commercial products." Quoted in "Nurseries Aide in City" *Los Angeles Times* (November 15, 1935) A3. Langdon also judged "modern" home designs in "2000 Home Designs in Prize Contest" *New York Times* (March 20, 1935) 24. She returned to consulting after World War II.
2. "While the equipment which preschool children need is relatively cheap for groups of children, it is expensive for individual families." See Lois Hayden Meek Stolz, "Why Nursery Education?" *Childhood Education* 11 (April 1935) 292–294. Approximately 53% of schools were located in towns and cities, 34% in small towns, and about 13% in villages and rural areas.
3. *Emergency Nursery Schools During the First Year, 1933–1934*, pp. 39–52.
4. Lee Vincent, "Why Physical Education in the Early School Years" *Childhood Education* 13 (March 1937) 301.
5. Paul Douglas, "The Impact of Recent Social and Economic Changes upon the Family" *Child Welfare Pamphlet* 38 (October 1934) 4. About 55% of WPA nursery school children came from families with three or fewer children, as reported in *Emergency Nursery Schools during the First Year, 1933–1934*, pp. 39–52.
6. Winifred Bain (WPA program supervisor in NC) called for peer play:

   > It is a good thing for children to come to know others of their own age, even as early as two years or before. . . . This can be done only by association with others of one's own age and by daily practice of social techniques which are necessary for living together, with someone always ready to teach these techniques when they are needed . . . the nursery school offers an opportunity for children to play together naturally and wholesomely, under the guidance of a teacher who can lead them little by little toward good social habits and understandings . . . a boon to a parent who cannot ordinarily have the house overrun with the neighbors' babies in order to provide social contacts.

   The quotation is from her award-winning book, *Parents Look at Modern Education* (1935).
7. Historian Robert Rydell's definition is especially applicable:

   > Because it built on the past, modernism in its American guise, would only enhance the possibilities for Americans to make progress out of the Depression and towards a better future. . . . American modernism, in short, was not

68 *American Modernism and the WPA*

just about style or a way of living; it was not just about surfaces. It was about the substance and meaning of modern life itself.

See his *Designing Tomorrow: America's World Fairs of the 1930s* (2010) 7–8. For other thoughtful discussions, see Martin Greif, *Depression Modern: The Thirties Style in America* (1975); Richard Guy Wilson et al., *The Machine Age in America, 1918–1941* (1986); Eric P. Mumford, *CIAM Discourse on Urbanism, 1928–1960* (2000); J. Stewart Johnson, *American Modern, 1925–1940: Design for a New Age* (2000); R. Roger Remington, *American Modernism: Graphic Design, 1920–1960* (2003); Christopher Wilk et al., *Modernism: Designing a New World, 1914–1939* (2008); and the following four exhibits www.moma.org/inter actives/exhibitions/2012/centuryofthechild/ (2012), www.clarkart.edu/Mini-Sites/Machine-Age-Modernism/Exhibition (2015), http://folkartmuseum.org/exhibitions/folk-art-and-american-modernism/ (2015), and www.theartstory. org/ (2009–present).

8. In *Women as World Builders: Studies in Modern Feminism* (1913), Floyd Dell argued: "A tremendous lot remains to be done in the way of cooperation for the management of households and the education of children before women who are wives and mothers will be set free to take their part in the work of the outside world." In *Were You Ever a Child* (1919), Dell gave his blueprint for children's education. In addition to celebrating progressive education, his futurist final chapter "Education in 1947 A.D." sounds remarkably similar to what the WPA nursery school program achieved, 1933–1943. See also Dell's *Love in the Machine Age* (1930). Secondary works consulted include Walter Kalaidjian, *American Culture Between the Wars: Revisionary Modernism and Postmodern Critique* (1992); Douglas Clayton, *Floyd Dell: The Life and Times of an American Rebel* (1994); Christine Stansell, *American Moderns: Bohemian New York and the Creation of a New Century* (2000, 1st ed.); Julia Mickenberg, *Learning from the Left: Children's Literature, the Cold War, and Radical Politics in the US* (2005); and Christina Simmons, *Making Marriage Modern: Women's Sexuality from the Progressive Era to WWII* (2011).

9. Floyd Dell, "Children and the Machine Age" *Child Welfare Pamphlet 35* (August 1934) 10.

10. George Stoddard, "What of the Nursery School?" *Progressive Education* 14 (October 1937) 447.

11. General Electric invited "Woman of the Week" Langdon to speak in part because of the favorable attention the WPA nursery school exhibit generated at the 1939 NYC World's Fair. The Fair's 'Nursery Education Day' was October 26, 1939.

12. Rebecca Reyher-Grace Langdon correspondence (April–July 1938) NARA. Langdon's two 1940 films were "A Day in WPA Nursery Schools" and "Activities in WPA Family Life Education." Extant movie clips include the WPA series, "A Better America" (1937), and Rose Alschuler's ACEI filmstrip, "What Has the Nursery School to Offer?" (1945).

13. See, for example, "Inventing Modernism" www.photographymuseum.com/modernism1.html and WPA nursery school photos http://newdeal.feri.org/. See also Peter Stearns, "The Dilemma of Children's Happiness" *Childhood in World History* (2017, 3rd ed.) 166–172.

14. Mary Dabney Davis, "Emergency Nursery Schools" *School Life* 19 (January 1934) 93.

15. Hopkins substituted "qualified and needy teachers" for women, and "needy and unemployed parents" for mothers, in his "Announcement of Emergency Nursery Schools" on October 23, 1933. See the reprint of his announcement in *Childhood Education* (December 1933) 155.

American Modernism and the WPA   69

16. NANE October 1933 proceeding, page 90. Written by Edna Dean Baker, Christine Heinig, and Ethel Waring.
17. Stoddard and White et al, *Bulletin #1: Administration and Program* (December 1933) 9, 21–22.
18. Ibid: 10.
19. Lois Meek Stolz, "What Is Home-School Cooperation?" *Childhood Education* 14 (December 1927) 147.
20. Nearly every WPA nursery school employed two full-time teachers for every 20–30 children, as well as a part-time nurse and a part-time cook. In addition, some schools employed dietitians, laundry workers, and janitors. Doctors and psychologists participated on an ad hoc basis, and NYA youth acted as teacher's aides. In "Report on Field trip to Michigan" (NARA, June 12, 1940), Langdon listed the advantages of using men as teachers: (1) gives man's point of view to the work, (2) helps children make contact with men as well as women, (3) disproves the "common idea that teaching young children is solely a woman's job," and (4) meets the problem of providing personnel.
21. Women generally earned more money working for the WPA than staying at home and receiving mothers' pensions (also called aid to dependent children [ADC]). WPA leaders Grace Langdon, Florence Kerr, and Aubrey Williams actively protested the mandatory removal of ADC women from the WPA nursery school program. See, for example, Aubrey Williams' (as Deputy Administrator) correspondence to regional field representatives on December 22, 1938. NARA. See also Jane Lannak, "Millie Almy: Nursery School Education Pioneer" *Journal of Education* 177 (1995) 39–55.
22. Grace Abbott, *From Relief to Social Security: The Development of the New Public Welfare Services and Their Administration* (1941) 275. The passage quoted above was a reprint from an introductory note to Abbott's *Child and the State: Dependent and Delinquent Child* (1938). Katherine Lenroot became CB Chief after Abbott.
23. Chase Going Woodhouse, "Some Trends in Women's Work" *Social Forces* 16 (May 1938) 548. Woodhouse served briefly as a Democratic congresswoman from Connecticut following World War II.
24. Walther Joel, "Praise of the FNST" [Federal Nursery School Teacher], *Los Angeles Nursery School News Bulletin* (March 1936), Rosalie Blau Collection, 1921–1987, California State University, Northridge: Urban Archives. Joel was a WPA nursery school psychologist.
25. Grace Langdon pointed out that one-third of those being trained as WPA nursery school teachers in California had college degrees at a time when less than 4% of American women were college-educated. See "Nurseries Aide in City" *Los Angeles Times* (November 15, 1935) A3. See also statistics in Grace Langdon's *Final Report of the WPA Nursery School Program* (1943) and Floyd Dell's *Final Report of the WPA* (1947). Consider also the woeful state of childcare professionals in the 21st century, as described by Jennifer Ludden in her excellent 2016 article www.npr.org/sections/health-shots/2016/11/07/500407637/poverty-wages-for-u-s-child-care-workers-may-be-behind-high-turnover.
26. Lifetime professionals who got their start in the Los Angeles WPA nursery school program include Rosalie Blau, Theresa Mahler, Mary Alice Mallum, Molly Morganroth, and Anne Nugent. Blau was the head teacher at the Breed Street School in Boyle Heights. After raising children in the 1920s, Blau completed child development coursework at Los Angeles City College. One of her professors, Dr. Elizabeth Woods, a WPA nursery school supervisor (whose husband had worked at Hull House with Jane Addams), recommended Blau for the job. Morganroth was LA City coordinator for WPA nursery schools. She later worked for the American Friends Service Committee in Chicago during World

70 *American Modernism and the WPA*

War II helping Japanese Americans. Afterwards, she founded Pacific Oaks College in Pasadena and spearheaded the cooperative preschool movement in Long Beach, CA. Theresa Mahler is featured in Natalie Fousekis, *Demanding Child Care: Women's Activism and the Politics of Welfare, 1940–1971* (2011), and a San Francisco Unified preschool is named for her. Nugent was showcased as head nursery school teacher at Van Nuys High School during World War II because Hollywood star Spencer Tracy helped pay the rent—see June Barth, "8-Hour Orphans" *Los Angeles Times* (July 18, 1943) G5.

27. As teachers in Los Angeles made explicit, "There is a great deal of ability within our own teaching group. We have decided to organize ourselves, study our problems and teach each other." Quoted in *Los Angeles Nursery School News Bulletin* (April–May 1936), Rosalie Blau Collection, 1921–1987, California State University, Northridge: Urban Archives (RB, CSUN).

28. Annette Bothman, *Reflections of the Pioneers on the Early History of the Santa Monica Children's Centers and Changing Child-Rearing Philosophies* (Unpublished Master's thesis, May 1976), RB, CSUN. The interviews focused on the creation of Lanham children's centers, which began in Santa Monica in 1943. All of the women interviewed, save one (Docia Zavitkovsky), had earlier worked in the WPA nursery school program.

29. For current research findings, see, for instance, David Kirp, "How to fix the country's failing schools" (January 10, 2016) *New York Times*; Jonathan Zimmerman, "Why Is American Teaching So Bad" (December 4, 2014) in *New York Review of Books*; and Amanda Ripley, *The Smartest Kids in the World* (2013) 216.

30. Dorothy Baruch and Mabel Rice, *Nursery School Before and After: Drawn by Lietta, 1938. Rosalie Blau Collection, 1921–1987* (Northridge: California State University, Urban Archives).

31. Bothman 1976: 5. Mallum taught at a WPA Nursery School on Fletcher Drive in Los Angeles. The *Los Angeles Times* profiled her in 1940. Mallum also collaborated with Rosalie Blau in Lanham children's centers during World War II.

32. *Emergency Nursery Schools during the First Year, 1933–1934*, pp. 39–52.

33. Floyd Dell defined modern education by quoting a bulletin of the newly formed Progressive Education Association (PEA) in *Were You Ever a Child* (1919) 199–202: "1) freedom to develop naturally 2) interest in all work 3) teacher to act as guide, not task—master 4) scientific study of pupil development 5) child's physical health addressed 6) parent—home cooperation, and 7) best practices shared with other schools." All of these tenets were achieved by WPA nursery schools.

34. Ruth Andrus, *Curriculum Guides for Teachers of Children from Two to Six Years of Age* (1936) 29.

35. The University of Maryland and the University of Utah, for instance, used their WPA nursery schools as laboratories to conduct courses in the care and education of preschool children. In addition, some teachers taught children in their own homes, and schools could also be found in mills, mining districts, and migrant camps. Patty Smith Hill's WPA nursery school in Harlem was housed in what had once been a building of the Jewish theological seminary. WPA nursery schools were also placed in housing projects in Ohio, Illinois, Indiana, and Minnesota. The one in the New Deal planned community of Arthurdale, West Virginia was one of the few schools designed and built especially for the program.

36. Douglas Haskell, "The Modern Nursery School" *Architectural Record* (March 1938) 84. Haskell maintained a lifelong interest in all forms of architecture deemed "modern." As Yale professor in 1952, he coined the term "Googie" to describe Disneyland's Tomorrowland. For more information

American Modernism and the WPA 71

on Haskell's significance to American Modernism in architecture, see excellent May 2015 article by Gabrielle Esperdy, "Architecture and Popular Taste" https://placesjournal.org/article/future-archive-architecture-and-popular-taste/.

37. See, for instance, the recommendations Amanda Hebeler made in "Learning to Face Reality: New Schools for Old" *Childhood Education* (February 1940) 269–271. Educated at Columbia University under William H. Kilpatrick (who admired the work of Patty Smith Hill), Hebeler directed Washington State Normal School's student teaching program, 1924–1956. See her 1966 oral History at: http://digitalcommons.cwu.edu/library_lectures/1/, in which she alludes to an elementary school that briefly housed a WPA nursery school in Ellensburg, Washington.

38. Rosalie Blau, *Los Angeles Nursery School News Bulletins* (March 1936; April–May 1936). RB, CSUN. Blau's WPA nursery school, Jewish Mothers' Alliance, was located at 244 North Breed St. in the Boyle Heights neighborhood of Los Angeles.

39. Drawing of a floor plan. In *WPA Bulletin #2: Housing and Equipment of Emergency Nursery Schools* (1933) 13. See also Rose Alschuler, *Children's Centers* (1942) 103. Her son, John, then an architecture student at MIT, drew this design. Her oldest son, Alfred, also an architect, worked closely with modernist Mies van der Rohe in Chicago. In an August 28, 1942 letter to Edna Noble White, Alschuler acknowledged that she revised WPA nursery school bulletins (1,2,5 adding "50% more") to create her 1942 work.

40. Marian Post Wolcott, *Fathers are Parents, Too! [FSA Photo]*. In *Children's Centers* (New York: Morrow, 1942) 85.

41. Nurses and/or teachers examined their eyes, ears, throat, and skin surfaces for any sign of infection. Children suspected of being sick were sequestered until their parents could pick them up. In the event of a medical emergency, teachers accompanied the children to the hospital and/or nearest doctor.

42. Nursery school schedule from WPA, *Federal Emergency Nursery Schools and Parent Education Activities in Minnesota, 1935–36.* Time analysis is based on composites taken from 10 different WPA nursery school schedules, 390–420 minutes at school daily. In seven sketches depicting young children playing, eating, resting, and attending to their bodily functions, Stolz presented the standard WPA nursery school schedule. See Lois Meek Stolz, *Your Child's Development and Guidance* [drawings by Lucia Manley] (1940) 38–42.

43. George Stoddard, "Emergency Nursery Schools on Trial" *Childhood Education* 11 (March 1935) 260. Although private nursery schools maintained daily inspections throughout the Depression, they minimized basic health needs because their wealthier clientele generally had access to medical care. Instead, private schools focused on behavior modification and/or habit training, such as establishing "healthy" toilet training routines. [See Dorothy Baruch, *Parents and Children Go to School* (1939) 171–185 and Jennie Haxton and Edith Wilcox, *Step by Step in the Nursery School* (1936)]. As characterized by Catherine Landreth of UC Berkeley's Child Welfare Center, children on relief needed immunizations and medical treatment; at private schools, children were under the care of a family doctor or pediatrician. See *Education of the Young Child* (1942) 19.

44. Dorothea Lange, *Rest time in nursery school for migrant children at Shafter Camp, California.* February 1939. Library of Congress, Prints & Photographs Division, FSA/OWI Collection, LC-USF346-T01-018816-E. This photo also found in the Helen Gahagan Douglas papers at the University of Oklahoma.

45. Questions included: when had the child last seen a doctor; had the child been a full-term birth; when was the child weaned; had the child had smallpox,

72 American Modernism and the WPA

diphtheria, scarlet fever, measles; and did the child have physical handicaps or disabilities.

46. *Emergency Nursery Schools during the First Year, 1933–1934* (compiled by John Anderson) determined children were in need of considerable health service: 43% had bad tonsils; 26% bad adenoids; 19.3% had teeth in poor condition; only 9.7% of the children rated as robust. See also Ruth Andrus, "The Nursery School, A Child Welfare Center" and Grace Langdon, "Coordination of Agencies in Carrying on WPA Nursery Schools" *Progressive Education* (October 1938) 469–484.

47. Height and weight measurements, especially, helped school staff detect malnutrition in children.

48. *WPA Bulletin #1* (1933) 19. The American Academy of Pediatrics, *Caring for Your Baby and Young Child: Birth to Age 5* states that those from two to three need 9–13 hours a day and those four to five need 10–12 hours a day. "Unless she routinely becomes irritable and overtired from lack of sleep, there's no reason to force a nap schedule on your child" (1998) 368. The fifth edition (2009) favors more structured daytime napping for ages 2 to 5—see pp. 347, 381, 842–844.

49. Grace Langdon, "Coordination of Agencies in Carrying on WPA Nursery Schools" *Progressive Education* 15 (October 1938) 475. When children did not fall asleep immediately, they rested or played quietly under watchful eyes. Children slept in individual cots whenever possible.

50. WPA, *Federal Emergency Nursery Schools and Parent Education Activities in Minnesota* (1935–1936) 15 mentions its surplus commodities as beef, rice, and prunes.

51. According to *WPA Bulletin #4* (1936) 99.

52. Mary Sweeny and Dorothy Buck, *How to Feed Children in Nursery Schools* (1936) 40. As these two authors remarked, "Any icing on cakes is undesirable for children. Plain cakes are low in fat and sugar, are very palatable and can be included in a child's menu" (39). Sweeny was colleagues with Edna Noble White at Merrill-Palmer, and worked with WPA nursery schools in Detroit. She pioneered in research on young children's nutritional needs and also worked with Stolz at the Kaiser Centers in Portland during World War II. See also Mary Sweeny and Marian Breckenridge, *How to Feed Children in Nursery Schools* (1944).

53. Private nursery programs served lunch but often had different reasons for doing so. UCLA's laboratory school served lunch to its children in order to help problem eaters modify their food habits and table manners. Campbell WPA nursery school in Oakland, however, served lunch because otherwise its young charges went hungry. See Barbara Greenwood and Charles Waddell, *A Six—Year Experiment with a Nursery School* (1931) 87–103 and Catherine Landreth, *Education of the Young Child* (1942) 57–68.

54. According to www.littletokyounplugged.org/prop40.aspx, Amelia Street School (1885–1952) was Little Tokyo's second public elementary school at 611 Jackson Street and educated children of Japanese, Chinese and Mexican immigrants. In 1936, Salisbury had one Chinese student. Two-thirds of the children were Japanese, and nearly one-third Mexican—ten students remained on the waiting list.

55. Helen Salisbury, *Los Angeles Nursery School News Bulletins* (March 1936; April–May 1936). RB, CSUN.

56. "Pupils Find Ideal Spots" *Los Angeles Times* (July 12, 1936) A.

57. Margaret Mead and Carl Guthe, *The Problem of Changing Food Habits* (Washington, DC, 1941–43) 141–149. See also Eunice Fuller Barnard, "Food Joins the 3 Rs" *Survey Graphic* 32 (November 1943). For more on school

American Modernism and the WPA   73

lunches, see Jane Ziegelman and Andrew Coe, *A Square Meal: A Culinary History of the Great Depression* (2016).

58. Russell Lee, *Children eating lunch at WPA (Work Projects Administration) nursery school at the Agua Fria migratory labor camp, Arizona. May 1940.* Library of Congress, Prints & Photographs Division, FSA/OWI Collection, LC-USF347-036141-D.

59. WPA, *Federal Emergency Nursery Schools and Parent Education Activities in Minnesota* (1935–1936) 49–50.

60. Ruth Andrus and Eugene Horowitz's study of children's feelings of insecurity in WPA nursery schools remains a case in point. In order to undermine the notion that "you can't change personality"—a view they believed was behind opposition to public nursery schools—they tried to show that the WPA programs enhanced children's sense of security. Their project was doomed from the start, however, because they were neither able to define security nor to collect data on children's positive emotional feelings. Instead, they focused solely on collecting data about children's negative (insecure) behaviors like "whining, crying and tattling to get attention." See Ruth Andrus and Eugene Horowitz, "The Effect of Nursery School Training: Insecurity Feelings" *Child Development* 9 (June 1938) 169–174. Their study was completed before Lawrence Frank's speech in November 1937.

61. Rosalie Blau and her former WPA nursery school colleagues in Los Angeles, for instance, talked about habit formation and the "Toronto School" ideas of William Blatz in Annette Bothman, *Reflections of the Pioneers on the Early History of the Santa Monica Children's Centers and Changing Child-Rearing Philosophies* (Unpublished Master's thesis, May 1976). The program was only mildly influenced by behaviorist John Watson, whose classic *Psychological Care of Infant and Child* was panned in *Progressive Education* 6 (January–March 1929) 77–79. Lois Meek Stolz said she never recalled him dominating the field as historians assumed he had. Stolz also asserted that Watson recanted his "no touching" directives after completing more research. See especially Stolz's oral history conducted by Ruby Takanishi, *An American Child Development Pioneer: Lois Meek Stolz* (Stanford University, 1978). Stolz provided an overview of how child psychologists changed their study of children's fears over time in *Our Changing Understanding of Young Children's Fears, 1920–1960* (1964). See also Grace Langdon's *Home Guidance for Young Children: A Parents' Handbook* (1946).

62. See William Burnham, "Mental Hygiene in the Preschool Period" *Progressive Education* (December 1934) 441–444 for its emphasis on self-reliance; Lois Murphy, "Emotional Development and Guidance in Nursery School and Home" *Childhood Education* (April 1936) 306–311 for emphasis upon emotional vibrancy; Josephine Foster and Marion Mattson, *Nursery—School Education* (1939) for emphasis upon appropriate emotional responses; and Alice Groth, "Sex Education: A Factor in Mental Health" *Childhood Education* (February 1935) 223–226 for emphasis upon healthy attitudes towards sex.

63. Langdon-Clark, *Child Welfare Foundation* (Long Beach, CA, July, 1939). Langdon's emphasis was that children develop at different paces. On October 6–7, 1940, Langdon also gave a talk for WPA teachers on "Individual Development of the Child" at a nursery school exhibit at Rutgers University. NARA.

64. As head of the Laura Spelman Rockefeller Memorial (LSRM) fund from 1923–28, Frank was the primary sponsor of pioneer nursery schools in the US (see Chapter 1). Frank also provided the seed money for the WPA nursery school program through another Rockefeller foundation, the General Education Fund in 1933. Frank's ground-breaking study, "The Fundamental Needs of the Child" *Mental Hygiene* 22 (July 1938) 353–379. The quote is from page

74 *American Modernism and the WPA*

377. Stolz stressed love as early as 1935, but Frank acted as the harbinger of change. Frank was also influenced at that time by Freudianism.

65. See, for example, Rose Alschuler, "Guidance Needed" *Progressive Education* (October 1938) 459–467; Lois Murphy, "The Nursery Years" *Progressive Education* (May 1941) 243–246; and Beth Wellman, "The Need for Nursery Education" *Progressive Education* 19 (March 1942) 147–149.

66. See Lois Murphy, "The Nursery School Contributes to Emotional Development" *Childhood Education* (May 1940) 404–407 and Claudia Lewis, *Children of the Cumberland* (1946) 26.

67. See, for example, Dorothy Baruch, *Parent and Child Go to School* (1939) 186–204. See also Catherine Landreth, *Education of the Young Child* (1942) 130–142 and Susan Isaacs, "Security" *Child Study* 15 (November 1937) 35–37. The notion of security took on added importance following the onset of World War II. See in particular, Jimmy Hymes, "Building the Post–War World Now" *Childhood Education* 19 (March 1943) 300–303; Katherine Whiteside Taylor, "Changing Family Life—Its Implications for Teachers" *Childhood Education* 20 (October 1943) 55–61; and Nancy Bayley, "The Emotions of Children: Their Development and Modification" *Childhood Education* 21–22 (December 1944) 156–159.

68. Dorothy Baruch, "Therapeutic Procedures as Part of the Educative Process" *Journal of Consulting Psychology* 4 (September–October 1940) 165–172. Baruch focused on the "developing personality" of young children in advocating play therapy. In April 1941, Lawrence Frank mailed eighty copies of this article to Langdon for her to distribute in WPA nursery schools. NARA. "Personality" remained the focus of the 1950 White House Conference on Children and Youth. Vice Chairmen of this conference included former WPA stalwart, George Stoddard. See Helen Leland Witmer and Ruth Kotinsky, *Personality in the Making* (1952) and Marilyn Irvin Holt, *Cold War Kids: Politics and Childhood in Postwar American, 1945–1960* (2014).

69. See, for example, Henry Jenkins, "The All-American Handful: Dennis the Menace, Permissive Childrearing and the Bad Boy Tradition" http://web.mit.edu/21fms/People/henry3/dennis.html. Jenkins refers to Baruch as well as to Jimmy Hymes. Grace Langdon, "How a Baby Learns" *Parents' Magazine* 19 (May 1944) is also cited in Julia Wrigley, "Girls, Boys, and Emotions: Redefinitions and Historical Change" *Journal of American History* 80 (June 1993) 36–74. See also Robert Genter, *Late Modernism: Art, Culture and Politics in Cold War America* (2011); John Burnham, *After Freud Left: A Century of Psychoanalysis* (2012); and Ann Marie Kordas, *The Politics of Childhood in Cold War America* (2013).

70. Lois Meek Stolz, *Your Child's Development and Guidance* (1940) 26–27.

71. Dorothy Baruch and J. Risser, "An Experiment with Posture Work in a Nursery School" *Child Development* 6 (December 1935) 269–276.

72. Arthur Rothstein, *Nursery School Playground* (Robstown camp, Texas. January 1942). Library of Congress, Prints & Photographs Division, FSA/OWI Collection, LC-USF34-024865-D.

73. Mary Murphy (WPA Nursery School Advisory Committee member), "Physical Health Needs—Suggested Ways of Meeting Them" *Childhood Education* 9–10 (1938–1939) 11–15.

74. Staff also believed exercise improved metabolism, relieved stress, and helped with motor development. See Lee Vincent, "Why Physical Education in the Early School Years" *Childhood Education* 13 (March 1937) 297–301.

75. George Stoddard, "What of the Nursery School?" *Progressive Education* 14 (October 1937) 443.

American Modernism and the WPA   75

76. As Winifred Bain phrased it in *Parents Look at Modern Education* (10),

> As the youngster gradually goes forth from home, he widens his horizon and builds up new ideas. He sees the world of many things—not too many at first—a world of pictures and books, and fire engines, and airplanes, all of which extend beyond his own backyard.

77. Training manuals placed little emphasis upon rote memorization and the 3 Rs. See, for example, *Workers' conference manual for WPA nursery teachers* (KY WPA and KY Dept. of Ed., 1936) and E. Embler, *Recreational Activities for the Pre-School Child* (NY: WPA Recreation Project, 1938). Many more examples could be added.

78. Lois Lenski's picture books were extremely popular with WPA preschoolers. See Rose Alschuler, *Children's Centers* (1942) 46 and Jean Cook, "Books for Nursery Schools" *Library Journal* 70 (January 1, 1945) 18–20. Lenski herself believed *The Little Auto* "was a little ahead of its time" because of its subject matter (the car) and because of its modernist streamlined look, which "told the story with the fewest possible words and illustrated it with the simplest possible drawings." See Bobbie Malone's thoughtful biography, *Lois Lenski: Storycatcher* (2016) 90–91.

79. Baruch specifically recommended *The New Poetry*, edited by Monroe and Henderson. For analysis of this work, see J. Marek, *Women Editing Modernism: "Little" Magazines and Literary History* (1995). On modernism in children's literature, see Karin Westman, "Children's Literature and Modernism: The Space Between" *Children's Literature Association* (2007) 283–286 and Anne Fernald's November 2015 article, www.publicbooks.org/blog/in-the-great-green-room-margaret-wise-brown-and-modernism, both of which identify modernist markers as love of color, joy in ordinary objects, and repetition with unexpected variation—all found in WPA nursery school libraries.

80. Dorothy Baruch, *Los Angeles Nursery School News Bulletins* (April–May 1936). RB, CSUN.

81. Dorothy Baruch, *Sung Under the Silver Umbrella: Poems for Young Children* (1935) 39. In 1940, Baruch wrote Walt Disney's *Pinocchio* and began writing for the "Dick and Jane" series.

82. MacCarteney co-wrote "Airplane Song" with Edith Newlin. Newlin's "Warm Kitty," also from MacCarteney's 1937 anthology, was featured on the 21st-century hit sitcom *Big Bang Theory*.

83. Free play was defined not as unsupervised play but that which was not formal or teacher directed. See *Nursery Education: White House Conference Proceedings* (1931) 124 and Rose Alschuler and Christine Heinig, *Play: The Child's Response to Life* (1936) 18. Teachers also encouraged preschoolers (and their parents) to create free—form modern art with paints, clay, crayons, scissors, paste, and blocks. In addition, program staff believed children learn most effectively through their own initiatives—by taking risks and by learning from mistakes. That children learn best through free play continues to be widely supported by early childhood specialists, although the debt owed to WPA nursery school leaders is rarely acknowledged. See, "Old-Fashioned Play Builds Serious Skills" (Feb. 21, 2008) www.npr.org and "Taking Play Seriously" (Jan. 29, 2018) www.nytimes.com.

84. Patty Smith Hill quoted in Charlotte Garrison, *Permanent Play Materials for Young Children* (1926), a widely used curriculum manual. See also *WPA Bulletin #2: Housing and Equipment* (1933), *WPA Bulletin #5: Nursery School Equipment* (1936), and Rose Alschuler, *Children's Centers* (1942).

76 American Modernism and the WPA

85. Photo credits, clockwise: Figure 2.7: Lewis Hine, Scott's *Run, West Virginia.* Interior of the Jere WPA nursery. March 19, 1937. National Archives photo no. 69-RP-103. Figure 2.8: Russell Lee, Children looking at picture books at the WPA nursery school at the Casa Grande Valley Farms, Pinal County, Arizona. April-May 1940. Library of Congress, Prints & Photographs Division, FSA/OWI Collection, LC-USF346-036294-D. Figure 2.9: Sing—Along Time: Negro [sic] nursery school at 280 Hickory Street, Buffalo, NY. 1936. National Archives photo no. 69-N-87-5165. Patty Smith Hill's "Happy Birthday to You" and Laura Pendleton MacCarteney's "Open-Shut Them" were two popular songs in WPA nursery schools. Hill's "Happy Birthday" (1893) is regarded as the most recognized song in the English language. Program leaders were also among the first to emphasize music education—children experimenting with rhythm, sound, and instruments in school.

86. Ilse Forest, *The School for the Child from Two to Eight* (1935) 51.

87. Christine Heinig openly acknowledged that many of the best ideas for crafting toys out of "waste" materials (e.g., making a wagon out of a packing box with pie tins for wheels) came from parents. In addition to writing *Bulletin #5,* Heinig also collaborated with Marie Muhlfeld [O'Donohue] to write *Bulletin #2, Housing and Equipment of Emergency Nursery Schools* (1933).

88. Drawing of a spool-doll. In *WPA Bulletin #5: Nursery School Equipment* (1936) 32.

89. *WPA Bulletin #5* (1936) 16, 31–32. See also ACE's best-selling book from 1939, *Uses for Waste Materials* and www.mpm.edu/research-collections/history/online-collections-research/wpa-milwaukee-handicraft-project.

90. See Mary Kellogg Rice, *Useful Work for Unskilled Women: A Unique Milwaukee WPA Project* (Milwaukee: Milwaukee County Historical Society, 2003) www.uwm.edu/People/lquinn/wpa.htm and Irma Hochstein, "A Brief Summary of Facts on Emergency Nursery Schools in Milwaukee County" undated (late 1930s?), 2 pages. NARA.

91. In this sense, program staff may have been trying to disentangle modernism from the conspicuous consumption that the historian Gary Cross outlines so well in *Kids' Stuff: Toys and the Changing World of American Childhood* (1997). In *Children at Play: An American History* (2007), the historian Howard Chudacoff argues the turning point in children's play occurred when commercial toys began to be advertised on television in the 1950s.

92. Christine Heinig (author of the two curriculum manuals on play for the program) quoted by Sally MacDougall in "Nursery Schools in 36 States Improve Children in Health and Spirit" *New York World-Telegram.* Reprinted in *Teachers College Record* 35 (May 1934) 73.

93. *Bulletin #4: Suggestions for Record Keeping in Nursery Schools* (1936) 44–55.

94. Rose Alschuler and Christine Heinig, *Play: The Child's Response to Life* (1936) 19 and Josephine Foster and Marion Mattson, *Nursery School Education* (1939) 253. See also Dorothy Van Alstyne, *Play Behavior and Choice of Play Materials of Pre-School Children* (1932); Ethel Kawin, *The Wise Choice of Toys* (1934/1938). All were highly recommended in WPA circles throughout the course of the program, 1933–43.

95. Rose Alschuler, *Children's Centers* (1942) 39. Most blocks used in WPA nursery schools were homemade.

96. Figure 2.11 [hammer/nails]: Helen Post, "Three and Four-Year Olds Work Together" in *Curriculum Guides: For Teachers of Children from Two to Six Years of Age* (New York: John Day, 1936) 165. Figure 2.12 [sand-box]: Russell Lee, Children of the nursery school at the FSA (Farm Security Administration)

American Modernism and the WPA 77

farm family migratory labor camp. Yakima, Washington. September 1941. Library of Congress, Prints & Photographs Division, FSA/OWI Collection, LC-USF34-070239-D.

97. Drag blocks, which children used outdoors, were hollow, larger, and had rope handles attached. Rose Alschuler, *Children's Centers* (1942) 124–127.

98. Throughout the 1930s, companies like Fisher Price successfully marketed unit blocks by changing Pratt's dimensions slightly. See Ruth Updegraff, *Practice in Preschool Education* (1938) 347.

99. In *Inventing Kindergarten* (2002), Norman Brosterman shows that Froebel's gifts also influenced the designs of architect Frank Lloyd Wright. Wright's son John created Lincoln Logs in 1916.

100. Schoenhut Toy Company, one of the finest toy companies of the era, manufactured Hill Floor Blocks.

101. Charlotte Garrison (with Hill introduction), *Permanent Play Materials for Young Children* (1926).

102. Harriet Johnson, *The Art of Block Building* (1933) 24. The creative potential of blocks continued to be emphasized for the duration of the program, as evident from Alschuler's *Children's Centers* (1942).

103. Josephine Foster and Marion Mattson, *Nursery School Education* (1939) 99. Some staff members also concluded that class differences persisted: children from professional backgrounds were more prone to fanciful play with blocks, while children from working-class backgrounds were more prone to realistic (fear-inducing) play with blocks. See Francis Markey (NYC), Teacher's College Record (December 1935) and also Claudia Lewis, *Children of the Cumberland*. However, only two WPA nursery school studies concluded that significant gender differences persisted.

104. Similar observations are noted by early childhood specialists today: See Martha Bronson, *The Right Stuff for Children Birth to 8* (1995) and Joe Frost, Sue Wortham, and Stuart Reifel, *Play and Child Development* (2011, 4th edition).

105. Figure 2.13 [outdoor play]: 2.13 Arthur Rothstein, Queens, New York. Nursery school at the Queensbridge housing project. Children playing with blocks. June 1942. Library of Congress, Prints & Photographs Division, FSA/OWI Collection, LC-USW3-004710-D. Figure 2.14 [indoor play]: Lewis Hine, Scott's Run, West Virginia. Interior of the Jero WPA nursery- These children are from unemployed miners' homes. March 19, 1937. National Archives photo no. 69-RP-86. See also hollow-block diagram, *WPA Bulletin #5* (1936) 23 and Schoenhut advertisement for Hill Floor Block in *Childhood Education* (November 1942) 144.

106. Until quite recently, construction materials like blocks and Legos were marketed as boy's toys. In *Frailty Myth* (2000), Colette Downing actually makes this plea: in the interests of girls' long-term physical and mental health, get them "out of the doll corner" and playing with blocks!" See also Adrienne LaFrance, "How to Play Like a Girl" *The Atlantic* (May 25, 2016) www.theatlantic.com/entertainment/archive/2016/05/legos/484115/.

107. Josephine Foster and Marion Mattson, *Nursery School Education* (1939) 98. In its stunning 2012 exhibit, "Century of the Child: Growing by Design," The Museum of Modern Art, *MOMA* (using very different source materials) concludes that the interwar material culture of early childhood also helped children learn through play:

If the built environment was central to shaping the larger awareness of modern society, the mental environment of the child also required attention. Interactive picture books and construction toys led children on spatial, temporal,

78 American Modernism and the WPA

and imaginative journeys into the wider world of things and ideas, preparing them to function as members of a modern industrialized society.
www.moma.org/interactives/exhibitions/2012/centuryofthechild/#/
timeline/light—air—health

108. Words of the narrator in the WPA nursery school film clip from "A Better Ohio" (1937). NARA.

109. New York World's Fair 1939 and 1940 Incorporated Records 1935–1945 http://archives.nypl.org/mss/2233, p. 8. The fair's emphasis on the World of Tomorrow is often regarded as the most spectacular celebration of modernism ever held in the United States, but little attention has been given to its WPA exhibit. See, for example, Barbara Cohen et al., *Trylon and Perisphere: The 1939 New York World's Fair* (1989) and Robert Rydell et al., *Designing Tomorrow: America's World's Fairs of the 1930s* (2010).

110. See R. Roger Remington and Robert Fripp, *Design and Science: The Life and Work of Will Burtin* (2007) 30. Philip Guston's mural in front of the WPA Building, "Advancing America's Skills," won first prize for outdoor murals at the fair. See https://digitalcollections.nypl.org/items/5e66b3e8-da10-d471-e040-e00a180654d7.

111. *WPA helps children and parents to be happier.* In *FWA 1940 New York World's Fair Report.* Library of Congress, Prints & Photographs Division, LOT 14178 (H).

112. "FWA 1940 New York World's Fair Report" www.loc.gov/pictures/item/2016647202/. "Nursery School Exhibit" photos in author's possession, courtesy of Lara Szypszak, Library of Congress, Prints & Photographs Division (December 2016).

113. See especially *WPA at 1939 Fair* https://digitalcollections.nypl.org/items/5e66b3e8-b8f3-d471-e040-e00a180654d7 and *Makers of cot, blankets & toys* http://archives.nypl.org/2233#detailed.

114. See Mary Kellogg Rice, *Useful Work for Unskilled Women: A Unique Milwaukee WPA Project* (Milwaukee: Milwaukee County Historical Society, 2003) www.uwm.edu/People/lquinn/wpa.htm and "The WPA Dolls of Milwaukee" http://newdeal.feri.org/dolls/index.htm.

3 The WPA Nursery School and the Community

Local communities played an important role in the program. They provided play equipment, clothing, transportation, and health services, and in so doing, turned schools into community projects, "something to which everyone can contribute and from whose services everyone can derive benefit."[1] One observer gave credit to such widespread involvement for helping turn "dirty, rickety, ragged and sullen" children into "clean, stronger, even smiling" toddlers. The schools affected the communities in turn:

> Parents, watching the change, have come into the school to see how the miracle is wrought. Somehow it has become their school. Mothers have met to sew on new curtains and towels for it, often under the tutelage of home economics teachers. . . . Out of barrels and boxes, fathers have built toys, cots and other equipment. And frequently more wholesome ways of living have penetrated the crowded homes. Often the whole community becomes interested.[2]

Community involvement on behalf of young children proved essential because the program received insufficient federal funding, a situation that worsened over time. For the first two years, states could use up to 20% of their WPA education budget for the nursery school program, which itself enjoyed designated federal funding until late 1938. Yet from the outset, Congress also demanded that WPA relief funds be used only for teacher salaries and food. Although the Civil Works Administration initially paid for furniture, equipment, and necessary remodeling, local communities generally bore all other expenses: rent (if charged), play equipment, and utility bills.[3] But funding declined after the November 1938 election, when a Congress hostile to the New Deal was elected, WPA Director Harry Hopkins left his post to become FDR's Secretary of Commerce, and the Dies Committee, which investigated un-American activities, accused the WPA of harboring communists.[4] Within months, staff salaries became one victim of an increasingly stingy Congress, and the program stopped paying for school lunches nationwide.

The program offset these cuts as it had earlier deficiencies—with community support. Local businesses, civic groups, and child welfare agencies volunteered time and labor, as well as money and supplies, to keep WPA

80 The WPA Nursery School and the Community

nursery schools running smoothly. In some cases, town councils picked up food expenditures. In other communities, local professionals, lay organizations, service clubs, and welfare groups banded together through central advisory committees that pooled contributions.[5] As a result, the number of WPA nursery schools did not decrease precipitously even when Congress forced Langdon to dismiss well-trained teachers.[6] Although not all local communities could sustain the program financially, the program endured because of strong local support:

> [Communities] wanted to keep the nursery schools. They weren't sufficiently well established that they were financially secure. . . . They had to have that Federal payroll and a good deal of supervision, but they were locally popular.[7]

This chapter examines the depth and breadth of the program and shows how WPA nursery schools became community schools. It examines the program's community outreach through parent education and looks at the schools as a space for community activism.

Community Schools

WPA nursery schools enjoyed widespread community support throughout the Depression, even as some public schools eliminated their kindergartens.[8] By 1936, the schools could be found in all forty-eight states.[9] On average, fifteen hundred schools were open at any given point from 1933 to 1943.

Table 3.1 Nationwide Distribution of WPA Nursery Schools[10]

Region	50 and over	25–50 schools	10–25 schools	10 and under
Northeast (12 states)	MA 165 New York 63 PA 52	Connecticut 25 W Virginia 48	R. Island 21 New Jersey 21 Maryland 18 Vermont 12 N Hampshire 12	Maine 6 Delaware 3
Midwest (12 states)	Ohio 98 Illinois 80 Michigan 51	Minnesota 35 Iowa 32 Indiana 31 Missouri 31	Kansas 22 Nebraska 14 N. Dakota 11	Wisconsin 10 S. Dakota 10
South (12 states)	Kentucky 67 Florida 54	Tennessee 35 Georgia 35 Virginia 31 N. Carolina 28	Alabama 23 Oklahoma 13 Louisiana 11	Arkansas 9 S. Carolina 8 Miss. 7
West (12 states)	California 62	Washington 35 Texas 32 New Mexico 31 Colorado 25	Arizona 19 Montana 17 Idaho 17 Oregon 15	Utah 8 Nevada 3 Wyoming 3

The WPA Nursery School and the Community 81

Distinct regional patterns emerged.[11] From 1933 to 1943, the Northeast consistently maintained high numbers of WPA nursery schools. The Midwest began with very high numbers, but overall growth fell sharply given the mandatory removal of single female teachers by the Midwestern WPA regional supervisor in 1938, which Langdon and her boss Florence Kerr protested but proved powerless to prevent.[12] The South witnessed a more gradual decline. Areas with large pockets of white poverty (Kentucky and Florida, for instance) operated many WPA nursery schools, and the program provided employment and education to African American women and children in most Southern states.[13] George Stoddard held out high hopes for the South, characterizing the growth of WPA nursery schools there as "a folk movement springing up from deeply felt but long-neglected needs on the part of the great mass of mothers and fathers who, having children, want to do well by them."[14] Nonetheless, the number of WPA nursery schools in the South had fallen by the early 1940s.

Steady upward growth marked the number of WPA nursery schools in the West.[15] Some growth was due to the Resettlement Division of the Farm Security Administration's having opened sixty-three nursery schools for migratory workers in the late 1930s.[16] Half of these were in California (11), Texas (7), Arizona (5), Oregon (5), and Washington (4).[17] In addition, growth may have been spurred because those involved with the program in Western states remained committed to the principle that "schools be open to children of every race and creed."[18] Grace Langdon noted how one form of racial prejudice broke down at Sawtelle Nursery School in Los Angeles when an African American boy enrolled. At first, "the parents of the other children (mostly from Oklahoma) objected but have now come to accept the situation. He was playing happily with other children when I visited." She also told that the mothers at Santa Barbara school "insisted that the negro assistant teacher, who was very capable, be made head teacher rather than close the school" after the head teacher was laid off.[19] Thank you letters to FDR, Harold Ickes, and others show that the parents of minority communities were often grateful for the schools.[20]

Yet not all school efforts to serve minority communities necessarily led to feelings of mutual goodwill. Despite the smiling faces of children in photos, it remains unclear, for example, how Native Americans felt about WPA nursery schools located on reservations or how Chinese Americans viewed their segregated nursery schools in San Francisco.[21] The voices of Japanese Americans remained largely silent.[22] Attempts to provide high-quality early childhood education to these children may not always have engendered goodwill, even as schools in New Mexico and Colorado, in addition to those in Southern California, opened their doors to all.

Figure 3.1 Manzanar Nursery School[23]

Psychologists on the east coast looked for ways their research with WPA nursery school children could help combat racial prejudice more widely. Anticipating what Dr. Martin Luther King, Jr. would later call "The Beloved Community," they crafted studies to explore how young children develop racial consciousness.[24] Their ambitious goal was to root out racism at its very beginnings in order to create a more tolerant, inclusive, and cooperative society.

In 1938, Ruth Horowitz (née Hartley) designed a study to determine the emergence of racial attitudes in young children.[25] Horowitz interviewed 24 children from ages two to five at an integrated WPA nursery school in New York City.[26] Using a set of pictures (photos and line drawings of white and African American girls and boys), she asked, "*Which one is you? Which one is—?*" She also asked the girls to identity "brothers," meaning siblings. Horowitz followed up by showing each child a set of ten portraits and asking "*Is this you? Is this—?*"

According to Horowitz, girls generally correctly identified those with their own skin color but were less certain about which boys ought to be regarded as brothers, sometimes choosing white and sometimes African American boys. The boys, meanwhile, were all over the place as to which pictures they related to themselves. Her tentative findings suggested that

The WPA Nursery School and the Community   83

African American preschoolers had a somewhat developed sense of racial identity, but that more research was needed to better explain the development of racial attitudes. That some of these children were used to racist language was clearly apparent. One four-year-old white girl asserted, "This is a nigger doll.—That ain't my brother, he's white." Horowitz posited that children learned this language at home.[27] She also noted that at least one African American boy resisted making skin color a primary form of identity:

> The possibility of conflict in the process of learning to accept that one is different from others was illustrated by one of the Negro boys. It was he who, when confronted with the set of four pictures, identified with *both* boys. In so doing he overlooked the more obvious pattern-component which the other children saw. The pattern he chose to interpret was more abstract and more difficult. Although this same lad identified correctly in the cases in which he had to make one of two choices, after one of these choices, he said quite spontaneously that the White boy was his brother. It was he, too, who objected when by accident he observed one of the White children point to one of the pictures and say, *"That's a black boy."* He shouted vehemently, *"No, it ain't; it ain't a black boy;—it's a big boy."*[28]

In 1939, Mamie Clark designed a set of experiments inspired by Horowitz and her own 1938 master's thesis at Howard University.[29] In collaboration with her husband, Kenneth Clark, she focused the scope of her inquiry on 150 African American children in segregated schools in Washington, D.C.[30] Like Horowitz, Clark found girls' responses to be inconclusive as to which boys should be considered a brother. Unlike Horowitz, however, she reported that boys' responses showed a marked age difference. In her much larger sample, three-year-olds showed a range of responses, but a clear majority of four-year-old boys correctly identified their race. She concluded that African American boys developed racial consciousness between the ages of three and four.[31] In a follow-up, the Clarks contrasted the segregated schools of D.C. with two integrated WPA nursery schools in New York City, finding "Racial identification as a phase of ego-consciousness develops comparatively later in the mixed nursery school subjects."[32]

Then, in what would become their most famous study, the Clarks devised a series of experiments with dolls in 1940.[33] The two psychologists tried to determine the racial preferences of 253 African American children from ages three to seven, using data from both integrated schools in the North and segregated schools in the South.[34] Results corroborated their earlier findings regarding racial identity: young children understood skin color literally but not yet as an abstract racial construct.[35] When asked to "Give me the doll that looks like you," 80% of the lighter-skinned children handed over a white doll while 81% of darker-skinned children chose the black doll. Yet in terms of racial preference, the Clarks discovered that nearly two-thirds

84 The WPA Nursery School and the Community

of these African American children chose the white dolls as the ones they would like to play with or thought looked nice. A marked increase in such a preference occurred around age four:

> It seems justifiable to assume from these results that the crucial period in the formation and patterning of racial attitudes begins at around four and five years. . . . At these ages these subjects appear to be reacting more uncritically in a definite structuring of attitudes which conforms with the accepted racial values and mores of the larger environment.[36]

In interpreting children's choice of white as a form of internalized self-hatred that increased with both age and segregation from the larger society, the Clark studies played a historically significant role in the landmark Supreme Court case of *Brown v. Board of Education* (1954).[37] The decision echoed the ways in which the earlier findings of Ruth Horowitz, Mamie Clark, and their husbands had helped WPA nursery schools fight Jim Crow. Langdon and other leaders had one more compelling reason to promote their program. To combat racism, children needed to be taught carefully, preferably in integrated nursery schools, during the formative stage of racial consciousness.[38]

Despite the WPA's success in creating integrated nursery schools, some localities resisted. The New Deal resettlement community of Arthurdale, for example, was home to one of the most publicized WPA nursery schools of the 1930s. Located in the Appalachian Mountains of West Virginia, Arthurdale became a pet project of Eleanor Roosevelt. Although she supported integration, Roosevelt and other high-profile New Dealers deferred to the wishes of the majority of impoverished miners who resided in Arthurdale, and the school remained open to white children only.[39]

Founder Elsie Clapp did not discuss segregation when recounting her experiences, but she did emphasize that the nursery school became "the heart and spring of community education at Arthurdale."[40] Arthurdale was "a school not only for, but of and by the community" because it offered toy-building classes for adults, discounted food and medical supplies for all families, and a clinic for babies.[41] In 1934, the head teacher offered evening classes to help parents craft Christmas toys for their children. "The parents were delighted. Husbands and wives came and worked together. The place was crowded with workers and onlookers."[42] On Christmas morning, parents helped teachers "collect from the families food, extra canned goods, and toys they could spare, for other people in the neighborhood less fortunate than they."[43] The staff also introduced well-baby clinics, inviting mothers to bring their babies to the nursery school for preventative care. On May 23, 1935,

> There were 23 babies, out of a possible 30, present. Dr. Timbres examined the children, and [Nurse] Plummer showed the mothers how to

wash the buttocks and put on a diaper. There were sample packets containing nose swabs, cotton, zinc oxide ointment, and talcum powder, for sale for five cents. Most of the mothers bought them.[44]

Because staples of the local diet (e.g., fresh pork, fried potatoes, green beans cooked with bacon, buckwheat cakes) lacked vital nutrients, staff urged mothers to feed their infants vegetables, fruit juices, and cod liver oil:

> At several of the clinics the doctor talked to the mothers about the use of Heinz strained baby foods [which] were placed on sale at the Arthurdale Co-operative Store. Many of the mothers have been buying these, and those who could not afford them have been shown how vegetables can be puréed for young children.[45]

Arthurdale nursery school came to function as a food cooperative, recreation center, and public health clinic.[46] It moved beyond rhetoric to become a true community school, helping young children and local families thrive in hard times.[47] Arthurdale residents, including those who participated in the WPA nursery school, continued to hold annual reunions long after the school's closing in 1941.[48]

Figure 3.2 Arthurdale Nursery School[49]

86 The WPA Nursery School and the Community

Parent Education

"Modern parents are confused, questing, thwarted. They ask for help," declared Lois Meek Stolz.[50] To help parents, "WPA nursery school leaders designed a program that educated parents about children's behavior, health and nutritional needs, and the services they could find at community agencies to assist them in caring for their children."[51] Working together, parents and teachers helped young children navigate between the cooperative ideals of school and the competitive nature of society.[52]

Yet it was not just for the children's sake that program leaders promoted parent education. WPA Director Harry Hopkins saw the participation of parents as a way to "raise their morale and that of the entire family and the community."[53] Similarly, teachers and parent-educators saw their job as a form of community outreach that focused on what parents needed and helped solve family problems by considering the circumstances that affected the adults.[54] Such home-school cooperation was meant to bring about a New Deal in education "that matters, that changes people significantly, that can in any way direct social change."[55]

Program leaders began by adopting the idea that adults needed education in order to become effective parents:

> It is as silly to trust the maternal instinct to bring up a child as to trust the acquisitive instinct to earn a living for the family. Instinct is at the base of all we do, but does not relieve us of the necessity of training.[56]

Leaders emphasized more than educating parents.[57] They set up parent observation and parent-teacher conferences, practices common to university (laboratory) nursery schools and cooperative nursery schools.[58] They also revived the tradition of home visits, which kindergarten reformers had used prior to World War I, and incorporated group meetings as "the best method" for educating parents.[59] Embracing both the approach progressive-era kindergarten reformers had taken with the poor as well as practices that had developed in upper-middle-class nursery schools and middle-class cooperatives during the 1920s, program leaders created a hybrid form of parent education to reach WPA families.

As creators of a hybrid model, program administrators and teachers relinquished their status as experts, no longer presuming that professionals knew best.[60] WPA nursery school staff learned to address parents' interests by consistently listening to their reports on their own children.[61] Working with parents also allowed a way to deal with some issues involving the school and local communities. In one neighborhood, a rumor that children were being doped emerged from the inclusion of daytime naps in the schedule. Teachers were able to put the story to rest by inviting parents to take turns helping the teacher and seeing for themselves what actually went on.[62] There was also a benefit in acknowledging to the parents that the teachers were

The WPA Nursery School and the Community   87

imperfect: "A willingness on the part of the educator to let the parent know her own weaknesses and faults, in other words, to be altogether human, will ease the parents and relieve tensions on both sides."[63]

Parents participated in WPA nursery schools in many ways: filling out forms about their children's home behavior, observing classroom activities, making hot lunches, building toys, and attending meetings. Although parent volunteers were always involved, WPA nursery schools were not parent cooperatives. They kept the idea of parent participation alive during the 1930s, but they never placed the burden of running the schools exclusively on parents' shoulders, nor did they require parents to underwrite school finances entirely.[64] WPA nursery schools gave many parents a much-needed break from their children. As one mother put it, "I can love 'em a lot when they ain't under foot all day."[65] Deliberately intent on creating good outcomes for both children and their parents, program leaders designed a new parent education program during the Great Depression. It aimed not at telling parents they were doing a bad job but to offer help "in the solution of home difficulties."

From 1933–1943, well over half of the WPA's formal parent education program took place through its nursery schools. Emphasizing visual learning devices such as charts and exhibits, educators rarely used lectures or textbooks.[66] Once they established trust, discussions moved beyond family issues to radio broadcasts, plays, movies, and current magazine articles. More than a year before Pearl Harbor, parent groups in Mississippi talked about whether the United States should declare war on Japan and how to combat racial prejudice at the local level. Hoping to improve the status of African Americans in Mississippi, one local parent educator suggested considering whether white Mississippians might improve their status by "raising the Education, Health, and Economic Level of the Negro." In reply, this leader remarked, "Ignorance is not good for any people or for any righteous cause. . . . It is not good for either race or for our beloved state that half of our population be denied the right of intelligence."[67]

Demand for this sort of parent education soon outstripped the resources of the WPA nursery school program. As a result, local WPA administrators adapted the nursery school model to such other forms of adult education as literacy instruction. In Iowa, adult educators focused their curriculum more broadly than on individual development "because the whole emergency education program had arisen out of a crisis that vitally affected families."[68] Vocational educators helped adults improve their skills in carpentry, sewing, and cooking by teaching them to craft toys and clothing and how to select and prepare food for children. By committing itself to meeting parents' needs, the WPA nursery school program maintained close ties to local communities. The WPA described the successful parent educator as:

> in very essence a community leader. She must be able to speak the idiom and understand the problems of the poor, yet at the same time

88   *The WPA Nursery School and the Community*

comprehend the workings of the more complex society in which they live. She must think with them through their blind groping for adjustment, yet be sufficiently objective to show them how to make use of available agencies of society in making that adjustment; and she must be able to enlist the support of those agencies.[69]

Hailed by WPA publicists as the most social and democratic of all WPA education activities, the WPA nursery school parent education program welcomed community involvement.[70] In this way it aimed "to provide that service to parents which can best guide them in the independent solution of their family problems."[71]

Community Activism

Wanting to make it harder for Congress to cut program funding, progressive educators, women's groups, and parents sponsored a national letter-writing campaign in 1935 to achieve more secure appropriations.[72] In November 1938, they organized an even larger campaign because school closures had become an issue. Extant letters to representatives and senators suggest that widespread community support for the program aimed at garnering bipartisan support on Capitol Hill.[73]

Parents wrote especially poignant pleas.[74] In April 1935, coal-mining parents in Oklahoma begged for schools to remain open: "if the Nursery School continues on thro the summer, which we, as a community, sincerely hope it will, our children will be sure of one real good meal a day, when otherwise they wouldn't be."[75] That November, the father of a three-year-old daughter wrote:

> I am a disabled war veteran, unable to contribute anything toward the support of my family and my wife works all day in an office in downtown Los Angeles and barely makes enough to pay car fare, rent, and for the food she and the child eat. . . . It is a great relief to us to know that while we may never do the things we should for our children, they will still get the start in life to which they are entitled.[76]

Late in 1938, a mother from the Bronx wrote:

> We send our children here because we love them, and want them to be kept off the streets. I am also speaking for the widows who send their children here because of their inadequate salary to have paid help. In the name of Humanity, we appeal to you, don't take this away from us, there is so much at stake, do not put this aside as a crank letter, because each and every mother has collaberated [sic] on this mission of mercy which has come from their hearts. Help us.[77]

The WPA Nursery School and the Community   89

Letters like these not only carried political clout, but with "so much at stake," as that mother put it, parent activism moved well beyond writing letters.[78] Mothers in Long Beach, California, for instance, took to the streets in November 1937 when the local WPA office threatened to close their nursery school because of budget cuts.[79] Obtaining the signatures of more than 100 businesses in their neighborhood, these mothers kept the school open and secured a second one that garnered national headlines in early 1942 because it served the widows and children of servicemen who had died at Pearl Harbor.[80]

Parents also looked for alternative funding sources. When Washington State's WPA education program closed temporarily in 1936, parents in ten communities protested so strongly that the schools were converted to kindergartens for the oldest children and became part of the public-school system.[81] Parents in Wyoming, Georgia, and Connecticut also petitioned for public kindergartens.[82] When the economy began to improve in the early 1940s, middle-class parents began parent cooperatives to give their children the opportunity to attend nursery school.[83] WPA parents, on the other hand, generally waited until federal funding ceased before finding an alternative.

Patty Smith Hill encouraged community activism.[84] On March 1, 1934, Hill opened a WPA nursery school at 123rd Street, in Harlem in New York City. Housed in the former Jewish Theological Seminary, Hilltop cared for children who came from the impoverished community just north of Columbia University. On the day Hilltop opened, nearly eighty children stood in line for the thirty spots. The teachers, hired from relief rolls, had been trained at Teachers College. Needing help to pay for the rent and upkeep of the building and equipment, Hill went door to door, and local businesses donated paint and other supplies.[85] She interested parents and other community members in the project.[86] One, Agnes Snyder, was an innovative teacher-education specialist.[87] During the summer of 1934, Snyder and eight of her students investigated the neighborhood in which Hilltop children lived. They took photos, made drawings, and did interviews, including some with young children, about how best to improve their community.[88]

Above all, the community wanted a program for children who were too old for nursery school. Accordingly, Hill and Snyder began a parent cooperative for WPA nursery school graduates.[89] The community also wanted an inexpensive form of family entertainment and opportunities to improve neighborhood race relations. In 1935, Hilltop parents and children staged family plays in which they celebrated holidays from their respective countries of origin and religious backgrounds. Through these plays, families learned to appreciate their Jewish, Protestant, and Catholic neighbors and those from diverse racial and socioeconomic backgrounds. Given a farm, the families also banded together to refurbish it. Working "each according to his ability," they made for themselves a beautiful vacation spot in Monticello, about seventy miles north of New York City.[90]

90   The WPA Nursery School and the Community

Hilltop Nursery School was forced to close its doors in 1937 when the roof caved in, but community activism continued even as Hill and Snyder became frustrated with the local WPA bureaucracy. They sponsored research that promoted integration.[91] After Columbia-affiliated participants drew accusations of being radical influences, Hilltop teachers, parents, and students established the Community Association for Cooperative Education (CACE) to keep their school going.[92] Like the WPA nursery school program itself, CACE believed "solutions of many a problem of education, health, recreation, home-making, and employment can be found" by working together. [93] CACE lived on for more than twenty years.

Community involvement like that achieved at both Arthurdale and Hilltop was a vital component of the program's overall strategy to achieve permanence in public schools.[94] Grace Langdon made this explicit in her October 1938 call for universal preschool:

> By its very nature, the nursery school under the relief set-up is essentially a community service agency . . . such cooperation is evidence of a determination that little children shall not suffer unduly because of devastating economic and social conditions over which they have not control. . . . It is a challenging glimpse of what combined effort might accomplish. It is a beginning. Dare we stop here? Must we not push on to wider understanding, to more self-forgetting cooperation, to a closer knit coordination—to the end that all young children and not merely a few may have their chance?[95]

Yet WPA critics in Congress made it harder to promote public preschools.[96] Especially problematic was the Dies Committee. On December 5, 1938, Langdon's boss, Ellen Woodward, testified on behalf of Federal One Projects (art, literature, and theater) in front of the newly formed committee, which was investigating the WPA for alleged subversive activity. Woodward came on her own, but by trying to be cooperative, she brought unwanted attention to the WPA nursery school program. During questioning about a Children's Theatre 1937 performance of *Revolt of the Beavers* in New York City, Woodward defended the play's worth by naming its consultants all "experts in their particular fields."[97] The first name she gave was that of WPA nursery school program leader Lois Meek Stolz who, in addition to her role as a radical progressive educator and nursery school pioneer, had voted the socialist ticket (as had John Dewey), traveled to the USSR to meet with Lenin's widow, and married a leftist New Dealer.[98] Woodward also confirmed that only three of the more than thirty consultants hired for the theatre program had even read the play, allowing committee members to criticize her inadequate oversight. Because she also admitted she herself had not seen the play, which told of downtrodden beavers who organize a union to overthrow their exploitative boss, the committee deemed her irrelevant

The WPA Nursery School and the Community 91

to their investigation, unfit to judge whether the play she called "fantasy" instead instigated social revolution.[99]

To the Dies Committee, it was obvious that the WPA was using its programs to indoctrinate young children with class consciousness and that child development specialists like Stolz were to blame. To make their point, they quoted influential theatre critic Brooke Atkinson of the *New York Times*, who remarked in his review of *Revolt of the Beavers*, "Mother Goose is no longer a rhymed escapist. She has been studying Marx; Jack and Jill lead the class revolution."[100] Stolz appeared never to recover from the negative publicity she received from Woodward's calling her the primary consultant for a play labeled "communistic."[101] In 1938, she left Columbia, divorced her New Deal husband to marry Herbert Stolz, and moved to the West Coast to reinvent herself as a psychologist. She resigned from the WPA nursery school advisory committee and worked primarily with private early childhood education.[102] Grace Langdon did not retreat, however. Taking the long view, she continued to push for program permanence despite the negative publicity generated by the Dies Committee.

Congress attacked the WPA still more broadly, with other committees joining in. In March 1939, the Appropriations Committee publicized a list of WPA personnel who made over $2000 a year. Taking a cue from the Dies playbook, anti–New Dealers like Congressman D. Parnell Thomas (R-NJ) insinuated that the WPA operated as a haven for leftists, whom he charged with sponging off the government to earn more than those in private industry. One of those he pointed to was Grace Langdon, whose salary of $4500 was higher than that of most men.[103] The agency's leadership also came under attack after Congress killed the Federal Theatre Program and required mandatory layoffs of many of those on work relief.[104]

For Langdon, one silver lining of the political tumult was that she gained a powerful ally in her new boss, Florence Kerr. Kerr managed to hold onto funding for the professional and services projects division of the WPA, even after the CCC and NYA were removed by the Reorganization Act of 1939.[105] Backed by Eleanor Roosevelt, Kerr gave detailed descriptions of WPA projects at the press conferences she held in her new capacity as WPA liaison to the White House. Echoing Langdon, Kerr generated favorable news coverage for the WPA. Shortly after Thanksgiving 1939, Kerr borrowed Langdon's language of community to highlight the benefits of the WPA at the local level:

It costs more to save a life than to provide a cheap coffin. . . . And it is through the white-collar projects of the WPA almost entirely, that a wide variety of professional and technical services have been provided to our communities. It is through the WPA that the children of the nation have been most extensively helped in these recent years. It is through the WPA almost exclusively that needy women with families dependent upon them have been given public employment in different

Figure 3.3 WPA Neighborhood Preschools[106]

kinds of work of value to our communities. In almost every kind of work done with Federal funds in assistance of our communities, the WPA has taken the leading part.[107]

In January 1940, Kerr singled out the WPA nursery school program. Like Langdon, she made community involvement a necessary precondition for achieving program permanence. To the Business and Professional Women's Club of Milwaukee, Wisconsin, Kerr declared:

> I hope you are acquainted with some of our WPA nursery schools. They are under the wing of expert school authorities in the localities where they exist, and I can assure you that they are as good nursery schools as you can find anywhere in this county. We do not have enough of them to make an impressive figure, but each one is important as a "demonstration program" in the locality. Our nursery schools need various kinds of assistance that the school authorities may not be able to give, and so we have Kiwanis Clubs, and Rotary Clubs and Lions Clubs and American Legion Posts as co-sponsors, pledged to help the school in some way. And every once in a while a committee of business men comes around

The WPA Nursery School and the Community 93

to see what it is all about. There is perhaps no human sight so enchanting as a nursery school. The committees usually never knew that such a thing existed, and they are charmed and thrilled, and they go away dazed—wondering why they can't have nursery schools like that for their own children. Well, they can, whenever they make up their minds to it, and someday we will have them in every community, not under the WPA but as a part of our regular school system. We are just carrying the torch, showing communities what they can do.[108]

Grace Langdon must have thought universal preschool just around the corner. With a supervisor who paid homage to the program's excellence, the future looked bright for program permanency.[109] Despite congressional attacks, the WPA nursery school program enjoyed widespread popularity precisely because Langdon and the staff at the federal, state, and local levels had succeeded in creating an innovative curriculum that clearly benefited young children and their families. As national director, Langdon encouraged communities to "make up their minds" to support local schools. Ignoring the politicking as best she could, she remained intent on achieving public preschool for all young children.

Notes

1. Grace Langdon, "Emergency Nursery School—A Community Agency" *Journal of Negro Life* 13 (February 1935) 50.
2. Eunice Fuller Barnard, "Before Reading and Writing" *Survey Graphic* 28 (October 1939) 646. She continued, "It is literally true that a little child has led town after town in these United States to a new community cooperation."
3. Grace Langdon, "The Facts About Emergency Nursery Schools" *Childhood Education* 11 (March 1935) 255–258.
4. In her testimony, the WPA's star witness, Ellen Woodward, defended Lois Meek Stolz. See HUAC, Investigation of Un-American Propaganda Activities in the U.S. Vol. 4, 75th Congress (December 5, 1938) 2810.
5. See Grace Langdon, "Nursery Schools Plus" *School Life* 26 (November 1940) 48–51; Edna Amidon and Muriel Brown, "Community Organization for Family Life Education" *School Life* 26 (November 1940) 38–40; Muriel Brown, "Wichita Program" *School Life* 26 (December 1940) 68–70, 77; Muriel Brown, "And Now Toledo" *School Life* 26 (February 1941) 140–143; and Lucile Emerson, "The Nursery School and Community Cooperation" *School and Society* 53 (April 12, 1941) 477–478.
6. Approximately 1,400 schools (slightly down from the average of 1,500) remained in operation in all areas of the country from 1938–1943.
7. Oral History Interview with Florence Kerr; 4200 Cathedral Avenue, N.W. Washington, DC; October 18, 1963; interviewed by Harlan Phillips for the Archives of American Art, page 34. Entire text available at http://archiveso famericanart.si.edu/oralhist/kerr63.htm.
8. Determining that WPA nursery schools enjoyed high approval ratings at the local level is the subject of Martha Cunningham, "Measurements of Attitudes Toward Nursery Schools" *Journal of Experimental Education* 3 (1935) 88–96 and Girdie Bruce Hutchison-Ware, "Attitudes Toward Emergency Nursery Schools in Oklahoma" (Master's thesis, Oklahoma Agricultural and

94 The WPA Nursery School and the Community

Mechanical College, 1936). See also David Tyack, Robert Lowe, and Elisabeth Hansot, *Public Schools in Hard Times: The Great Depression and Recent Years* (1984).

9. Schools also developed in Washington, D.C., Puerto Rico/Virgin Islands, and Hawaii.

10. Table 3.1 was created using statistics found in Doris Campbell et al., *Educational Activities of the Works Progress Administration* (Washington, DC: US Government Printing Office, 1939) 110 and Catherine Landreth, *Education of the Young Child* (1942) 13.

11. Regional distribution of WPA nursery schools reflected population patterns. The Northeast had the most schools (31%), followed by the Midwest (29%), the South (22%), and the West, including Texas, (18%). Among the states, Massachusetts averaged the greatest number of schools (165); Delaware, Wyoming, and Nevada averaged the fewest (3). See Bureau of the Census, *Statistical History of the US from Colonial Times to the Present* (1965).

12. December 1938 field reports of Florence Kerr vividly show the effect of budget shortfalls on nursery school personnel in the Midwest (in Nebraska and the Dakotas in particular). Isabel Robinson (Langdon's assistant) reported in July 1940 that the program in Iowa had suffered seriously from this mandatory removal of women (30% of the workforce was affected).

13. See Grace Langdon, "Emergency Nursery School—A Community Agency" *Journal of Negro Life* 13 (February 1935) 49–52; James Atkins, "The Participation of Negroes in Pre-School and Adult Education Programs" *Journal of Negro Education* 7 (July 1938) 345–356; and Myrtle Thompson, "Trends in Nursery School Education in the US with Special Reference to the Negro Schools" (Master's thesis, Teachers College of the University of Cincinnati, 1939).

14. George Stoddard, "What of the Nursery School" *Progressive Education* (October 1937) 441–451. See also Morris Mitchell, "Watch the South" *Progressive Education* 16 (September 1939) 342–346.

15. The lone exception was Washington state. Although it had a large number of schools (72) until the late 1930s, the state supervisor quit soon afterwards, and the program was reduced to twelve schools by 1940.

16. According to Langdon, "[FSA] is finding the nursery school an excellent nucleus for the community centers which constitute the heart and soul of the subsistence unit." Director Grace Langdon worked closely with FSA staff, J. O. Walkers and Molly Flynn, in California's Central Valley, for instance.

17. Statistics from Catherine Landreth, *Education of the Young Child: A Nursery School Manual* (1942) 13. See also Eva Evans, "Uncle Sam's Migrant Children" *Childhood Education* 18 (April 1942) 362–366; Susan Fleisher, "Preschool Education for Migrants" *Childhood Education* (December 1943) 181–183; and Mebane Martensen, "Care for Migrants' Children" *Survey Midmonthly* 80 (May 1944) 152–154. Texas also experienced a sharp increase in the early 1940s because of the rise of WPA nursery schools associated with its fledgling defense industry. See Lorena Laas, "A Study of Nursery Schools for Children of Mothers in Wartime Employment" (Master's thesis, Southwest Texas State Teachers College, August 1944).

18. "CWA Nursery Schools for Children" *Literary Digest* 117 (February 24, 1934) 21.

19. *Langdon to Walter Kiplinger: Southern CA Field Report* (July 1941), 11 pages, p. 8. See also "Nursery Like Small World Court" *Los Angeles Times* (June 26, 1944) 12.

20. Colorado letters at the National Archives (RG 69) include: Paul Goffman [concerned citizen on behalf of African American working parents]to Harold Ickes, Secretary of Interior. Colorado Springs, CO. June 13, 1935; Mrs. D. G.

The WPA Nursery School and the Community   95

Green [mother] to Harry Hopkins. Colorado Springs, CO. May 20, 1936 and Mrs. Williamina Adair [mother] to Harry Hopkins. Colorado Springs, CO. May 19, 1936. New Mexico letters include: Earl Mcdaniel [Superintendent of public schools: advocate for his bilingual nursery school children] to Tom L. Popjoy, Director NYA in Santa Fe, NM. Mosquero, NM. May 11, 1936. and Mrs. Mary Margaret Webb [African American working mother] to President Roosevelt. Roswell, NM: February 9, 1939.

21. "Indian Education" *School Life* 21 (October 1935) 34 and Eleanor Roosevelt's "My Day" column (March 16, 1938). See also *The WPA is operating a nursery school project in the YMCA for Chinese children in the Chinatown district of San Francisco. Planned supervised play teaches the children the elements of getting along with their companions* (June 19, 1940). National Archives photo no. 69-N-23614, and *Indian boys enjoy free reading in Vineland, Minnesota,* National Archives photo no. 69-N-22078.

22. Wanda Robertson, curriculum advisor at Topaz, wrote. "It is hoped that the varied kinds of experiences shared by these children will build constructively toward that kind of social maturity so essential to the future citizens of the world. . . . Mothers volunteered part-time service when the shortage of teachers threatened the closing of one of the nursery school centers" (70). Wanda Robertson, "Developing World Citizens in a Japanese Relocation Center" *Childhood Education* (October 1943) 66–71. See also Marian Robertson Wilson, "Wanda Robertson: A Teacher for Topaz" *Utah Historical Quarterly* 69 (2) (2001) 120–138. Chapter 4 of Blythe Hinitz, *The Hidden History of Early Childhood Education* (2013) includes a link to Keiko ['K'] Uchida's depiction of the Topaz nursery school, "Donald Goes to School" *All Aboard* (Spring 1944) 41–42, http://ddr.densho.org/ddr-densho-142-428/. Keiko became an early childhood educator, and her sister (Yoshiko Uchida) wrote an award-winning account of their World War II experience, *Desert Exile: The Uprooting of a Japanese-American Family* (1982). Early childhood specialist Susan Matoba Adler is currently comparing the impact of internment on families and children in Hawaii and Manzanar, CA, where her parents and grandparents were sent.

23. Francis Stewart, *Manzanar Relocation Center, Manzanar, California. Little girls of Japanese descent at nursery school. Evacuees of Japanese ancestry are spending the duration at War Relocation Authority center.* May 28, 1942. National Archives photo no. 210-G-D519.

24. According to www.thekingcenter.org/king-philosophy:

> The Beloved Community is a term that was first coined in the early days of the 20th Century by the philosopher-theologian Josiah Royce, who founded the Fellowship of Reconciliation. However, it was Dr. Martin Luther King, Jr., also a member of the Fellowship of Reconciliation, who popularized the term. . . . Dr. King's Beloved Community is a global vision, in which all people can share in the wealth of the earth. In the Beloved Community, poverty, hunger and homelessness will not be tolerated because international standards of human decency will not allow it. Racism and all forms of discrimination, bigotry and prejudice will be replaced by an all-inclusive spirit of sisterhood and brotherhood. In the Beloved Community, international disputes will be resolved by peaceful conflict-resolution and reconciliation of adversaries, instead of military power. Love and trust will triumph over fear and hatred. Peace with justice will prevail over war and military conflict.

25. Ruth Horowitz, "Racial Aspects of Self-Identification in Nursery School Children" *Journal of Psychology* 7 (1939) 91–99.

96   The WPA Nursery School and the Community

26. Study participants included eleven white boys (ages 3–5), five African American boys (ages 3–4), six white girls (ages 2–5), and two African American girls (age 3).
27. Like Horowitz, Evelyn Helgerson in "The Relative Significance of Race, Sex, and Facial Expression in Choice of Playmate by the Preschool Child" *Journal of Negro Education* 12 (Autumn 1943) 617–622, found that racial prejudice was "generally attributed to the parent." She studied preschool and kindergarten-age children in Minneapolis'—18 of 168 attended a WPA nursery school.
28. Ruth Horowitz, "Racial Aspects of Self-Identification in Nursery School Children" *Journal of Psychology* 7 (1939) 98.
29. Mamie Clark, "The Development of Consciousness of Self in Negro Pre-School Children" (Master's thesis, Howard University, 1938).
30. To these 150 children in five WPA nursery schools, one private nursery school, and one public kindergarten (75 boys and 75 girls, ages 3–5), Clark showed "a series of lined drawing of white and colored boys, a lion, a dog, a clown, and a hen." The boys were asked the same two questions Horowitz used: Show me which one is you. Which one is——? Girls were asked: Show me which one is——? ("using name of brother, boy cousin or boy playmate)."
31. Kenneth Clark and Mamie Clark, "The Development of Consciousness of Self and the Emergence of Racial Identification in Negro Preschool Children" *Journal of Social Psychology* 10 (1939) 591–599.
32. Kenneth Clark and Mamie Clark, "Segregation as a Factor in the Racial Identification of Negro Preschool Children: A Preliminary Report" *Journal of Experimental Education* 8 (December 1939) 161–163. Quote from p. 162.
33. Kenneth Clark and Mamie Clark, "Racial Identification and Preference in Negro Children" *Readings in Social Psychology* (1947) 169–178. The Clarks completed their research in 1940 and 1941, with sponsorship from the Julius Rosenwald Fund.
34. Of these African American children, 119 (47%) attended integrated WPA nursery schools or grades K-1 in the public schools of Springfield, MA. The other 134 (53%) attended segregated WPA nursery schools or grades K-1 in the public schools of Hot Springs, Pine Bluff, and Little Rock, Arkansas. In both regions, most of the children were in kindergarten or first grade. 47% of the children in Massachusetts attended an integrated WPA nursery school, and 37% of the children in Arkansas attended WPA nursery schools. Girls (137) slightly outnumbered boys (116).
35. Kenneth Clark and Mamie Clark, "Skin Color as a Factor in Racial Identification of Negro Preschool Children" *Journal of Social Psychology* 11 (1940) 159–169.

> In this study, Mamie Clark and her husband, Kenneth Clark, focused on how these 150 children of DC defined skin color. Their finding: light-skinned children consistently identified as white while medium and dark-skinned children more commonly defined themselves as colored. Concluded Mamie and Kenneth Clark: "Consciousness of self as different from others on the basis of observed skin color precedes any consciousness of self in terms of socially defined group differences in these Negro children."
>
> (161)

36. The Clarks, "Racial Identification and Preference in Negro Children" *Readings in Social Psychology* (1947) 177.
37. Interviewed in 1985 for *Eyes on the Prize*, Kenneth Clark recalled, "We did the study fourteen years before *Brown*. . . . we did not do it for litigation. We did it to communicate to our colleagues in psychology the influence of race and color and status on the self-esteem of children." The Clark studies have been criticized in recent years for questionable conclusions. See especially, Gwen Bergner,

The WPA Nursery School and the Community 97

"Black Children, White Preference: *Brown v. Board*, the Doll Tests, and the Politics of Self-Esteem" *American Quarterly* (2009) 299–232; and Robin Bernstein, *Racial Innocence: Performing American Childhood from Slavery to Civil Rights* (2011) especially Chapter 5, "The Scripts of Black Dolls." Bernstein sees rejection of black dolls not as victimization or internalized racism but as resistance against a long history of violent play involving black dolls.

38. Grace Langdon called for federal funds to be distributed directly to local schools (as opposed to via block grants to states) as a means to avoid segregation. Former program leaders also conducted studies of perceptions of skin color after World War II. See especially, Catherine Landreth et al., "Young Children's Responses to a Picture and Inset Test Designed to Reveal Reactions to Persons of Difference Skin Color" *Child Development* 24 (March 1953) 63–80. For recent commentary on the benefits of integration, see Thomas Edsall, "Integration Works: Can It Survive the Trump Era?" www.nytimes.com/2017/02/09/opinion/integration-works-can-it-survive-the-trump-era.html.

39. The NAACP, for example, protested Arthurdale's segregation. While this vote for segregation indicated racial prejudice, it also reflected a particular local resentment: African Americans had earlier been brought to the area as strikebreakers during bloody labor struggles. See observations by American Friends Service Committee, Lorena Hickock, and Daniel Perlstein, "Community and Democracy in American Schools: Arthurdale and the Fate of Progressive Education" *Teachers College Record* 97 (Summer 1996) 625–650.

40. Elsie Clapp, *Community Schools in Action* (1939) 216. The press often referred to Arthurdale as a grievous example of a New Deal boondoggle. Clapp founded the Arthurdale nursery school in 1934 after having directed Ballard Memorial, a progressive rural school near Louisville, Kentucky. Following her stint at Arthurdale, she served as editor of *Progressive Education* and promoted integration. See also her *New York Times* obituary (May 18, 1976) M34.

41. The community school and the modern nursery school were rich and interrelated veins of interwar progressive education. See especially, Winifred Bain, "Prospective Teachers Learn to Live with Their Neighbors" *Childhood Education* (February 1938) 245–251; Grace Langdon, "Coordination of Agencies in Carrying on WPA Nursery Schools" *Progressive Education* 15 (October 1938) 472–484; Elsie Clapp, *Community Schools in Action* (1939); Grace Langdon, "Nursery Schools Plus" *School Life* 26 (November 1940) 48–51; Edna Amidon and Muriel Brown, "Community Organization for Family Life Education" *School Life* 26 (November 1940) 38–40; and Lucile Emerson, "The Nursery School and Community Cooperation" *School and Society* 53 (April 12, 1941) 477–478.

42. Elsie Clapp, *Community Schools in Action* (1939) 185.

43. Ibid: 103.

44. Ibid: 190.

45. Ibid: 373.

46. As food cooperatives, WPA nursery schools often bought food in bulk to keep costs down for both the schools and the families they served. Staff, especially those with a home economics background, made home visits to help parents develop recipes to stretch the food dollar even further. As recreation centers, the schools hosted adult activities in the evenings—swimming, gym, pottery, metal, woodwork, dancing, music, art, and photography—in the hope that parents would pass on this "education for leisure" to their children. Toy classes proved especially popular: "Carpenters have been brought into some classes to show how to make toys out of waste materials or to make furniture for the children at home out of boxes and crates." A WPA nursery school in Oakland, California, found that regularly staged plays, with parents, children, and staff

98 *The WPA Nursery School and the Community*

performing the starring roles, proved more popular than inviting Federal One troupes to the school. Latino mothers, for instance, designed skits celebrating their heritage. According to Landreth 1942, the director believed these skits transformed apathetic parents into ones "joyous to take part in the school." As public health clinics, WPA nursery schools promoted programs for better housing, community sanitation, and adequate community medical services. They taught parents to understand not only the fundamental requirements of healthy children, but also how children should be guided to build adequate habits along these lines. Schools also gave treatment for tuberculosis to children and their families, and provided dental exams and free immunizations for illnesses like smallpox and diphtheria.

47. See Lois Meek Stolz, "The Relation of Family and School Life in the Education of Children" *Teachers College Record* 36 (January 1935) 271–278 and "Why Nursery Education?" *Childhood Education* 11 (April 1935) 291–294; MN WPA Guide 1935–36; Sweeney and Buck 1936; Grace Langdon, "Parent Education at First Hand" *Journal of Adult Education* 10 (1938) 45; Ruth Andrus, "The Nursery School, A Child Welfare Center"; and Elizabeth Vincent, "What Can the Nursery School Teach Us?" *Progressive Education* 18 (March 1941) 145–152.

48. Nancy Hoffman interviewed WPA nursery school teacher's assistant and Arthurdale resident Glenna Williams for *Eleanor Roosevelt and the Arthurdale Experiment* (2001). See also Douglas Haskell, "The Modern Nursery School" *Architectural Record* (March 1938), Catherine Landreth, *Education of the Young Child* (1942), and www.arthurdaleheritage.org/.

49. Elmer Johnson, *Children at Play in Nursery School* (Reedsville, West Virginia. April 1935). Library of Congress, Prints & Photographs Division, FSA/OWI Collection, LC-USF34-001084-C.

50. Lois Hayden Meek Stolz, "The Relation of Family and School Life in the Education of Children" *Teachers College Record* 36 (January 1935) 277.

51. "Emergency Nursery Schools" *School and Society* 41 (January 26, 1935) 118–119.

52. Christine Heinig, "Social Development at Home and School" *Childhood Education* (May 1934) 403–405, 444. Program leaders like Heinig also argued that family life would improve once parents developed awareness of their influence upon children: "changed adults in the home will mean changed children."

53. Harry Hopkins, "For Nursery Schools" *School Life* 19 (November 1933) 57. National Council of Parent Education director, Ralph Bridgman lauded the program, calling it the best form of parent education yet devised. He considered the program to live up to Hopkins's goal: "The program should be of immediate use in relieving parents from their anxiety due to inadequate home provisions for their young children, and should be permanently beneficial both to the parents and to the community." See "Parent Education in the Emergency Nursery School Program" *NANE Conference Proceedings* (October 1935) 80–84.

54. LeRoy Bowman, "Putting the Parent in Parent Education" *Progressive Education* 11 (April–May 1934) 300. See also letter from LeRoy Bowman to Harry Hopkins (October 31, 1935) and "Doing a Parents' Job" *Childhood Education* 14 (December 1937) 16.

55. Ernest Osborne, "New Duties of Parents and Schools" *Progressive Education* 12 (April 1935) 270–274.

56. Woolley is quoted by Lois Hayden Meek Stolz, "The Nursery School as a Center for Parent Education" *Childhood Education* 4 (January 1928) 218. A year later, Stolz predicted that: "Three names will go down in the history of education in the United States as leaders in this [early childhood] research: Bird T. Baldwin (Iowa Child Welfare Research Station), Arnold Gesell (Yale Child Development

The WPA Nursery School and the Community 99

Clinic), and Helen Thompson Woolley (Merrill-Palmer and Columbia)." See Lois Hayden Meek Stolz, "The Preschool Movement" *Progressive Education* 6 (January–March 1929) 3–10. Echoed Langdon in 1935, "One is not just born with knowledge of how to raise children. It has to be learned." Langdon studied with Woolley while a doctoral student at Columbia and is quoted in Alma Whitiker, "Sugar and Spice" *Los Angeles Times* (November 16, 1945) A5.

57. Although 1920s nursery schools provided an unparalleled outpouring of attention aimed at teaching parents of young children, it was education geared toward the middle and wealthy classes. See Steven Schlossman, "Before Home Start: Notes toward a History of Parent Education in America, 1897–1929" *Harvard Educational Review* 46 (August 1976) 436–467; Julia Wrigley, "Do Young Children Need Intellectual Stimulation? Experts' Advice to Parents, 1900–1985" *History of Education Quarterly* 29 (Spring 1989) 41–75; Julia Grant, "Modernizing Mothers: Home Economics and the Parent Education Movement, 1920–1945" in Sarah Stage and Virginia Vincenti, eds., *Rethinking Home Economics: Women and the History of a Profession Edited* (1997) 55–74; Julia Grant, *Raising Baby by the Book: The Education of American Mothers* (1998); Elizabeth Rose, *A Mother's Job: The History of Day Care, 1890–1960* (1999); and Paula Fass, *The End of American Childhood: A History of Parenting from Life on the Frontier to the Managed Child* (2016). According to Dorothy Baruch, 1930s private nursery schools aimed to help parents "gain a greater measure of security." See her *Parents and Children Go to School: Adventuring in Nursery School and Kindergarten* (1939).

58. University nursery schools and parent cooperatives developed along parallel lines during the 1920s. Their concerns merged in the WPA nursery school program.

59. Sidonie M. Gruenberg, "Parental Education: Its Materials and Methods" *Childhood Education* 4 (January 1928) 225.

60. As Lois Murphy (psychologist active in WPA nursery schools) argued, "Nursery schools should 'cooperate' with families, instead of expecting families to cooperate with them" (311). See her "Emotional Development and Guidance in Nursery School and Home" *Childhood Education* (April 1936).

61. Grace Langdon, *Home Guidance for Young Children* (1931/1946). Lois Meek Stolz wrote the 1931 preface. See also Grace Langdon, "The Nursery School as a Family Aid" *Child Welfare Pamphlets—Iowa Child Welfare Research Station* #57 (December 26, 1936). One parent-educator from Chicago commented, "No one who has been on a picnic with a group of Mexican mothers can continue to think of Mexico as a torrid land inhabited only by bandits." Quoted in Foster and Mattson, *Nursery School Education* (1939) 310. Original study cited: Chicago Board of Education and the WPA, *Nursery School Parents* (1937). See also "Dr. Langdon of WPA, Defining Needs of Child, Puts Home First in Meeting Them" *New York Times* (February 22, 1940).

62. Grace Langdon, "Parent Education in the Nursery School" *Parent Education* 3 (April 1937) 32–33.

63. Quoted in Rose Alschuler, "Guidance Needed" *Progressive Education* 15 (October 1938) 459–467.

64. Parents did not take over even during the dramatic tightening of the labor market in the early 1940s, although they kept many WPA nursery schools afloat. See Jim Marshall, "Babies Aweigh" *Colliers* 110 (August 29, 1942) 58.

65. George Stoddard, "What of the Nursery School?" *Progressive Education* 14 (October 1937) 447.

66. Discussion topics included: childcare and guidance, child rearing, use of community agencies for the family, family health (both physical and mental); family

100 *The WPA Nursery School and the Community*

recreation, budgeting, meal planning, clothing, family furnishings at low cost; and household management and home arrangement as they affect family life. Visual learning devices included colorful posters, homemade toys, children's furniture, and play equipment. In early October 1940, Langdon attended a parent meeting in New Rochelle, New York. According to Langdon, the fifteen parents, all African Americans, talked about painting by children: "It was a pleasure to see the work in the two schools visited and to find such rich experiences being provided for children, teachers, and parents." By contrast, Lois Meek Stolz mentioned study groups (lectures and reading and discussing works on child development), not larger meetings, in her "The Nursery School as a Center for Parent Education" *Childhood Education* 4 (January 1928) 217–220.

67. *Forum Handbook: Conference for the Education of WPA Teachers of Adults and Nursery Schools, July 19–August 5, 1940* (Mississippi: WPA, 1940) 22, 24. See also "Introductory Training for Nursery School Workers" *Bulletin #8* (IL: WPA and State Department of Public Instruction, March 1942) 48 pages—Rose Alschuler Papers.

68. Grace Langdon and Isabel Robinson, "Parent Education in the WPA Education Program" *Parent Education* 4 (December 1937) 64. See also *WPA Nursery School Bulletin #3* (1936) 98–105.

69. Doak Campbell et al., *Educational Activities of the Works Progress Administration* (Washington, DC: US Government Printing Office, 1939) 119.

70. Ibid: 116.

71. Grace Langdon and Isabel Robinson, "Parent Education in the WPA Education Program" *Parent Education* 4 (December 1937) 61–69, 113.

72. NARA letters/telegrams include: School Officials: Maude Firth to Hon. Mr. Disney, Senator of Oklahoma. Tulsa, OK. October 21, 1935. [director of Home Economics Education, Tulsa Public schools]; Earl Franklin to Dr. Grace Langdon. St. Paul's, NC. May 21, 1935. [Superintendent of public schools]; Harry Clark to President Roosevelt. Knoxville, TN. October 18, 1935. [Superintendent of public schools: TN; J.H. Hope to President Roosevelt (telegram). Columbia, South Carolina. October 14, 1935. [state superintendent of education]. Women's Organizations: Elizabeth House to President Roosevelt. Stillwater, OK. October 15, 1935. [State pres. of WCTU]; Jeannette Kelly to President Roosevelt (telegram). Williamsburg, VA. October 18, 1935. State Secretary of AAUW; Mrs. William Kletzer to Harry Hopkins. Portland, OR October 15, [1935] [PTA]. Even women's groups not particularly receptive to New Deal politics (i.e. the Junior League and the American Legion auxiliary) supported WPA nursery schools at the local level. WPA advisory committee members also took part in this 1935 campaign. Edna Noble White, for instance, requested earmarked funds from Harry Hopkins, Eleanor Roosevelt and Representative Ralph Church (R-IL). Church then wrote a letter of program support to FDR on October 22, 1935.

73. According to NARA archivist, many WPA letters still need to be indexed. Northeast: Sen Augustine Lonergan (D-CT); Rep Isaac Becharach (R-NJ), Patrick Boland (D-PA), Harry Haines (D-PA), and Mary Norton (D-NJ). Midwest: Rep Chester Bolton (R-OH), Ralph Church (R-IL), and George Dondero (R-MI). South: Sen Wesley Disney (D-OK) and Josh Lee (D-OK); Rep Wilburn Cartwright (D-OK). West: Rep Florence Kahn (R-CA), Compton White (D-ID), WD McFarlane (D-TX). Along with pro-New Deal Texan, Maury Maverick, McFarlane lost to anti-New Deal Texan Democrats (e.g. Fritz Lanham and Martin Dies) during the Nov 1938 election. See L. Patrick Hughes, "West TX Swing: Roosevelt Purge in the Land of the Lone Star" www2.austin.cc.tx.us/lpatrick/his2341/West Texas_Swing.html.

The WPA Nursery School and the Community   101

74. Extant letters in NARA from local parents help explain the program's durability for nearly ten years even when the New Deal itself began to wane in popularity. In *Growing Up in 20th-Century America: A History and Reference Guide* (1996), Elliot West refers to the program as one of the most popular New Deal programs (p. 152). There is no record of what primary evidence he used to support this claim. In "Attitudes Toward Emergency Nursery Schools in Oklahoma" (Master's thesis, Oklahoma Agricultural and Mechanical College, 1936), Girdie Bruce Hutchison-Ware found that the program was most popular among mothers whose young children attended the schools.

75. Mr. and Mrs. T. Brashears to Mr. John Vaughan. Panama, OK. April 1, 1935.

76. Ed. Belderef [WWI vet] to Harry Hopkins. Los Angeles, CA (Sawtelle Nursery school). November 25, 1935.

77. Ethel Katz to Harry Hopkins. The Bronx, NY. 1938.

78. As Edna Kelley, WPA nursery school supervisor in Texas, asserted, "The more interested parents became in the free [WPA] nursery school movement, the more queries came as to how a community might avail itself of these government schools." See Edna E. Kelley, "Uncle Sam's Nursery Schools" *Parents' Magazine* (March 1936) 24–25; 48–49.

79. Long Beach was not especially supportive of the New Deal. Local history archival holdings at the Long Beach Main library suggest that the regional WPA office was interested primarily in public works projects. Yet the conservative local paper, the Long Beach Press-Telegram gave these mothers sympathetic coverage. See "WPA Nursery School Closing Is Protested" on November 18, 1937. Mrs. Fred Bixby, a wealthy local philanthropist, helped underwrite the costs for this school.

80. See " 'Door-Key' Children Offer Big Problem: WPA Nursery School Director Tells of 'War' Mothers" *New York Times* (July 15, 1942) 22:8. Congresswoman Mary T. Norton (D-NJ) mentioned this Long Beach school in congressional hearings in support of the WPA in June 1942. See also Bess Settle, "Work Starts on Nursery at Navy Housing Project" *Long Beach Press Telegram* (Spring 1942) from Historical Society of Long Beach's presentation, "Long Beach Remembers Pearl Harbor—75th Anniversary" (December 2016), the *Los Angeles Times* (December 23, 1943) A5 and Nona Baldwin, "America Enlists Its Women" *Independent Woman* (September 1942).

81. Grace Langdon, "Development in Field of Emergency Nursery Schools: How These Developments Are Becoming a Part of Permanent Programs" *School Life* 23 (March 1938) 242–243, 246.

82. In Cheyenne, Wyoming, WPA nursery school mothers successfully petitioned for a kindergarten in 1938. In May 1939, WPA nursery school teachers reported to Langdon, "We are working diligently to educate the public to demand kindergarten education throughout the state." Adeline Missal to Grace Langdon. Bristol, CT. September 27, 1935. After a steep decline throughout the 1930s, kindergarten enrollment started to rise in the early 1940s. See Mary Dabney Davis, *Schools for Children Under Six: A Report on the Status and Need for Nursery Schools and Kindergartens* (1947).

83. Mothers in Brooklyn, frustrated that a mid-level family income rendered their children ineligible for WPA nursery schools, banded together to form the Stuyvesant Park Mothers' Association parent cooperative. The nursery campaign director, Mrs. Ted Allan, said in February 1942:

> These children should not be denied the benefits of nursery school, and their mothers have much to offer our community life, particularly in defense activities. Therefore, what we want are WPA nursery schools admitting children of

102   The WPA Nursery School and the Community

both low and . . . middle income groups, or schools otherwise supported but maintaining a standard equal to that of WPA schools.

See also Robyn Muncy, "Cooperative Motherhood and Democratic Civic Culture in Postwar Suburbia, 1940–1965" *Journal of Social History* 38 (Winter 2004) 285–310.

84. As Hill remarked to a biographer in the late 1930s: "First I thought of education as child-centered; later, as family-centered; and now I think of it as community-centered including the total environment, physical and social" Ilse Forest (unpublished manuscript on Hill at Filson Club in Louisville, Kentucky) 159.

85. WPA funds paid only for the salaries of the two teachers, a part-time cook, and a part-time nurse.

86. See Patty Smith Hill, "The University Reaches Out: Neighborhood Study as Basis for Plan of Improvement Is Sponsored by Columbia" *Teachers College Record* 35 (February 1934) 431–434.

87. With George Counts' encouragement, Snyder completed a PhD at Johns Hopkins. In the 1920s, she was fired from Towson State, Maryland, because she was too "theoretical and radical in education." Snyder became a major architect of an experimental teacher education program at Columbia, New College, which ran from 1932 to 1938. She worked with Tom Alexander (Grace Langdon's dissertation advisor) and wrote curriculum with William Withers, published as *Current Social Problems* in 1936. HUAC called Withers to testify in the 1950s. Snyder did not include Current Social Problems under an extensive list of publications. See "A Note too—Serious Vita" (January 14, 1962), ACEI archives. See also Gracia Caines, "Dr. Agnes Snyder's Life Has Influenced Many" *Evening Journal, Wilmington, Delaware* (February 4, 1971) and "History of New College" *Teachers College Record* 38 (October 1936). Right before she died in May 1973, Snyder wrote what is still the most accessible biography on Hill in *Dauntless Women in Childhood Education, 1856–1931* (1972) 233–280.

88. In September 1934, the students took their impressionistic summer survey and transformed it into a piece of urban anthropology by including the scholarly work of many of their professors. "Area #14" was widely distributed at Columbia University. See also Agnes Snyder. "A Teachers College Becomes Part of Its Neighborhood" (January 29, 1939). Manuscript at ACEI archives.

89. For two years, Snyder coordinated activities with Hilltop parents gratis, although she made only modest mention of this role in her account of Hilltop in *Dauntless Women in Childhood Education, 1856–1931* (1972). See also Hill's depiction in "Hilltop—A Community Experiment" *Childhood Education* (January 1937) 201–205.

90. Flyer on Hilltop family farm (early 1940s), ACEI archives, University of Maryland, College Park. Patty Smith Hill donated the funds to buy the farm from "Happy Birthday" royalties.

91. New York City personnel were stingy and did not always give free rein in hiring staff. See Snyder-Hill correspondence—Hilltop, 1935–1942, ACEI and Patty Smith Hill correspondence re: Hilltop in William Russell Papers, Teachers College Special Collections. In 1942, Hill and Snyder also sponsored research that addressed how young children develop racism and anti-Semitism. No doubt inspired by their Columbia colleagues, Ruth Horowitz and Mamie Clark, Hill and Snyder sponsored Evelyn Brandon of Alabama State Teachers College (who had been recommended by Kenneth Clark) through a fund, administered by the ACE, until Hill died in 1946.

92. New College's closing at Columbia University became a cause célèbre. A huge outcry erupted among students and teachers, and James Wechsler of *The Nation* took up their banner. He suggested that money had little to do with

The WPA Nursery School and the Community 103

New College's demise. Rather, it was the radicalism of New College's faculty and students that caused the school's closure. See his "Twilight at Teacher's College" *The Nation* (December 17, 1938). People around Snyder became targets of HUAC, including New College colleagues Goodwin Watson, Leo Huberman, and her 1936 co-author, William Withers. Although Snyder's relationship to the far left remained complex, George Counts, on the other hand, became an anti-communist. See, for example, his reply to Wechsler, "Whose Twilight?" *Social Frontier* 5 (1938–39) 137, and George Counts and John Childs, *America, Russia, and the Communist Party in the Postwar World* (1943).

93. CACE named its nursery school after Snyder. Anthropologist Gene Weltfish raised money for Snyder's school in the early 1940s. After Weltfish was red-baited in 1948 (see chapter five), Hilltop participants retreated into their private lives and gave up on their dream of creating community-centered nursery schools at public expense. Snyder remained in early childhood education but kept a low public profile for the rest of her life.

94. On January 12, 1937, for instance, the WPA nursery school advisory committee agreed:

> That all efforts should be directed toward the eventual complete assumption by local communities of responsibility for the continuance of nursery schools, recognizing that there must be a transition period during which time WPA will continue to give support, with a gradual shifting of local responsibilities as communities are ready to take them over. ENW.

95. Grace Langdon, "Coordination of Agencies in Carrying on WPA Nursery Schools" *Progressive Education* 15 (October 1938) 469–484.

96. For overviews on critics, see Nick Taylor, *American-Made: Enduring Legacy of the WPA: When FDR Put the Nation to Work* (2009) and Sandra Opdycke, *The WPA: Creating Jobs and Hope in the Great Depression* (2016).

97. HUAC, Investigation of Un-American Propaganda Activities in the U.S. Volume 4, 75th Congress (December 5, 1938) 2810.

98. See Ruby Takanishi's oral history of Lois Meek Stolz, *An American Child Development Pioneer* (Stanford University, 1977) and Cedric Fowler, "They Train the Young" *New Outlook* 165 (February 1935) 36–37.

99. HUAC, Investigation of Un-American Propaganda Activities in the U.S. Volume 4, 75th Congress (December 5–6, 1938) 2809–2860. In January 1939, Woodward exited the WPA to join the Social Security Board.

100. Brooks Atkinson, "Mother Goose Marx, Under WPA Auspices" *New York Times* (May 21, 1937) 19.

101. *The Washington Post, Life Magazine,* and *Saturday Evening Post* also published negative reviews of *Revolt of the Beavers*. Soon thereafter, Stolz proved "unable" to attend the October 1937 NANE conference in Nashville, and allowed her NANE membership to lapse. For more detailed analysis of the play itself, see Leslie Frost, *Dreaming America: Popular Front Ideas and Aesthetics in Children's Plays of the Federal Theatre Project* (2013) Chapter 2.

102. Stolz and Langdon remained friends after this move until the Battle of 1943 permanently soured their relationship (see Chapter 4). In a March 18, 1940 letter, for instance, Stolz urged "My Dear Grace" to visit California, mentioning that her soon-to-be-published *Your Child's Development and Guidance* contained WPA nursery school photos from Connecticut and New York. Langdon replied soon thereafter and visited Stolz while on a field trip for the WPA. For overviews of Stolz's work with privatized nursery schools during World War II, see James Hymes, "The Kaiser Child Service Centers: An Interview with Lois Meek Stolz" in his *Living*

104   *The WPA Nursery School and the Community*

History Interviews 2, pp. 26–56 and http://kaiserpermanentehistory.org/ latest/wartime-shipyard-child-care-centers-set-standards-for-future/.

103. Investigation and Study of the WPA before the subcommittee of the Committee on Appropriations, House of Representatives, 76th Congress, 1st [3rd] session, acting under House Res. 130, (March 1939) 1242.

104. In August 1938, HUAC accused John Carmody (soon to be head of the FWA) of being a member of the American League of Peace and Democracy, allegedly a communist-front organization. In 1939, Representative Andrew May (D-KY) accused him (as former head of Rural Electrification) of leading a leftist "wrecking gang" engaged in "Socialist warfare" against private power industry. In October 1939, HUAC also listed 500 federal employees as members of the American League for Peace and Democracy. Forty of these came from the WPA. See HUAC, Investigation of Un-American Propaganda Activities in the U.S. Volume 10, 75th Congress (October 25, 1939) 6404–6417. Susan B. Anthony II was one staffer named at this time. Although forced out of her position at the NYA, she remained a staunch supporter of Langdon's program. See Chapters 4 and 5.

105. This Act was the first major planned reorganization of the executive branch since 1787. Details follow in Chapter 4.

106. WPA Education, Recreation and Nursery School. Nursery School children play at Whittier School in Denver, Colorado. October 1938. National Archives photo no. 69-N-11-20050-C.

107. "Strengthening America's Economic Dykes" (November 24, 1939) 11. Floyd Dell Papers, Newbery Library, Chicago.

108. "Bridging the Economic Gap (January 16, 1940) 13. Floyd Dell Papers, Newbery Library, Chicago.

109. Many saw Kerr as a rising political star. See especially, Eleanor Roosevelt, "Women in Politics" *Good Housekeeping* (January–April 1940) http://newdeal.feri.org/er/er13.htm.

4   In Time of War

In the last years of the 1930s, the nation moved out of the Depression as it began preparing for war. After the enactment of Roosevelt's governmental Reorganization Act of 1939, the WPA moved into the new Federal Works Agency (FWA), seen as the home for construction, rather than the new Federal Security Agency (FSA), to which the president gave responsibility for health and welfare.[1] In December 1941, active belligerency against Japan, Germany, and Italy began. Throughout this period, old issues about the role, organization, and permanence of the WPA nursery schools remained. And a new issue emerged—how to provide and use childcare to maximize the workforce and assure full mobilization for World War II.

Mobilization and War

Two months after the fall of France on August 22, 1940, as US involvement in hostilities grew more likely, the acting deputy administrator of the WPA, Howard Hunter, explained that the agency would give "rigid priority" to programs that were potentially of "military value."[2] On the same day, Langdon called for the establishment of *Child Development Centers*—nursery schools, neighborhood groups, and daycare centers—to contribute to military readiness.[3] After FDR won an unprecedented third term in November 1940, his administration intensified efforts to create an "arsenal of democracy" to provide Great Britain with military supplies for its war against Nazi Germany. Langdon organized a conference in Chicago to "redirect the nursery school program in light of impending war needs."[4]

But the timing could not have been worse. Florence Kerr, her immediate supervisor, had been sidelined by Eleanor Roosevelt's repeated requests she create a blueprint for the Office of Civilian Defense.[5] Kerr turned to her new duties just as the WPA Recreation Division, capitalizing on the reputation of Langdon's program, began calling its preschool play groups, *WPA Nursery Schools*. Emboldened by White House rhetoric on recreation as a national security measure, the division's personnel suggested that anyone could work with young children.[6] Away from her Washington office, Langdon could no longer give the program the institutional support and political backing

106   In Time of War

it needed. Hiring workers with little to no background in early childhood education not only meant a program of lesser quality but undermined Langdon's authority at the WPA and hurt the program's reputation with outside professional groups, especially ACE, one of its three original sponsors.[7]

Frustrated that Kerr could not help with damage control, Langdon wondered aloud where her program ought to be housed in a government mobilizing for war. In mid-January 1941, she thought about the possibility of moving into the Office of Education (OE) so the schools could be housed in a Federal agency, which might be a stronger anchor.[8] Later that month, however, she learned that Katherine Lenroot, CB Chief at the Department of Labor, had been appointed children's advisor to Paul McNutt, the new administrator of the FSA. That meant that Lenroot would have to be consulted if the OE, an FSA agency, took over. At Langdon's behest, Edna Noble White, chair of the WPA nursery school advisory committee, met with John Studebaker, the OE director, and Kerr, at that point WPA assistant commissioner, to figure out what to do.[9] On March 11, White counseled patience to Langdon. Labeling the program "a defense measure," Langdon replied, was the only way "to stabilize our family life program."[10]

Given bureaucratic reshuffling at the WPA, Kerr's dual focus, and agency rivalries between the FWA and FSA, Langdon busied herself with field visits while she waited to see what happened.[11] White, meanwhile, met with Will Alexander, who might offer a home through the reactivated Council of National Defense.[12] On March 20, she gave him a detailed version of Langdon's August 1940 proposal, "Protection of Young Children in a Defense Program."[13] When Alexander left government to direct the Julius Rosenwald Fund, that potential home disappeared.[14] Compounding matters, Walter Kiplinger (the chief of public activities for the WPA) called Langdon back to the capital given changes "incident to reductions in projects and administrative employment."[15] Langdon then worried about the very survival of her program:

> In the states in which I visited the program is strong and the support for it is fine. However, this Washington situation is having more effect in the states than it has any time before. They feel the unsoundness and insecurity of it all and no one dares protest for if they do, the one who protests is out summarily.
>
> The only solution which I can see which will safeguard the program is to get it tied in with Katherine Lenroot's coordinated activities for defense.
>
> What I wish most of all is that it could be lifted out of the mess to someplace where we could push ahead with the things which need to be done. I can see from my field trip just how big a thing we could do if we could only get out of this petty mess. People believe in the nursery schools and support them and we could go places if a few strings could be untied.[16]

In Time of War 107

White, too, worried about the program's future. With Kerr gone, prospects at the WPA looked shaky. Wanting desperately to find a permanent home inside the federal government and having struck out with both Studebaker and Alexander, White used Lenroot's competition with Kerr and the longstanding rivalries between the CB and the WPA over the best way to care for young children. White feared that WPA nursery schools might be lodged in the WPA Recreation Division, which she saw as fatal to the program and wanted forestalled.[17] At that point, Katherine Lenroot suddenly showed great interest in WPA nursery schools.

When Fiorello LaGuardia, director of the Office of Civilian Defense, fired Kerr in July, she went back to her WPA office and supported Langdon's nursery school program.[18] At the end of the month, Lenroot held a Conference on Day Care of Children of Working Mothers. Representatives from various governmental as well as private agencies, including Grace Langdon, attended. Although Lenroot and others called for foster care for the children of women defense workers, the conference as a whole recommended using the WPA nursery schools as a model for providing childcare services for women working in defense industries.[19] Once Lenroot indicated her willingness to contribute CB money and personnel to a national program based on the WPA nursery experience, Kerr called Langdon and asked her to write up a project proposal.[20] Langdon worried that a new federal project would endanger local support for WPA nursery schools, which she called "one of the strongest features of the program." But cautiously optimistic that "a WPA project sponsored by CB and OE" might have more advantages than disadvantages, she advised Kerr to "secure a special congressional appropriation or allocation" to augment the program.[21]

In presenting "A Nation-Wide Project for the Daytime Care of Children during the National Emergency" in early September, Langdon called for tripling the size of her program from 1,500 to over 4,000 schools.[22] Determined to maintain program continuity, Langdon argued her project would serve mothers and migrant workers in industry, rural migrant workers, families in trailers near military bases, and low-income families struggling as post-Depression prices rose. Nursery schools catered to low-income mothers, public childcare centers to employed mothers with low incomes, and child development units to military-base and industrial-defense workers.[23] The CB would contribute guidance, field staff consultants, and money from Title V of the Social Security Act. The OE would offer advisory services and facilitate cooperation with state and local school officials to find more public-school buildings.

Langdon also made explicit her intention to maintain the course towards permanence, setting up this national project "with a long-time view to the services which might later also serve peacetime needs." Anticipating that it would cost nearly $20 million annually, Langdon called for making use of the WPA administrative structure at the state level, "with emphasis upon local support." Langdon concluded: "As written, this project provides for

108   *In Time of War*

the care of only about 135,000 children, which is only a small part of the total need."[24] Langdon and Kerr met with representatives from the WPA, the CB, and the OE over the next weeks to finalize plans.[25] About concerns that the WPA was "shrinking rapidly," Florence Kerr said the WPA was "not going to disappear and would still be able to carry on these programs."[26] Yet she also indicated the WPA leadership was disinclined to move forward with yet another national program given that Congress had just killed federal projects in theater, art, and music and was still investigating the WPA for alleged subversion. Immediately, Langdon offered an alternate proposal, declaring it "unwise" to launch anything new because doing so "sacrificed the local initiative and support."[27] She suggested an inter-agency committee create schools for young children through state and local channels.[28] Elected chair of this Joint Planning Board on Day Care for Children, Langdon held regular meetings and freely exchanged information about WPA nursery schools with CB and OE affiliates.[29] She also gave photos of WPA nursery schools to CB staff and fact-checked an article on early childhood education for the OE.[30]

"Decentralized control" became Langdon's preferred method for achieving program permanence as she worked in the context of a fragile alliance between erstwhile rivals at the FWA and FSA and continuing external opposition. When John Carmody, the FWA administrator, was named a communist sympathizer by the Dies Committee in mid-October 1941, Langdon hoped she could safeguard her program through outside channels.[31] She called for a new national commission to help federal agencies coordinate their childcare policies "during this National Crisis."[32] Sponsors included NANE, ACE, the PEA, and the AAUW. Langdon meant for this new National Commission for Young Children to operate "as a free-lance, completely non-governmental, advisory group."[33]

When reports appeared from the field after the attack on Pearl Harbor, Langdon realized the magnitude of creating child development centers at the local level.[34] On December 11, she wrote that the "WPA nursery school program ought to be able to move ahead without being delayed by all manner of procedural clearances and similar red tape."[35] Edna Noble White, the recipient of those words, asked Kerr to mobilize the WPA nursery school program in the context of war: "No other agency in Washington has the facilities, with the supervisors in every state who are thoroughly familiar with the state assets and liabilities and it seems to me it would be a great pity not to see that they are used."[36] Describing young children living in squalor near army camps, Langdon exhorted progressive educators to act, declaring, "The young ones need defense!"[37] In early March 1942, she wrote White a glowing letter describing how Kerr had reorganized the WPA, ensuring that Langdon was in charge of all early childhood education, including the former WPA Recreation play groups. She saw nothing to hinder the program's expansion and mentioned her new program title, "Child Protection." Added Langdon, the "CB is making a desperate effort"

In Time of War 109

to get administrative control of all programs for children, but the effort had been "blocked."[38]

In spearheading a new national commission, Langdon had hoped to protect her beloved program from both CB interference and uneven funding by the WPA.[39] Yet despite renewed support from Kerr, she faced the politicking of Rose Alschuler, the commission's newly appointed president. Alschuler did not use back-door channels to get things done.[40] Although she shadowed Langdon on field trips and openly acknowledged Langdon's excellence as childcare consultant and family life specialist, Alschuler, a political novice, undermined Langdon's authority in Washington.[41] More damaging still, she publically broke ranks with Langdon, parroting the CB line: "As Miss Lenroot said several times yesterday—The problems are far too large and complex to be taken care of by any one agency."[42] In spring 1942, Alschuler took sides in the public rivalry between the WPA and CB as Langdon, in collaboration with White and Kerr, proceeded to expand access to the WPA nursery school program by working behind the scenes to ensure renewed congressional funding.[43]

Representative Mary Norton (D-NJ) soon defended the WPA nursery schools. In congressional hearings, she made such a powerful case for their value that Congress earmarked $6 million for childcare, the only time it singled out a specific WPA program.[44] Norton's defense came during the final year of WPA appropriations hearings. Given that workers were in great demand, various members of Congress emphasized allegations of WPA waste, poor management, corruption, and worker "laziness."[45] Nonetheless, on June 30, Congress approved the Norton Amendment, which mandated "not less than six million dollars be expended for day nurseries or nursery schools for children of employed mothers."[46] Langdon then created three types of WPA nursery schools, all for two- to four-year-olds. One, for children from low-income families, was free. Another was intended for the children of all employed workers in areas with defense industries. These parents paid half the cost. Finally, children of parents in the armed forces or defense industries also enrolled at half the cost.[47]

Reorganization and the Community Facilities Act

Acting in his capacity as FSA Administrator, Paul McNutt began making life more difficult for Grace Langdon. Pundits assumed that FDR had given the "tall, tan and terrific" career politician the FSA position to occupy his time and dissipate his strength as a political rival.[48] Following the November 1940 election, possibly to reward McNutt for his faithful campaign stumping, FDR put him in charge of the Office of Defense Health and Welfare Services (ODHWS), making him responsible for all policies and programs related to people's well-being and recreation as they affected national defense.[49]

110   *In Time of War*

When FDR determined in early 1941 that defense workers needed community facilities in addition to housing, McNutt made a case for why the FSA, not the FWA, should oversee a bigger share of funding allocated to the Community Facilities Act.[50] He hired Charles Taft, son of the former president and brother of Senate Minority Leader Robert Taft, as his assistant. In February 1941, Taft invited Langdon and others to join his Family Security Committee. Taft asked those present to advise him on their respective defense preparations because he would be in charge of domestic matters relating to defense.[51] A month later, in March 1941, Taft held that the FSA should oversee community facilities and services for defense workers.[52] McNutt argued in late April that the FSA was the proper agency to deal with defense-related health, education, and welfare programs.[53] At the May 1941 hearings on community facilities, both men continued making their case.[54]

McNutt asserted that the FWA, a mere "construction" agency, could not possibly cope with the widespread migration of families to defense areas, whereas the FSA was better able to provide community facilities like schools. Taft suggested amending the Community Facilities Act to move such authority away from the FWA and give it to the FSA. Although Congress kept community facilities in the FWA, McNutt's description of the facilities the FSA could ably administer proved so convincing that the FWA agreed to consult the FSA about the allocation of Lanham funds through the Community Facilities Act.[55] On June 28, 1941, Congress expanded its definition of public works to include schools in order to enhance military preparedness in "war-torn" areas and appropriated $150 million for public works related to defense.[56] It did not then include nursery schools.[57]

When early childhood educators argued that Lanham funds should be extended to nursery schools, McNutt approached the CB and asked Lenroot for a childcare liaison to his national defense assistant, Taft.[58] Lenroot recommended Charles Schottland, a social worker and lawyer who had been the Director of the California Relief Administration during part of the Great Depression. Schottland attended Lenroot's Daycare Conference in July 1941 and, in the fall, became one of three CB representatives on Langdon's Joint Planning Board on Day Care for Children.[59] Through him, McNutt and Taft learned of Langdon's efforts to double the size of her program through inter-agency cooperation, her assessment that doing so would cost $20 million annually, and her interest in obtaining funds to create more nursery schools. Days after Pearl Harbor, their testimony and that of FWA officials succeeded in getting nursery schools included under the act's public works rubric.[60] In early January 1942, McNutt sent a directive to Florence Kerr, asserting that WPA nursery schools, although a part of the FWA, might well be granted Lanham funds through the updated Community Facilities Act. Eligibility would nonetheless need approval from the FSA's OE in consultation with Charles Schottland.[61]

While the FSA was wrangling with the FWA over funding, Eleanor Roosevelt stepped down from her role in the Office of Civilian Defense volunteer

In Time of War 111

program after allegations that she had "taken the old WPA crowd, plus some communist recruits and promoted them into the OCD office."[62] McNutt's lukewarm defense of her work (coupled with his attempt to usurp Kerr's authority over the Community Facilities Act funding) led the president to keep him in check. In April 1942, he gave McNutt an additional high-profile position, one with headaches galore, as chair of the War Manpower Commission.

McNutt did not let go of childcare, however. Shortly after Representative Norton's congressional testimony in support of WPA nursery schools, he staged a preemptive strike by taking over the role of Langdon's Joint Committee on Day Care. Suggesting that her group "continue in advisory capacity," McNutt established a section on daycare services for children in the ODHWS, naming his CB liaison, Charles Schottland, its new director.[63] On June 23, McNutt presented his plan "to solve the problem of day care of children of working mothers" to an audience drawn from eight federal agencies (including the WPA), and outlined four goals for the administration of daycare: (1) bringing together all available information, (2) coordinating all federal agencies involved with the task, (3) motivating them to prepare technical materials, and (4) allocating funds.[64] Although he mentioned various childcare services, McNutt abandoned Langdon's plan for a federally sponsored system of nursery schools. He proposed instead that federal funds be issued as block grants to states, that the CB and OE work through state public welfare and education departments, and that daycare services emphasize foster-family care and mandatory counseling for working mothers.[65]

So even as Congress bestowed recognition on WPA nursery schools in June 1942, outsiders nearly seized control.[66] McNutt knew very little about early childhood education but saw the daycare program as a potentially powerful vehicle for wielding authority in a nation undergoing massive mobilization. Reorganization made his hostile takeover bid possible. So did the ambiguous language of the Community Facilities Act.

Langdon took McNutt's takeover attempt in stride. She had invested nearly nine years developing the WPA nursery school program into an outstanding model of early education. In the *New York Times* of July 15, 1942, she modestly offered her "adequate nursery system" as the solution for the rise in "door-key" children—those with keys around their necks because their mothers worked in war industries and did not get home before they did.[67] As War Manpower Commissioner, McNutt issued a directive a few weeks later contradicting Langdon's intent for WPA nursery schools to be available to all door-key children:

The first responsibility of women with young children, in war as in peace, is to give suitable care in their own homes to their own children. In order that established family life may not unnecessarily be disrupted, special efforts to secure the employment in industry of women with

112 In Time of War

young children should be deferred until full use has been made of all other sources of labor supply.[68]

FDR, worried that war would require ever-larger numbers of mothers to become defense workers, executed three quick decisions aimed at closing the rift that had developed between the FSA and the FWA. On August 20, he put Kerr in charge of all applications for funding under the Community Facilities Act. She would be responsible for both Lanham children's centers and WPA nursery schools. The next day, he issued an order that rival agencies refrain from criticizing each other in public, and a week after that, he gave McNutt $400,000 from the President's Emergency Fund "for the promotion and coordination of programs for the care of children of working mothers."[69]

In the meantime, Langdon had set up a process for reviewing applications and allocating funds. Regarding inter-agency squabbling, she noted that:

> Some of the other agencies are taking this assignment of Mrs. Kerr's very hard. Particularly the Federal Security Agency is frothing at the mouth for it was a plum they had wanted terribly.
>
> Just before this happened we had moved ahead on our working out relationships with the Office of Educ. . . . We hear via the grapevine that they are pretty well "het up" about our handling the Lanham applications. They don't need to be because we will work with them if we have a ghost of a chance and their dockets are moving for the first time.
>
> Another angle is that Mr. Schottland has had two bursts of very unfortunate publicity in which he is quoted as saying that foster home care is the only answer to the problem of children—that there are psychological barriers to the WPA nursery schools, etc. . . . I think he is saying words that are put into his mouth and it is my prediction that he will not stay long in the job for I think they are using him as the goat.
>
> Now it appears that the Children's Bureau is out to push the foster home program in a big way as the only solution. . . . Of course it is a desperate effort to try to get hold of something.[70]

Langdon spent the rest of 1942 speeding up the application process for Lanham children's centers (she issued the first to Arnold Gesell days later).[71] She also explored how WPA nursery schools could become Lanham centers if WPA appropriations gave out and worked to get WPA nursery schools reinstated into the Washington, D.C. public schools.[72] As she had predicted, Schottland left the ODHWS in late September and joined the army.[73]

With their $400,000, McNutt and Taft began to send OE and CB agents into the field through state education and welfare channels.[74] CB agents, acting as consultants, emphasized the harm mothers caused their "eight-hour

In Time of War 113

orphans" by working and continued to present foster home care as the preferable option:

> No informed American needs a psychologist to tell him that children separated from home ties and without competent care during their most impressionable age are the troublemakers, the neurotics, the spiritual and emotional cripples of a generation hence.[75]

OE field agents, however, felt pulled in all directions. On record as being very much in favor of public nursery schools, they nonetheless had to contend with their director, Studebaker, who remained embittered that the WPA/FWA controlled the Lanham application process.[76] Paralyzed into inaction, state education officials no longer cooperated with WPA nursery school staff at the local level, even in defense areas, like Childersburg, Alabama, that were in desperate need of daycare for working mothers.[77]

With the war economy booming, Florence Kerr, as Assistant WPA Administrator, believed WPA nursery school leaders like Langdon to be safely ensconced in Lanham's permanent headquarters at the FWA, and decided it was time to call for "an honorable discharge" for the WPA. On October 30, 1942, she did just that in the *New York Times*, devoting most of her column space to detailing the "dire need for nursery schools."[78] When the November 1942 elections resulted in a more conservative Congress, FDR also saw the handwriting on the wall. He signed the death warrant for the WPA on December 4, using the words Kerr had spoken weeks earlier: "With the satisfaction of a good job well done and with a high sense of integrity, the Works Projects Administration has asked for and earned an honorable discharge."[79] On December 30, Langdon and Kerr met with FWA Administrator Philip Fleming, who assured them he would do his utmost to keep as many WPA nursery schools open as possible by using Lanham funds.[80] Confronting newly open hostility from the FSA and CB (as well as from New Deal opponents like Senator Pat McCarran), Langdon confided to White: "I think it will not all be smooth sailing. I think there is a fight on our hands of the first order but I believe that we have the means of seeing it through."[81]

The Battle of 1943

The year 1943 began on a good note. FDR issued an executive order making all WPA nursery schools in defense areas eligible for Lanham funds, and Langdon subtly subverted McNutt's August 1942 argument that mothers with young children should stay at home. To the readers of *Parents Magazine*, she advised:

> Of course, this does not in any way infringe upon the right of each mother to decide whether she will or will not seek or accept employment outside her home, but it does indicate that the government will

114 *In Time of War*

not undertake active recruitment of women with infants until such time as is absolutely necessary.[82]

By substituting infants for young children, Langdon implicitly endorsed the right of all mothers with preschool-age children to work. She also questioned the notion that separating mothers and children caused harm:

> It is not the actual number of hours in a day that a parent is with [the child] that gives him this feeling of security which is the foundation of his life, it is the feeling that his parents love him and can be depended upon.

While Langdon was transferring WPA nursery schools to Lanham funding before the end of the WPA on April 30, Taft effected an immediate takeover on February 17. With Lenroot and James Brunot (Schottland's replacement) at his side, he unveiled plans for an ODHWS childcare program to subsume programs then funded under the Community Facilities Act. Taft wanted to maintain the roughly 1,500 extant WPA/Lanham nursery schools in public-school buildings and spend an equal amount of money developing a foster daycare program that would allow young children to remain at a home where, by implication, they belonged. In essence, his plan was a containment strategy for federally sponsored nursery schools. Taft quickly acceded to requests that his plan be considered a temporary war measure, while Lenroot exploited fears about federal control through the WPA/FWA. FWA legal counsel Alan Johnstone headed off this stealth attack. Still, his testimony underscored the difficulties Langdon would face in achieving program permanence through the Community Facilities Act. Although he saved Langdon's program in the short term, Johnstone emphasized the temporary nature of defense money and assumed that working mothers would eventually shoulder the costs for childcare.[83]

The situation worsened. Langdon indicated her dismay when she learned Taft had succeeded in getting his takeover bid onto the Senate floor. Known as the Thomas Bill after one of its sponsors (Senators Carl Hayden of Arizona and Elbert Thomas of Utah), the measure would establish an ODHWS wartime childcare program for working mothers.[84] In addition, Langdon proved unable to save all the WPA nursery schools from mandatory closure on April 30, largely because the OE refused to approve more Lanham funds until after the Thomas Bill hearings, slated for early June, settled nursery school jurisdiction.[85] From mid-March through early June, as WPA nursery schools closed, Lanham applications piled up and local communities, much to the CB's and OE's political advantage, directed their outrage at Langdon's office.[86]

Especially troubling to Langdon was that NANE parted company with her, its former president, over the Thomas Bill.[87] NANE's support for the Thomas Bill reflected a pragmatic consideration of events. WPA nursery schools had not been made permanent. Indeed, Langdon was in the midst

In Time of War 115

of closing some 550 schools. NANE members also worried that the Community Facilities Act would not allow permanent nursery schools within the public-school system, a concern that an assistant to the FWA administrator did nothing to allay, saying that "We have no interest in children except to see that they have care so that mothers can work in the war effort."[88] Weighing their options, prominent leaders, most notably Rose Alschuler, Mary Dabney Davis, and Ruth Andrus, publically opposed Langdon at the FWA. Those like Edna Noble White, who had an inside track on the story, did not.[89] The stage was set for a full-scale battle.

At hearings on June 8, no one declared themselves against childcare for working mothers.[90] But the wording of the Thomas Bill couched childcare as a temporary war measure that would end six months after hostilities ceased. The Thomas Bill also stipulated that funds be distributed through block grants to states.[91] By contrast, the FWA's Community Facilities Act left funding to the president's discretion and had no mandated end date. It required local control of federal funds and bypassed state channels altogether.

Once again, Florence Kerr proved a strong advocate for the FWA childcare program. She spoke of creating childcare centers for a million children in six months if she could get the funding.[92] Other FWA officials backed her and argued that the debate was really about who controlled the purse strings. They intimated that their issue with the Thomas Bill was that it put Taft, Lenroot, and Studebaker in charge. Stay the course with Kerr, they counseled. In defense of the FWA position, Eleanor Fowler of the CIO Women's Auxiliaries testified at the hearings that she preferred federal appropriations to block grants to states because states could delay funding. She also asked for more money on the ground, arguing that $20 million was simply too small a sum for the number of nursery schools required. Thomasina Johnson, spokesperson for Alpha Kappa Alpha, an African American sorority, castigated both the CB and OE as organizations that had discriminated against blacks, whereas the WPA/FWA childcare program had not.

Langdon's concerns during the summer of 1943 proved prescient.[93] Even though Congress funded the Community Facilities Act (albeit with a clause that all Lanham centers would fall under the OE and CB should the Thomas Bill pass), Langdon correctly predicted that continued feuding would permanently destroy chances for public nursery schools. She also wondered aloud whether or not she and the labor movement should float a bill incorporating her vision of universal preschool.[94] Langdon did not love the Community Facilities Act's provisions, but she did consider them better than those of the Thomas Bill. At the same time, she talked about being weary of the fight and wished aloud she could move over to the Office of Civilian Defense, where she felt she might have a better chance at promoting nursery schools for all children even though that office was "letting people go."[95]

Taft at the ODHWS would not let up the attack, however.[96] In pursuit of a containment strategy for public nursery schools, he kept insisting that the FWA was incompetent, insinuating it was filled with subversives who had

116   *In Time of War*

formerly worked for the WPA.[97] J. Edgar Hoover raised the specter of "wild children" running about because their mothers worked.[98] In late August 1943, Taft stopped his attacks because McNutt, his boss, was failing in his duties at the War Manpower Commission. Although FDR brokered another truce, the damage was done as far as public nursery schools were concerned.[99]

Langdon survived this battle in that she was not completely destroyed.[100] A critical mass of WPA nursery schools remained open as Lanham centers, and most remained excellent.[101] As media accounts depicted, families took full advantage of the centers.[102] In addition, Susan B. Anthony II, who had worked with Langdon to safeguard WPA nursery schools in D.C., published a well-reviewed account of Langdon's program.[103]

Anthony (great-niece of the suffragist) called on the federal government to provide childcare to ensure full mobilization for the ongoing war:

> The first responsibility of the War Manpower Commission, charged with mobilizing millions of mothers as well as childless women to win the war, is to provide a vast network of approved, low-cost nursery schools and other child-care programs, so that the children we cherish will not be among the growing list of war casualties.[104]

Calling for a federally subsidized system based on the WPA model, Anthony described three groups battling over wartime childcare. Langdon and other WPA nursery school program leaders represented "win-the-war forces."[105] They were opposed by the champions of keeping children at home, political reactionaries opposed to the New Deal in general and, more specifically, to federal aid to education of any kind.[106] In the middle, Anthony placed the "park 'em any place" contingent: Washington insiders in the CB and FSA, who saw the need for childcare but assumed "mothers would rather park their children with a neighbor upstairs."[107] Anthony pronounced Langdon's program "the most spontaneous and important demand of women workers since the fight for suffrage."[108]

Influential nursery school leaders also continued their support. Dorothy Baruch, for instance, wrote an investigative eight-part series on Lanham centers that was published in the *Journal of Consulting Psychology,* basing much of her research findings on centers in Southern California but also obtaining information from around the country. Her activism was one reason California remained the only state with publicly subsidized childcare centers after World War II.[109] Although Kerr nixed the idea of Anthony becoming a member, Langdon's advisory committee remained powerful with White as its chair, reflective of the rise of both CIO and African American support and the removal of OE representation.[110]

But the nursery school movement itself, an unprecedented interdisciplinary coalition of men and women, with children and without, and both professionals in the field and not, fragmented over the Thomas Bill, and program leaders around the country began to go their separate ways.[111]

In Time of War 117

Figure 4.1 Langdon's Advisory Committee[112]

Lois Meek Stolz moved away from the nursery school movement soon after her directorship of the Kaiser Child Care Centers ended.[113] Women's reform networks fragmented over the Thomas Bill, and the CIO split over whether to fight for a reasonable family wage or on behalf of working women's right to decent childcare. Taft and McNutt could rest assured—public nursery schools were now prevented from coming into being.

Despite another round of elected women politicians going to bat for Langdon in early 1944, she never got to 4,000 nursery schools, a number that was itself greatly insufficient given need and demand.[114] Under continued heavy attack from child welfare groups and McNutt, Taft, Studebaker, and Lenroot, she barely held on to the 1,500 with which she started—the same number on average as there were WPA nursery schools.[115] By the same token, the CB never got its foster care centers or mandatory counseling for working mothers.[116] Langdon did not approve funding for these services. And, as journalist Katherine Close admitted in *Survey Graphic*, a journal for social workers, working women wanted neither foster care nor counseling. What they wanted were more childcare centers.[117]

Katherine Lenroot took a parting shot on the final day most Lanham centers were open. Although her own office had been inundated with

Figure 4.2 Politicized Childcare[118]

requests to keep them in operation, Lenroot issued a press release on March 1, 1946:

> Twice as a country, we have done something about day care, but never in terms of what children need. In the depression years, centers were

In Time of War 119

maintained with Federal assistance in order to provide employment for adults. In the war years, they were maintained in order to get women on the job. Perhaps some time in the future, the problem will be considered in terms of the welfare of children.[119]

And so the end began. In the postwar years, continued bitterness from the 1943 battle brought the swift erasure of program accomplishments. With the birth of the Cold War, a veil of silence descended on consideration of using public expenditures for the education of young children in the United States. Program leaders and supporters retreated into their private lives during the Red Scare. Increased specialization in academic disciplines resulted in a willful amnesia concerning the first federally funded early childhood education program in American history. Images of babies crying while strapped to their working mothers' backs replaced images of preschoolers playing happily in community-centered nursery schools. WPA nursery schools became a buried treasure. Surely Langdon could not have foreseen all of this when she wrote to Edna Noble White on March 15, 1943: "In all the time I have been in Washington I have not known such a battle between agencies."

Notes

1. Reorganization took effect on July 1, 1939. FDR spearheaded this move to streamline the federal government. Engineer John Carmody was the first FWA director. General Philip B. Fleming headed the FWA from December 1941 until it was abolished in 1949.
2. He continued, "and probably will in some places go to the extent of closing down other projects that are not directly related to national defense." "Hunter Press Conference, 8/22/40" http://newdeal.feri.org/workrelief/hun04.htm.
3. Grace Langdon "How Family Life Education Can Contribute to a Defense Program" (August 22, 1940). WPA nursery schools were also known as the family life program after Langdon suggested to Carmody that a Family Life specialist coordinate work with young children and families for all of the FWA. See December 28, 1939, Langdon to White.
4. The conference took place from January 6 to 11, 1941. Isabel Robinson helped with organization, and WPA nursery school staff from around the country attended. Quote is from Grace Langdon and Isabel Robinson. *The Nursery School Program, 1933–1943: Record of Program Operation and Accomplishment* (1943) x.
5. According to historian Matthew Dallek, Eleanor Roosevelt began conceptualizing the Office of Civilian Defense following the November 1940 election. See his *Defenseless Under the Night: The Roosevelt Years and the Origins of Homeland Security* (2016). See also Jean Edward Smith, *FDR* (2008) and Ira Katznelson, *Fear Itself: The New Deal and the Origins of Our Time* (2013) for how FDR became preoccupied with events abroad.
6. Recreation Director, G. Ott Romney, a former college football coach (and distant relative of Mitt Romney), apparently condoned this action.
7. Langdon met with ACE's Pres. Olga Adams, a University of Chicago professor at her January defense conference in Chicago. See January 23, 1941, Langdon to White: "[she] is concerned about the Recreation play groups."
8. January 18, 1941, Louise Stanley to White (confidential): "need to have nursery school tied to 'some permanent Federal agency having to do with education.'"

120   *In Time of War*

Stanley read this letter over phone to Langdon because of the confidential nature of McNutt's new program. January 6, 1940, Langdon to White: "Bess Goodykoontz has just told me that Studebaker is about to ask Paul McNutt (recently named head of FSA) to transfer nursery school program over to OE. Langdon likes this idea, but worries that direct approach will backfire."

9. January 31, 1941, White to Goodykoontz: "I was concerned at [Studebaker's] apparent lack of realization that a program such has been developed under Dr. Langdon's direction could be split up in parts and placed in several different categories." White was also frustrated by Kerr's preoccupation with Office of Civilian Defense preparations: she can't "afford to have people like Miss Lenroot and professional groups like the ACE and many others, condemning the WPA program because of the large number of preschool groups with untrained [WPA Recreation] teachers."

10. March 11, 1941, White to Langdon and March 14, 1941, Langdon to White.

11. March 14, 1941, Langdon to White: "Hunter (new WPA Director) hates Kerr, but I think she is solid so long as Hopkins is near the White House." Kerr continued to sing the program's praises whenever she had the opportunity. In a speech given to the Americans Women's Voluntary Services, she asserted:

> I don't need to tell you of the value of [WPA nursery schools]. I think you will agree with me that such nursery schools should be and someday will be, a part of our regular school system, for the benefit of all our children. In the meantime, there is certainly need for more community services of this kind, and it is an important field for volunteer work.
>
> "Total Defense and Community Service" (March 14, 1941) 10-H.
> Floyd Dell Papers, Newbery Library, Chicago

In a handwritten note at the end of speech, Dell said Kerr's address was close to his own personal views.

12. FDR had reactivated the Council of National Defense in May 1940. Its new advisory committee (NDAC) consisted of seven experts in specific areas of the national economy, with responsibility to recommend defense materials needed and the means of obtaining them. Will Alexander became the NDAC specialist on Minority Affairs in July 1940. (He had just left his position as director of the Farm Security Administration to accept a position with the Julius Rosenwald fund but came back to D.C. to help with mobilization). FDR placed all NDAC activities under supervision of the Office for Emergency Management on January 7, 1941, but all activities were indefinitely suspended on October 21, 1941. See NARA RG 220.5.5 and Wilma Dykeman and James Stokely, *Seeds of Southern Change: The Life of Will Alexander* (1962).

13. In this March 20, 1941, memo, Langdon called for mobilizing all extant nursery schools to serve defense needs. She also recommended using the well-trained teachers and supervisors already in place with the WPA nursery school program in "practically every state." Alexander (recommended earlier by Kerr) was interested in achieving civil rights. In addition to showing enthusiasm for Langdon's idea on March 20, Alexander expressed interest in supporting what would become *Encyclopedia of the Negro* when he met with W. E. B. DuBois on March 21, 1941.

14. April 15, 1941, Kerr to White: "I want us all to meet to figure out a way to protect both nursery schools and pre-school play groups." Kerr and other FWA administrators expressed support for the WPA nursery school program when they testified in mid-May hearings. Langdon stayed busy with field trips.

15. Kiplinger telegrammed Langdon, June 19, 1941. Langdon then telegrammed White, "nursery school program in jeopardy; am cutting visit in CA (in SF) short, and heading back to DC—more info to follow."

In Time of War 121

16. June 24, 1941, Langdon to White, written two days after Hitler began Operation Barbarossa against USSR.
17. June 30, 1941, White to Lenroot.
18. Women's groups cried sexism in the national press. See, for instance, "Discrimination Against Women Is Seen by Mrs. Whitehurst in Civilian Defense" *New York Times* (July 31, 1941), *Indianapolis Star* (July 31, 1941) 6, *Arizona Republic* (July 31, 1941) 49, and *Louisville Courier-Journal* (August 1, 1941) 24.
19. Sonya Michel, *Children's Interests/Mothers' Rights: The Shaping of America's Child Care Policy* (1999) 128–132. Appendix B of this book lists the participants, which included the CB, OE, and WPA.
20. August 15, 1941, Lenroot to Kerr: "Care of Children of Working Mothers Conference" Lenroot offered CB funds generated by Title V, parts 1 and 3 of the Social Security Act, for doctors and nurses in this new federal project.
21. Langdon to Kerr, "Possible Federal Project for the Care of Children" (August 19, 1941) 7 pages. Quotes are from pages 1 and 5.
22. Langdon and Robinson, "Memo 1: A Nation-Wide Project for the Daytime Care of Children During the National Emergency" (September 4, 1941) 10 pages; Langdon and Robinson, "Memo II: Analysis of Federal WPA Project Proposal for Daytime Care of Children During the National Emergency" (September 4, 1941) 10 pages.
23. Langdon also suggested cooperative play groups, cooperative neighborhood groups (parents taking family life/parent education classes), temporary shelter care, and individual home care, particularly for infants.
24. Langdon and Robinson, "Memo 1" (September 4, 1941) 4, 5, and 9.
25. Representatives at these meetings included: CB: Katherine Lenroot, chief: Dr. Ellen Potter, Director of Medicine, Dept. of Institutions and Agencies, Trenton, NJ; Dr. Martha Eliot, assoc. chief of CB; Charles Schottland, Asst. to Chief, CB; OE: Dr. N.S. Light, CT Dept. of Education; Dr. Arnold Gesell, School of Medicine, Yale; Miss Bess Goodykoontz, asst. commissioner, US OE; Dr. John Lund, asst. to Goodykoontz, OE; WPA: Dr. Grace Langdon, Miss Isabel Robinson; Mrs. Florence Kerr; Mr. Amory, Southern CA Director of WPA; Miss Van De Vrady, WPA.
26. Office of Children's Bureau, "Conference on Day Time Care of Children of Working Mothers" (September 6, 1941) 6 pages.
27. Langdon to Kerr, "Minutes of Meeting on Day Time Care of Children in Defense Preparations on 9/17/41" (September 18, 1941) 4 pages.
28. Langdon and Robinson, "A Suggested Alternate Plan" (September 5, 1941) 2 pages.
29. Joint Planning Board on Day Care for Children (August 1941–June 1942). Regular meetings combined services of "three agencies most directly concerned with services to children." The members included: Mrs. Florence Kerr, Assistant Commissioner, WPA; Dr. Grace Langdon, Chief Child Protection Program, WPA—chair; Isabel J. Robinson, Assistant Child Protection Program, WPA; Dr. Bess Goodykoontz, Assistant Commissioner, OE; Dr. John Lund, OE; Miss Olga Jones, OE; Katherine Lenroot, chief of CB; Emma Lundberg, CB; Charles Schottland, CB. See Grace Langdon and Isabel Robinson, *The Nursery School Program, 1933–1943: Record of Program Operation and Accomplishment* (1943) 90.
30. WPA-CB cooperation: October 31, 1941. Langdon outlines certain photos given to CB; Two from California: San Francisco (Chinese); Hemet (water play). WPA-OE cooperation: November 19, 1941. Langdon fact-checked Mary Dabney Davis, "What is the Federal Government Doing for Children?" *Childhood Education* 18 (November 1941) 105–109. "In sum, lots of government agencies working on behalf of children: OE in FSA; CB in Dept. of Labor; Bureau of Home Economics and Extension Service in Dept. of Agriculture;

122 In Time of War

US Housing Authority; WPA (Family Life, Recreation program, Housekeeping Aide, School Lunches); NYA; Farm Security Administration."

31. "Dies Charges 1,124 in Federal Posts Help Communists" *New York Times* (October 20, 1941) and "Sea Unions Protest Naming of Carmody as Member of Maritime Board: Red Leanings Charged" *New York Times* (December 7, 1941). See also Landon Storrs, *The Second Red Scare and the Unmaking of the New Deal Left* (2013) 256–257, 270.

32. Langdon desired this commission "To safeguard in all nation, state, and local planning the health, education, and general well-being of young children; To stimulate and help further programs of action designed to safeguard young children wherever they may be." November 3, 1941, Langdon to White and November 10, 1941, Langdon memo to NANE.

33. "Report of First Meeting of Commission" (November 8, 1941) 10 pages. Members present: Rose Alschuler, Lawrence Frank, Harriet Houdlette, Alice Keliher, George Stoddard, Edna White, Ruth Updegraff and Grace Langdon. William Carr, John Anderson, Frederick Redefer and Allison Davis join soon thereafter.

34. On December 2, Kerr sent letters to state WPA supervisors in 12 'defense area' states (PA, AR, AL, FL, IN, CT, VA, MO, CA, WA, TX, NJ), asking for information on the "acute" need for daycare. Replies came back from mid-December 1941 through February 1942. A December 11 and 16, 1941 response from a Missouri administrator, for instance, talked in terms of the desperate needs of both "underprivileged" children and working mothers.

35. December 11 and 12, 1941, Langdon to White. On December 12, Langdon stated, "I want to make sure our program is kept and used; child care is a vital defense requirement . . . I'm concerned about Rose . . . I can only do what I can as myself and as a WPA person (she's trying to run a 1-woman show) . . . what is clear is that CB wants to take over child care services . . . I understand on the QT that Miss [Eloise] Davison [at Office of Civilian Defense] has told Mrs. Roosevelt that positively the responsibility cannot go into the Children's Bureau."

36. December 15, 1941, White to Kerr.

37. Langdon, Grace. "The Young Ones Need Defense" *Progressive Education* 19 (February 1942) 118–119.

38. March 2, 1942, Langdon to White. In a March 12 memo on the WPA service division, Langdon is called Child Protection "Chief (nursery schools, public child service centers, child development group units in defense areas; and pre-school play groups formerly under the Recreation program)."

39. October 4, 1941, Langdon to White.

40. Alschuler moved to Washington in late 1941. See, for example, the following letters from ENW:

> November 19, 1941 White to Langdon: "Just had a telephone conversation with Eloise Davison [at Office of Civilian Defense]: we need to slow Rose Alschuler down a bit"
>
> November 24, Langdon to White, "Tell Rose that: 1) Things cannot be pushed, 2) Administration is none of her affair—she is working on a program; 3) Alschuler also came in to Kerr's office and talked about not using the WPA. Mrs. Kerr thinks that some pressure may be brought on her or may already have been, which would make her fall in with that trend even though she herself might not feel so. (She was also maligning WPA state supervisors, who I then supported . . . Rose is so earnest, and well-meaning, but does not know her way around Washington."
>
> November 24, White to Alschuler: [following Langdon's advice] "no need to sell commission to governmental people (they're already sold). This type

In Time of War 123

of program cannot be forced. Your discussion of program with Mary Davis before talking over with Bess Goodykoontz was not politically a deft maneuver . . . Let states decide on the state supervisors (including picking WPA people—most of whom are good)."

November 28, Langdon to White: can't you come down to help out? "I think it would be fatal for the commission to be tied up with any one governmental agency (especially the CB)."

December 4, White to Langdon: "Based on telephone conversation with Alschuler last night, I'm concerned about Commission. Don't feel that Alschuler is manageable—she just throws her money around. . . . I don't have time to deal . . . so I'm not coming to Washington to work out situation with Eloise Davison (who's in direct communication with Eleanor Roosevelt) or CB's Lenroot and Dr. Martha Eliot."

December 4, Ruth Updegraff to White: "Alschuler is trying to force the issue with Office of Civilian Defense—concerned about not having 'official status' with Eleanor Roosevelt, although she has an office and authorization to work in volunteer capacity. What should we do?"

December 5, White to Ruth Updegraff: "I too am disturbed about the Commission; Rose called me (on December 3) and is intent upon pushing OCD sponsorship which will not work—she has no real plan. She should take her trip to Arizona, you Ruth take your trip to California, and let's all meet in Washington in the early part of 1942. I'm hopeful that a good program can emerge (as it did in 1933)."

December 5, Alschuler to White (paraphrase): met with CT NANE; Bennington College—interested in getting government support for an experimental children's center to be placed in the one of the defense housing areas. [no mention of anything else].

December 6, White to Rose Alschuler: "I certainly agree that we cannot tie ourselves to one Government agency and that may mean that we will have to develop independently of any of them as we did before. Let's just wait a bit until situation clarifies somewhat (especially as it relates to Dr. Martha Eliot at CB)."

41. Alschuler to Commission, "First Report" (March 5, 1942) 10 pages. In this report, Alschuler mentions that she is working with Carleton Washburne, Lawrence Frank, and Dr. Pearl Bretnall. She also followed around 'Dr. Langdon' on a WPA field trip in Louisiana, Texas, Arkansas, Oklahoma, Arizona, and California and met with individual members of the AAUW—she is interested in starting a "cooperative" in Defense Housing Units (9). In Baton Rouge, "Mr. Perry, State Director of Civilian Defense+ Chairman of Dept. of Public Welfare "frank about the fact that they are tired of newly-formed committees" (3). Alschuler asserts,

> There has been in every state that I have visited thus far a very real need for someone to come in from the outside to point out objectives as they now exist. . . . Barriers between health, education and welfare departments and organizations exist, but there is evidently a very real desire to join forces in order to meet the urgent needs of the present situation.

42. Alschuler to Commission, "Second Report" (March 18, 1942) 9 pages.
43. In a handwritten note to White (June 26, 1942), Alschuler asserts, "I heard from a completely outside source that it was you who primed Mrs. Norton. If Grace [Langdon] knows this, she has certainly given no inkling of it—nor did I think it wise to open up the subject with her. . . . Perhaps this letter should be destroyed."

124   In Time of War

44. House Committee on Appropriations, "Work Relief and Relief for FY43: HJ Res. 3242" 77th Congress (June 1–2, 1942). See also Norton's testimony in Congressional Record.
45. As Jed Johnson (OK), Compton White (ID), Mary Norton (NJ), and Jerry Voorhis (CA) emphasized in their testimony, WPA critics conveniently ignored the plight of older people, women, and migrant workers.
46. Emergency Relief Appropriation Bill, fy43 (June 22, 1942) 31.
47. August 6, 1942, Langdon to White: "Enclosed minutes of July 5, 1942 meeting," 8 pages. According to Grace Langdon and Isabel Robinson, *The Nursery School Program, 1933–1943: Record of Program Operation and Accomplishment* (1943), "Emphasis changed from service for children from low-income families to service for children of working mothers" on July 1, 1942.
48. Paul McNutt had moved up the political ladder by aligning himself with the American Legion. Although intent on moving into the Oval Office, McNutt lost the 1940 Democratic nominations for both president and vice president. See Harold Zink, *The American Politician* (1938), Israel George Blake, *Paul V. McNutt: Portrait of a Hoosier Statesman* (1966), and Dean Kotlowski, *Paul V. McNutt and the Age of FDR* (2015).
49. By January 1941, his program included family security and education, which brought in Langdon, coordinator of FWA "family life education." McNutt's position underwent subtle name changes. For purposes of consistency, I use ODHWS throughout this book.
50. Congress passed the original act in October 1940 as a measure to build housing for defense workers. Written by Fritz Lanham, a conservative Democrat from Texas, the original language mandated local control and put the FWA in charge. Precedent for using this act's funds for community facilities was "the contribution the WPA had made to the expansion of local facilities in practically every community in the nation." See Donald Howard, "The Lanham Act in Operation" *Survey Midmonthly* 79 (February 1943) 38.
51. Langdon-Kerr, "First Meeting of Family Security Committee" (February 20, 1941) 7 pages. Public Agencies: WPA-FWA, Veteran's Administration, FSA/ Dept. Of Agriculture (no representative), OE/FSA (no representative) CB/Dept. of Labor: Bureau of Employment Security, Bureau of Old-Age, and Bureau of Public Assistance, Social Security Board; Surplus Marketing Administration, Dept. of Agriculture, CCC/FSA, Railroad Retirement, & NYA. Private Agencies: American Red Cross, Family Welfare Association, Travelers Aid, National Catholic Welfare, Council of Jewish Federations, Amer. Association of Social Workers, Amer. Assoc. of Medical Social Workers, Amer. Assoc. of Psychiatric Social Workers, American Public Welfare Assoc., Community Chests, Salvation Army, Amer. Association of Schools of Social Work, Child Welfare League of America, and National Urban League.
52. House committee on Public Buildings and Grounds, Public Buildings and Grounds: HR 3213, HR 3570, 77th Congress (March 4–7, 12, 13, 1941).
53. McNutt allowed his OE representatives to fret publicly that federal aid to education (even when designed to bolster national defense) meant loss of local control for school districts. In this manner, he began the process of dismantling both the CCC and the NYA. See Senate Committee on Education and Labor, Educational Finance Act of 1941: SB 1313, 77th Congress (April 28–30, 1941) and W. C. B. Bagley, "Is the Liquidation of the NYA Both a Protest and a Portent?" *School and Society* 58 (July 10, 1943) 21–22.
54. Senate Committee on public buildings and grounds, Acquisition and Equipment of Public Works Made Necessary by the Defense Program: HR 4545 and SB 1375, 77th Congress (May 19–20, 1941).

In Time of War 125

55. At these hearings, FWA attorney Alan Johnstone succeeded in showing that Senator Robert Taft (as well as Charles Taft) misquoted and distorted the testimony of FWA Administrator John Carmody. In *Defense and war years history, development and progress of War Public Services, Division 2, Bureau of Community Facilities, Federal Works Agency* (Washington, DC: Bureau of Community Facilities, 1946), Mary Moon asserts that a "gentleman's agreement" was reached between the FSA and FWA.

56. Funding obtained from the Senate Committee on Appropriations, Second Deficiency Appropriation Bill for 1941, 77th Congress, June 26, 27, 1941 and House committee, June 2–7, 10–13, 16–19, 1941. As reported by Ward Keesecker, Educational Measures Before the 77th Congress, First Session, 1941 *School Life* 27 (October 1941) 23–26.

57. Although best known as the law that made it possible for federal funds to be used for the childcare of children of working mothers in early 1942, crucial components of this June 1941 bill included the new consulting role of the FSA, the need for presidential approval on projects and the local control requirement. As stipulated by Fritz Lanham himself, federal auditing was allowed, but not federal oversight of Lanham funds.

58. *Childhood Education* mentioned the efforts of early childhood educators following passage of the Community Facilities Act (aka HR 4545 or Title II of Lanham) in June 1941.

59. The other two were Lenroot and CB assistant chief, Dr. Martha Eliot.

60. On November 8, 1941, Langdon urged her new commission to "facilitate the local priming" (drum up local support) for nursery schools at upcoming Senate hearings. See Senate Committee on Education and Labor, "Defense Housing and Community Facilities: HR 6128" 77th Congress (December 18–19, 1941). General Fleming and M. E. Gilmore represented the FWA (Carmody had resigned days earlier). Paul McNutt and Charles Taft represented the FSA. According to Barbara Harned, "testimony before a Senate subcommittee on Education and Labor in connection with the Defense Housing and Community Faculties Bill in December 1941, laid the foundation for use of Lanham funds for day care" in "Relationships Among the Federally Sponsored Nursery Schools of the 1930s, the Federally Sponsored Day Care Program of the 1940s and Project Heat Start" (PhD dissertation, Rutgers University, 1968) 495.

61. Henry Martin to Kerr, "Supplementary assistance to take care of children under the Lanham Act" (January 15, 1942) 2 pages. Martin referred specifically to "Title II, Section 202, article C." Two days later, Bess Goodykoontz, assistant commissioner of the OE, requested a meeting with Langdon to coordinate her office with the WPA. As a member of Langdon's advisory committee, Goodykoontz seemed intent on maintaining a positive relationship. Her OE colleague, H. F. Alves admitted to Langdon that many of the Lanham applications the OE received were for nursery schools. See Langdon to Walter Kiplinger, "Meeting in Mrs. Kerr's Office" (January 17, 1942) 2 pages.

62. Words of Representative John Taber (R-NY); quoted in Polenberg 1972: 187. In May 1941, NYC mayor Fiorello LaGuardia was put in charge of the Office of Civilian Defense. He showed little interest in organizing volunteer participation in civilian defense or the social welfare programs Eleanor Roosevelt believed should be part of the program. Nonetheless, she became his assistant, and "facilitated an interagency agreement on providing federal funds for day care and support for maternal, child-health, and child-welfare services." Briefly, Kerr worked there as well. For political reasons, both LaGuardia and Eleanor Roosevelt resigned in early February 1942. James Landis, the man Eleanor Roosevelt had gotten FDR to appoint following Pearl Harbor, had

126   In Time of War

already been labeled pink in the press. Anti-communist attacks weakened the Office of Civilian Defense, and Truman terminated the office on May 2, 1945.

63. Katherine Close, "While Mothers Work" *Survey Midmonthly* 78 (July 1942) 196–198.

64. The eight agencies were the CB, OE, WPA, National Housing Agency, Farm Security Administration, US Employment Service, Recreation Division of the ODHWS and Bureau of Public Assistance. According to Langdon 1943: "Certain conflicts among agencies arose and meetings were delayed and postponed and finally the Joint Planning Board ceased to function although there was no formal disbandment" (91).

65. In June 1942, McNutt emphasized this approach when he spoke in front of the American Legion. Emma Puschner, director of the American Legion National Child Welfare Division, introduced him.

66. FWA Administrator, General Philip Fleming, derisively referred to McNutt and Taft as "the health and happiness boys." See December 30, 1942, Langdon to White.

67. "Door-Key Children Offer Big Problem: WPA Nursery School Director Tells of War Mothers" *New York Times*, (July 15, 1942) 22:8.

68. McNutt had modified the proposals offered at the CB Day Care conference the summer before (reprinted in The Child, August 1941). Here instead are his three proposals:

   1. "Appropriate care should be provided for children while their mothers work.
   2. Mothers of preschool children should not be called upon to do essential work until other sources of labor have been tried.
   3. In consideration of the welfare of mothers and children, the idea should be stressed that a mother of young children may consider it her patriotic duty to remain at home to care for her children."

69. For confirmation of Kerr's appointment, see August 20, 1942 Langdon to White. See also FDR's August 21, 1942 letter to each federal department and agency on public disagreements between federal officials. On August 28, FDR directed the ODHWS to work in an advisory, not operational, capacity. He also stipulated that the $400,000 be transmitted through OE and CB channels. FDR issued a warning: "The need for child care grows out of increasingly acute problem of labor supply. I believe that much can be accomplished locally toward meeting such needs as may arise provided stimulation and co-ordination of efforts are achieved" (Grace Langdon and Isabel Robinson, *The Nursery School Program, 1933–1943: Record of Program Operation and Accomplishment* (1943) 197.

70. August 20, 1942, Langdon to White.

71. The New Haven Lanham center opened its doors to children in early October 1942. See Arnold Gesell, "The New Haven Child Care Center" *Childhood Education* (April 1943) 366–370.

72. Langdon kept Denver's WPA nursery schools intact though Lanham funds. She wrote to White in August: "We think we are getting the bottleneck in DC uncorked so that we may be able to have nursery schools here again. We are going over to the Hill about it this morning." See also unpublished hearing in front of Senate Committee on District of Columbia, "Day Nurseries and Nursery schools: HR 7522" 77th Congress (December 5, 1942). Powerful committee chair Pat McCarran held up funding. See Michael Ybarra, *Washington Gone Crazy: Senator Pat McCarran and the Great American Communist Hunt* (2004).

73. Schottland, who joined the military in October 1942, served as a lieutenant colonel with Eisenhower. In later years, he talked about the "terrible

In Time of War 127

jurisdictional battles" that took place during his stint as daycare liaison/
director of the ODHWS, but gave no further details [Earl Warren oral history
project]. On September 15, 1942, Langdon wrote White, "I think Mr. S. is
honestly trying to do the job he is put there to do but I think he is being used
by other people who are more interested in politics than in the job to be done."
After the war, Schottland worked as Commissioner of Social Security. For a
brief biography, see https://socialwelfare.library.vcu.edu/people/schottland-
charles-i/. James Brunot, his successor as day care director of ODHWS, helped
develop Scrabble in the late 1940s.

74. September 15, 1942, Langdon to White: "[Housing] having the same difficulties that we are with FSA. In fact just about everyone is. It apparently is an
over-ambition for power and more power."

75. Grace Thorne Allen, Maxine Davis and Warner Olivier, "Eight-Hour Orphans"
Saturday Evening Post 215 (October 10, 1942) 20–21, 105–106. CB staff also
encouraged their field staff to stall for time by surveying all needs before putting in any applications for day care—based on Lenroot's congressional testimony in February 1943.

76. Office of Education, FSA, Nursery Schools Vital to America's War Effort
(1943)12:

> The provision of nursery schools for young children of working mothers is
> no longer just a pleasant, kindly thing to do out a sense of human decency,
> justice, and kindness to children: it is a grim, unsentimental necessity in a
> nation geared to the production of tanks and more tanks, bombs and more
> bombs, planes and more planes. . . . Nursery schools in America may mean
> victory in Europe, in Asia, in Africa, and on the high seas. For the time
> being, at least, nursery schools have achieved the status of front-line defense.

As historians David Tyack and Paula Fass have noted, Studebaker consistently
fought to have the NYA and CCC placed under his jurisdiction as well. He
proved a spoilsport when that did not happen either.

77. What OE officials did do is focus on their Extended School Service Program,
the before and after school programs for children of school age. They did not,
as a rule, work with Lanham children's centers.

78. "Work Relief Seen Nearing Its Finish—WPA Official Would Give It Honorable
Discharge" *New York Times* (October 30, 1942). At this time, Kerr was WPA
Assistant Administrator, Director of WPA Community Services, and FWA
Community Facilities Director.

79. "FDR to Federal Works Administrator Discontinuing the WPA" (December 4,
1942) www.presidency.ucsb.edu/.

80. December 30, 1942, Langdon to White:

> Meeting with General Fleming was very satisfactory. He speaks of the
> ODHWS as "the health and happiness boys." It appears that there is no
> danger of any other agency getting the six million [Norton appropriation].
> Smith, director of the Bureau of the Budget is on Harry Byrd's committee
> which is committed not to leave a vestige of WPA. Of course we beat them
> to it by being in liquidation before Congress met. But it means that Smith
> as a member of that committee does not dare do anything to perpetuate any
> WPA fund or anything connected with it. So that is out. General Fleming is
> very ready to do anything possible to keep nursery schools in war areas open.
> I also spoke to George Field; creating an interim operation through FWA for
> all nursery schools now open or nearly ready to open in war affected areas;
> they can stay open. General sending out telegram to all FWA regional direc-
> tors telling them "that child protection applications have the first priority

128 *In Time of War*

over every other application" and that he wants them to get them moving. The General showed real understanding and great confidence in Mrs. Kerr. She has laid some good groundwork with some others and is following right up. But I think we are going to need you next week if you can come. There is so much which cannot be written.

81. Ibid. As for the number of WPA nursery schools in late 1942, one source indicates 1,250 WPA nursery schools, caring for 55,000 children in October 1942; another source lists 944 WPA nursery schools, serving about 39,000 children in December 1942; still another (Kerr) says 1,600 left. I now realize that the CB and OE had a vested interest in deflating WPA numbers, but whether Kerr also included Lanham centers in her figure is unknown.

82. Grace Langdon, "Uncle Sam Takes Care of His Youngest" *Parents Magazine* (January 1943) 34–35+.

83. Testimony from Committee on appropriations, US House of Representatives, 78th congress, 1st session, Hearings on the First Deficiency Appropriation Bill for 1943 (February 4, 6, 8, 10, 13, 15–19, 1943) 782–783.

84. March 15, 1943, Langdon to White:

> ODHWS request did get through. I was there for entire hearing. There was four hours debate and many speeches. I never heard so much misinformation bandied about as there was in those speeches. Hayden from Ariz. presented the motion for suspending the rules and later presented the bill. He did his level best to push it through. He had evidently been coached by Rose Alschuler and he did his best for her. He gave all sorts of wrong information. He used Lanham figures to show how little is being done by WPA. Knew nothing about any of the real facts.

85. Langdon's sadness in closing schools is evident in her 1943 history. Langdon remained focused on quality control—she went over each new Lanham application with a fine-toothed comb because the Community Facilities Act did not allow for federal oversight, only auditing.

86. At this point, New York City's public schools talked about funding nursery schools. Alice Keliher and Elinor Gimbel led this new NYC daycare committee. See Alice Keliher papers, NYU Archives.

87. In addition to supporting the Thomas Bill, ACE and NANE filed letters of endorsement during SB 637 hearings on April 7, 1943. Senator Robert Taft shut down this first federal aid to education legislation to reach the Senate floor in over fifty years by using race, religion, and fears of federal control as his calling cards. See especially, Gilbert Smith, *The Limits of Reform: Politics and Federal Aid to Education, 1937–1950* (1982).

88. Mary Leeper, "The Cooperative Effort for Children During Wartime: Federal Programs for the Care of Children in Wartime." Unpublished manuscript, ACEI archives (April 1943) 4 pages.

89. Langdon telegrammed White on June 1, 1943: "Thomas Bill is same old scheme dressed up. Proposed overall bill not being pushed until way is clearer." Both women realized McNutt and Taft had initiated a power play, not a good-faith effort to achieve universal preschool.

90. Senate Committee on Education and Labor, Wartime Care and Protection of Children of Employed Mothers Hearings: SB 876 and 1130, 78th Congress (June 8, 1943).

91. OE representatives continued to raise the bogeyman of "federal" control of local schools if the FWA stayed in charge of Lanham children's centers. See House Committee on Public Buildings and Grounds, Amendment of Title II

In Time of War   129

Housing in Connection with National Defense, 78th Congress (June 3, 4, 8, 1943).

92. These appropriations did not materialize. See decisions reached after hearings, Senate Committee on Public Buildings and Grounds, "Community Facilities" 78th Congress (June 29, 30, 1943).

93. The Thomas Bill passed in the Senate, but not the House, before the summer recess. According to Langdon, "Taft's outfit" was confident the bill would pass if it came up for a vote again in the fall. Anticipating a takeover, OE's Studebaker confused the issue further by announcing "funding for child care services" was ending. He meant the ODHWS $400 million had expired, but local Lanham people, in agitated fashion, thought it meant the schools themselves were ending, not just the advisory services by state welfare and education personnel. See Langdon—White letters.

94. On July 10, 1943, Langdon wrote the following extraordinary handwritten note to White, "What do you think of pushing our other bill now—it is much more in line with what is needed—what would you think of your state [CIO] committee coming forth with it and begin to roll up support for it." Earlier in the year, Langdon had expressed hope that her program "would survive to become a permanent legacy and after the war, because we have acquired this habit, it may be that all of the children, all of the time, may have the food they need, the health care they need, to become the best person each of them can be."

95. Langdon to White, July 16, 1943. The Office of Civilian Defense had a hiring freeze because, like the WPA, it had become an anti-communist target.

96. At the Thomas hearings, Taft made explicit his two-year effort to wrest control from the FWA.

97. In letters to White in July 1943, Langdon accused Taft of giving misinformation to major news outlets. Another ODHWS ally said,

> There is a positive aversion to group care of children in the minds of working women. . . . To some it connotes an inability to care for one's own; to some it has a vague incompatibility with the traditional idea of the American home; to others it has a taint of socialism. Group care violates the mores and sentimentalism that has grown up around the young.
> Wayne Coy, "The Federal Government and a Child Care Program" (November 5, 1943)

98. J. Edgar Hoover, "Wild Children" *American Magazine* 136 (July 1943).

99. Mary Moon et al., *Defense and War Years History, Development and Progress of War Public Services, Division 2, Bureau of Community Facilities, Federal Works Agency* (Washington, DC: Bureau of Community Facilities, 1946).

100. Langdon began to travel again, but her job, on paper at least, had been whittled down to an auditing service.

101. See, for example, J. W. Edgar, "The Story of Jimmy" *Progressive Education* 22–23 (October 1944) 33–34.

102. See, for example, Ethel Huggard, "The Nursery School—A Foundation Stone in Our National Defense" *Journal of Educational Sociology* 16 (March 1943) 417–420; Grace Thorne Allen, "Adults Tomorrow" *Woman's Home Companion* 71 (October 1944) 38, 114; Rose Kundanis, "Rosie the Riveter and the Eight-Hour Orphan: The Image of Child Day Care during WWII" in M. Paul Holsinger and Mary Anne Schofield, eds., *Visions of War: WWII in Popular Literature and Culture* (1992) 138–148; and references cited in Doris Weatherford, *American Women during World War II: An Encyclopedia* (2009).

130 *In Time of War*

103. In *Out of the Kitchen and Into the War: Women's Winning Role in the Nation's Drama* (1943), Anthony made a three-part argument that built on her experience as New Dealer, journalist, and CIO women's auxiliary leader. First, children were safer at school than at home. One day in December 1942, recounted Anthony, two sisters left their young children with their elderly and infirm mother to work in a Tulsa, Oklahoma aircraft company. Unbeknownst to their mothers, the children started to play with matches near the stove at home: all in the house burned to death. Motivated by their tragic loss, the mothers helped get a childcare program started for other working mothers in their factory. Second, nursery schools gave children and mothers a much-needed break from each other. Anthony cited psychologist Leo Kanner, who studied the effects of "mother-child separation" on those who attended nursery school and found the results beneficial for both children and their mothers: "it decreased friction, quarreling and nagging on the part of the mother and gave the child little encouragement to show off" (126). Third, federal subsidy was essential. Anthony advised American women: "Put your energy into starting twenty public nursery schools rather than one private nursery school. . . . Nurseries are, in the last analysis, a national problem" (137, 139, 140).

104. Ibid: 130. "I will not blame Mr. McNutt personally. . . . Personalities are not at issue. The story, much more complicated than that, is that Mr. McNutt has responded to heavy pressures in and out of Government. Like all politicians, he has had to appease certain groups, whether or not their policies coincided with the prosecution of the war" (131).

105. "Dr. Langdon reports that her office was deluged for weeks after the order with telegrams, letters and telephone calls from women and employers throughout the country" (141).

106. Anthony argued that "hostility to group care on the part of a few highly placed members of the Catholic hierarchy, ignoring or overriding the obvious needs of their own Catholic workings mothers, has been more at the root of the McNutt directive than we realize. . . . The work of 'short-sighted' and I believe, non-representative Catholics," convinced that nursery schools were an attempt to separate mother from child during vital formative years (134).

107. Ibid: 132.

108. Ibid: 144. Anthony accused Taft of sabotaging Langdon's program by deliberating falsifying information at the local level and trying to dismantle it through federal legislation: "From the Washington power-politics point of view, Mr. Taft and his agency are obviously seeking to crowd the FWA child care program out of the picture."

109. Except for Tuttle 1993 (who cites one) and Hewes 1998 (who cites another), Baruch's eight-part series is not cited in secondary works. The first of these was Dorothy Baruch, "Child Care Centers and the Mental Health of Children in This War" *Journal of Consulting Psychology* 7 (November–December 1943) 252–266.

110. April 27, 1944, Langdon to White: "I am particularly anxious to have Margaret Mead serve. She is so forthright and direct—has the ear of the White House—stands well with the professional groups—and I think it would counter some of the things the ACE and other groups are doing." On May 15, Kerr wrote White: Keep Mead, but "We have given further thought to the matter of a publicist on the committee. . . . I suggest that we leave that place unfilled. This will remove Susan Anthony's name from the tentative list which Dr. Landon gave you."

In Time of War 131

111. In a letter to White after the October 1943 NANE conference in Boston, Langdon asserted that Rose Alschuler, Ruth Andrus, and N. Searle Light convinced all at NANE gathering to promote Thomas Bill. After the Thomas Bill died in the House, membership fell at NANE. NANE splintered further after Light and Arnold Gesell testified against Langdon's program at the Senate Committee on Education and Labor, Wartime Health and Education, Part 1: Juvenile Delinquency, 78th Congress (November 30, December 1–3, 1943). Membership declined anew after Light became the first person to become NANE president without a background in early childhood education, 1943–1945.

112. Photo of FWA Advisory Committee on Child Care. November 14–15, 1944. Merrill-Palmer Institute: Edna Noble White Records, Walter P. Reuther Library, Wayne State University. The caption reads: "In the picture, Mrs. Florence Kerr, FWA director of War Public Services, is seated at her desk. To her right is Dr. Edna Noble White, director of the Merrill-Palmer School, Detroit, chairman of the National Advisory Committee. Standing, left to right are: C. F. Ramsay, superintendent of the Michigan Children's Institute, Ann Arbor; Mrs. Irene Murphy, director of the Department of Public Welfare, Detroit; Monsignor John O'Grady, Secretary of the National Council of Catholic Charities, Washington, D.C.; Miss Mary E. Murphy, director of the Elizabeth McCormick Memorial Fund, Chicago; Dr. Margaret Mead, of the National Research Council; Dr. A.W. Dent, president of Dillard University, New Orleans; Dr. Esther Crane, of the Department of Education and Child Development, Goucher College, Baltimore; Dr. Irene T. Heineman, assistant superintendent of public instruction of the Department of Education, Los Angeles; Dr. H. Councill Trenholm, president of State Teachers College, Montgomery, Ala.; Ralph B. Bridgman, president of Hampton Institute, Hampton, Va.; Miss Addie B. Bishop, principal personnel assistant to the industrial relations officer of the Mare Island, California, Navy Yard; and Dr. Herbert Bruner, superintendent of the Oklahoma City (Okla.) city schools." Members of advisory committee, but not in photo: Angela Babace, Representative of International Ladies' Garment Works' Union, AFL, Dr. Grace Langdon, Child Care Consultant, War Public Services, FWA, Mr. George Nickel, Exec. Secretary, Childcare Committee for Women in Industry, Los Angeles, Victor Reuther, Assistant. Director War Policy Division, UAW-CIO, and Miss Isabel Robinson, Child Care Consultant, War Public Services, FWA. See also "Agenda, Reports, Minutes: National Advisory Committee on Child Care," Florence Kerr papers, Grinnell College (November 14–15, 1944) 144 pages.

113. See, for example, Miriam Lowenberg, "Shipyard Nursery Schools" *Journal of Home Economics* (February 1944) and James Hymes, "The Kaiser Answer: Child Service Centers" *Progressive Education* 21 (May 1944): 222–223, 245–246.

114. See House Committee on Appropriations, First Deficiency Appropriation Bill for 1944: HR 4346, 78th Congress (February 16, 1944). The six supportive Representatives were: Mary Norton (D-NJ), Frances Bolton (R-OH), Edith Rogers (R-MA), Margaret Chase Smith (R-ME), Clare Boothe Luce (R-CT), and Winifred Claire Stanley (R-NY).

115. In secondary literature, statistics on Lanham extended school services (before and after school care for primary children) are often mistakenly mixed with statistics on Lanham children's centers. Only the Lanham children's centers dealt with preschool-age children.

116. Still fuming that her agency had not gained full control of government-sponsored childcare, Lenroot began to make blanket statements that a

132   In Time of War

mother's place was in the home. See her testimony at December 1943 Juvenile Delinquency Hearings and Kerr's tart rejoinder.
117. Katherine Close, "After Lanham Funds, What?" *Survey Midmonthly* 81 (May 1945) 131–135.
118. Rosie the Riveter with Child. Unsigned illustration in G.G. Wetherill, "Health Problems in Child Care Centers" *Hygeia* 21 (September 1943) 635. Hygeia, 1923–1950, was published by the American Medical Association.
119. Dorothy Bradbury, Four Decades of Action for Children (1912–1952), "Children of Working Mothers" section https://socialwelfare.library.vcu.edu/programs/child-welfarechild-labor/childrens-bureau-part-ii-4/.

5 Buried Treasure

The FWA's childcare program provoked controversy for three reasons, the anthropologist Margaret Mead wrote in January 1945.[1] The recommendation of Langdon's advisory committee to provide federal aid to local communities to ensure access to poor and minority children offended professional groups like the ACE because it bypassed state powerbrokers with whom they worked.[2] In addition, Langdon's program threatened those who believed mothers had a moral duty to stay home with their children.[3] Finally, Mead pointed to the professional rivalry between federal agencies over whether young children were better served by early childhood education or custodial care. Here, she directed her ire at actions taken by the CB. Chief Lenroot continued to insist that foster care was preferable. She had earlier denigrated Langdon's program, intent on having the CB control all defense programs involving young children.[4] Mead recognized the political calculation involved but was appalled that Lenroot turned away from science to make her point. Referring to the British experience, which clearly showed young children suffered when moved to foster homes, Mead wrote, "when evacuated children are put into nursery schools with teachers who continually refer to their homes and parents, family ties are less apt to breakdown than when they are put into foster homes where there is a new parental situation."[5] Mead, an expert on international child rearing and the working mother of a preschooler, resisted Lenroot's blanket assertion that foster care was superior to nursery school.[6]

Although many factors contributed to the demise of Langdon's childcare program, anti-communist attacks played a huge role in burying the program's accomplishments. Congressional hearings at the end of World War II politicized the program as the country began to demobilize. Program leaders and supporters were red-baited. By the time Langdon created preschools as an element of the War on Poverty in the 1960s, her New Deal program had been forgotten.

Congressional Hearings

In Langdon's quest to find a permanent home for nursery schools inside the federal government, 1943's battle scars left her little desire to collaborate

134   *Buried Treasure*

with the CB. Encouraged by Florence Kerr's assessment that she faced a "seller's market," Langdon hoped Senator Claude Pepper's (D-FL) much-anticipated report, *Wartime Health and Education*, would offer a blueprint for moving the program to a new agency devoted to demobilization, especially after the CIO's Dorothy Hayes supported that solution before Pepper's subcommittee.[7] In consultation with Margaret Mead and advisory chair Edna Noble White, Langdon sent her proposal to Pepper's staff with a letter from White that advocated a new agency receive federal funds to be allocated locally. The program would cover all children (not just those of working mothers).[8] But the January 1945 Pepper Report did not include support for Langdon's childcare program.[9] Instead, it offered recommendations that focused solely on improving health care.[10]

Langdon next placed hope in the Full Employment Act of 1945, but that was futile, too. After Senator James Murray (D-MT) introduced the full employment bill in January, its plans for labor, industry, and government working together in the postwar world underwent significant revision even before hearings. When subcommittee hearings opened, CIO President Philip Murray was the only witness to mention Langdon's program, and indirectly at that:

> The American people will soon be asking: Why are the good things a part of war; why can't we have them in peacetime as well? Our people have seen infant care and child care. . . . Are we concerned about the health and care of mothers and children only when the husband and father is being killed or mutilated?[11]

The hearing's attention to childcare concluded with an eerie foreshadowing when Congressman Carter Manasco (D-AL) read Article 122 from the Soviet Constitution:

> Women in the USSR are accorded equal rights with men in all affairs of economic, state, social, and political life. The possibility of exercising these rights is assured to women by granting them an equal right with men to work, payment for work, rest and leisure, social insurance and education, and by state protection of the interest of mother and child, [prenatal] and maternity leave with full pay and the provision of a wide network of maternity homes, nurseries, and kindergartens.[12]

For Manasco, equal rights, paid labor, and nursery schools were tainted by the communist Russians' adoption of them as ideals. Intent on discouraging federal support for the employment of American women outside the home, Southern Democrats and conservative northern Republicans opposed public nursery schools.[13] They also opposed federal aid to education more generally given that it threatened federal intervention in local issues, including segregation.[14]

Buried Treasure 135

Still, some saw the new federal aid to education bill (SB 181) as the way to address the nursery school program and achieve universal preschool.[15] Yet politics remained a problem. ACE, for example, endorsed SB 181 in February 1945 on grounds that echoed the more general conservative opposition to national education funding—because the text ruled out federal grants "directly to local communities, as is now the practice of the Federal Works Agency."[16] It was about "stemming invasion from within."[17] The CB remained neutral toward legislation establishing or aiding public preschools but suggested a new federal department of health, education, and welfare could use federal funds to promote programs—like foster care— that it considered to be truly in the best interests of children.[18] After the introduction of another federal aid to education bill in April (SB 717), calls for universal preschool intensified. But the bill sparked controversy because its funding could be used by both private and public schools "to raise the educational level of the nation."[19] For some, this portended federal aid to religious schools and would violate the First Amendment.[20] The CIO nonetheless endorsed it, arguing that nursery schools should "be encouraged and multiplied."[21]

In spite of growing opposition to federal funding, the fight to make the FWA's Lanham children's centers permanent continued. Once Claude Pepper's Senate subcommittee on education and labor began its final deliberations, Eleanor Roosevelt came out strongly in favor of Lanham centers, focusing on the federal government's responsibility to provide childcare for working mothers:

> These children are future citizens, and if they are neglected in these early years it will hurt not only the children themselves, but the community as a whole. . . . [W]here state help is needed, it should be given; and when states are incapable of giving sufficient help, it should be forthcoming on a national scale as it has been in the war years.[22]

Representative Helen Gahagan Douglas (D-CA) marshaled evidence of the centers' value. Newly elected, the movie and theatre star placed letters from her Los Angeles constituents into the *Congressional Record* in late September 1945. They showed that working mothers—often servicemen's wives— appreciated that Lanham centers were non-discriminatory and that their children had "better care than many children that are with their mothers all day."[23]

Roosevelt and Douglas underscored the point made earlier by the CIO's Elizabeth Hawes—that mothers wanted to work as long as their children attended "well-run nursery schools."[24] Hawes generated favorable headlines in Detroit when she declared:

> Just a job for everyone who wants it, a thirty-hour work-week, hot school lunches and nursery schools, and we've started toward every

136 *Buried Treasure*

American man having a good wife, every American wife having a good husband, and all American children having two good parents.[25]

She then helped launch Eleanor Roosevelt's effort at the Office of Civilian Defense to create public nursery schools, but anti-communists attacked her nationwide Committees for the Care of Young Children in Wartime.[26] Continuing to face intense political scrutiny, Hawes—like Mead and Roosevelt—focused on other endeavors after 1945.

Protests were widespread as Lanham centers closed.[27] Langdon traveled non-stop to help local communities figure out alternative funding. Her most straightforward approach was to persuade local service clubs, like Kiwanis chapters, to pick up the tab for any portion of the 1945–1946 school year not covered by the FWA.[28] Langdon also participated in local brainstorming sessions when public schools ran out of federal funds. In November 1945, she attended a meeting in York, Pennsylvania, at which activists requested state aid. She found it "very gratifying to find a community so interested in its children."[29]

Although assumed to be stopgap measures, necessary only until Congress enacted permanent legislation, the halt in federal funding was permanent—not just a brief hiatus. Claude Pepper's Subcommittee voted 10–9 on December 8, 1945 not to send a federal aid to education bill to the Senate floor. At the same time, local politicians began to red-bait Lanham center supporters.[30] Douglas tried to stem the tide, proclaiming on the House floor, "I am jealous for the school system we have built under democracy, and I do not want its extension, including fair salaries for teachers, day nurseries, school-lunch programs, and Federal aid to education, called communism."[31] Langdon, meanwhile, hunkered down to write a history of the Lanham children's centers, articles for *Parents Magazine*, and a complete revision of her 1931 bestseller, *Home Guidance for Young Children*.[32] In April 1946, she headed west to teach school for the summer.

Understanding that the political ground had shifted precariously, Langdon stopped discussing strategy on how to achieve universal preschool.[33] The words she spoke to an African American teachers' union in late 1944 take on added poignancy given the national stage she might have enjoyed if Congress had passed federal aid to education and not denounced childcare advocates as "un-American":

What these next steps will be is of vital importance. Will they be dictated by selfish interests? Will they be dominated by those who would use the schools for their own selfish ends? Or will they be taken in light of a genuine desire to further both the individual and the common good? . . . Let us hope that the steps we take will be those that lead forward to more and broader educational opportunities for all people.[34]

Retreat

As Lanham centers closed everywhere save California, Langdon ended her activism on behalf of public nursery schools. Returning to New York, she opened a consulting business, Langdon-Cromwell Services, at the same address where she had operated her Education Advisory Service before World War II.[35] By December 1946, she called herself a "consulting child psychologist."[36] Langdon also advised the United Nations (UN) Nursery School created by Lea Cowles, her former Columbia student and WPA nursery school teacher.[37] For a brief period after World War II, Langdon continued to argue that establishing nursery schools would cultivate world peace through religious tolerance and the "preservation of cultural values of each nationality while practicing the ideals of international understanding and cooperation."[38]

In December 1947, Langdon announced she had become the child development advisor for the American Toy Institute, a new agency created by the Toy Manufacturers of the United States, and would "conduct research on the importance of play in child development and promote American-made toys."[39] She wrote a widely distributed Associated Press article on age-appropriate toys for the upcoming holiday season.[40]

Her opponents also remained active. In addition to congressional red-baiting, Langdon's adversaries from 1943 wrote vicious revisionist histories. In early 1946, Arnold Gesell, nursery school pioneer and WPA-Lanham participant, raised the specter of "totalitarian regimentation" if Langdon's program continued and focused on how un-American it would be to institute universal preschool.[41] Lenroot, meanwhile, asserted that neither WPA nursery schools nor Lanham centers addressed children's needs and asked why the talk of permanence. Both Gesell and Lenroot ignored the ongoing nationwide protests over Lanham closures, but their critiques proved influential.[42] Attention to the successes of Langdon's program vanished, and soon little trace remained of Langdon's leadership in NANE.[43] NANE's postwar bulletin mentioned her only in passing.[44] The organization failed to recognize her advocacy of developmentally appropriate toys to a mass audience as well as her accomplishments as New Dealer and World War II childcare specialist.

NANE leaders who had worked closely with Langdon to achieve public nursery schools at the end of World War II also lost national standing. Dorothy Baruch gained two brief notices for books written after the war, but NANE distanced itself from its pre-war modernist embrace of psychoanalysis, at least if written by Baruch. Moreover, it paid no attention to her groundbreaking *Glass Hall of Prejudice* (1946), a template for how to improve race relations.[45] Edna Noble White's 1954 NANE obituary did not mention her involvement in the CIO, her integrated Merrill-Palmer Camp for Detroit children, her creation of the Detroit Youth Council (labeled a communist front in 1947), her advisory chair position in Langdon's program, or her postwar activism on behalf of public nursery schools in Michigan.[46]

138 Buried Treasure

After World War II, some NANE leaders, like James Hymes, became more conservative.[47] Instead of thinking about changing the social order, they focused on doing no more than holding onto what had been achieved.[48] Especially striking about NANE's postwar positions is that Langdon's dream of federally funded nursery schools disappeared. In its published discussions of legislation, NANE ignored the nursery school bills that Helen Gahagan Douglas and Claude Pepper sponsored in the very late 1940s.[49] George Stoddard's fiery 1949 UN speech on behalf of universal preschool provoked little response.[50]

NANE's retreat resulted in large part from the very real threat of red-baiting, which loomed large over the entire nursery school movement once HUAC re-emerged after World War II and Congress began to associate public nursery schools with the Soviet Union. Postwar progressive educators, a community that included NANE, were actively engaging in self-censorship "in the face of Red scares."[51] Langdon had past ties to the WPA, a former HUAC target, and to the Progressive Education Association (PEA), which had been named a communist front.[52] She also had links to a tightly woven web of networks that included many people investigated by HUAC and the FBI for alleged subversion. In addition to progressive educators, these overlapping networks included New Dealers, leftist feminists, the CIO, liberal Democrats in Congress, and child development researchers.

Langdon's political vulnerability grew after the 1946 midterm elections brought in an anti-communist Republican majority hostile to the New Deal. In March 1947, under political pressure, President Truman established loyalty boards designed to root out communist influence inside the federal government. In June, Congress passed the Taft-Hartley Act, which, among other provisions, prohibited radicals from holding positions of union leadership. And in late spring 1948, the Attorney General added the Congress of American Women to its list of subversive organizations.[53]

A cloud of suspicion also hung over several people with whom Langdon had worked closely as both WPA and Lanham director. Floyd Dell, who had been Florence Kerr's speech-writer, retired rather than endure an investigation into his radical past by the newly formed Loyalty Review Board. His own WPA narrative underlined the successes of Langdon's program and might have served as an effective counterweight to revisionist attacks but got buried in the archives.[54] Richard Nixon, who had labeled Helen Gahagan Douglas a communist sympathizer, vaulted onto the national stage with his investigation of Alger Hiss.[55] Former New Dealers had to worry about being branded disloyal.[56] Florence Kerr's 1974 assertion that "anyone in the relief business had no political future" describes the effect of the Red Scare in sending many New Dealers, especially women, into obscurity.[57]

Prominent social justice advocates and left-leaning feminists were further weakened when the CIO was attacked for harboring communists.[58] When Congress forced the CIO to purge itself of its most radical members, it sidelined some of Langdon's most devoted supporters.[59] Eleanor and Cedric

Buried Treasure 139

Fowler moved to the New Jersey countryside and eked out a living selling produce from their family farm.[60] Dorothy Hayes left Washington but continued to be red-baited in Chicago for being a progressive social worker. She and Eleanor Fowler participated in the Women's International League for Peace and Freedom (WILPF) together, but they gave up promoting public nursery schools.[61] Elizabeth Hawes, who had feistily declared factory life would be fine once all working mothers and fathers had a thirty-hour week and access to public nursery schools, gave up on union activism altogether. Blacklisted when she tried to return to the fashion industry, her career ended.[62]

The recently organized Congress of American Women fought back when it was named a subversive organization in mid-1948. National president Gene Weltfish demanded a retraction and apology from the attorney general. She received neither, but HUAC jumped in with its own criticism. The group's founding as a left-feminist and integrated organization in March 1946, combined with its support for Lanham children's centers and its assertion that the "Soviet Union is the only nation in the world where care for children constitutes one of the most important aspects of governmental and public activities," made all members vulnerable to being labeled un-American.[63] Elinor Gimbel and Susan B. Anthony II, vice-chairs as well as Langdon's friends and supporters, were among those caught in the right-wing's crosshairs as the Congress of American Women dissolved.[64]

This background helps frame Langdon's next professional move at the American Toy Institute. In November 1948, she created a Christmas-toy advertisement that pledged loyalty to the United States. Santa Claus was depicted in Uncle Sam attire with his arms around two children. The ad urged parents to "Buy American." For ten years, it ran in the mid-November issue of *Life*, the most popular magazine in the United States.[65] In a glossy spread of photos and descriptions of the latest American toys, Langdon listed American companies by name and embedded herself in postwar consumer capitalism on behalf of young children.[66]

Such an embrace of "well-made and safe toys" by American companies stood in stark contrast to the ingenuity and creativity of the open-ended and often homemade play materials Langdon advocated as director of WPA nursery schools and Lanham children's centers. Others also changed their tunes after the war, however. Mary Dublin Keyserling, who had earlier worked on childcare issues at the Office of Civilian Defense, embraced the postwar capitalist order as an economist at the Commerce Department once she underwent loyalty investigations.[67] Thomasina Johnson, the first African American registered lobbyist in D.C., retreated from her support of Langdon's program and focused instead on promoting black-owned businesses.[68] Langdon, a once-savvy Washington insider, may have thought that encouraging parents to "buy American" (rather than the cheaper imports flooding in from the former Axis powers of Germany and Japan) provided a relatively painless way to prove loyalty during the Red Scare. In 1949 and

140 Buried Treasure

1950, Langdon honed this message, linking patriotism to American toys in articles she wrote for the popular *Parents Magazine* and *Christian Science Monitor*.[69]

Nor was Langdon alone in shedding her WPA past. Just as she did not refer to herself as a New Dealer after 1948, postwar NANE leaders who had begun their careers in the WPA did not include it in their profiles, especially after Richard Nixon red-baited Helen Gahagan Douglas in the infamous California US Senate race of 1950.[70] Taking a page from the playbook of the successful anti-communist campaign against Senator Claude Pepper (D-FL) earlier that spring, Nixon hired far-right journalist Edna Lonigan of *Human Events* to dig up dirt on Douglas.[71] He then manipulated that evidence and won in November. Nixon disingenuously asserted that Douglas had a voting record similar to New York City's leftist congressional representative Vito Marcantonio and emphasized her advisory role in the WPA, her reluctance to fund HUAC, and her strong support of unions, minorities, working women, and integration. He and his wife, Pat, passed out thimbles with the slogan "Safeguard the American Home."[72] James Hymes, on the other hand, may have been as leery of Jim Crow politics as he was of red-baiting when he moved to Tennessee and neglected to claim not only his WPA past, NANE presidency (1945–1947), and recent consultation with UN representative George Stoddard, but also ignored his commitment to integration.[73]

In 1951, Langdon began collaborating with Irving Stout, an education professor at NYU, focusing on what today might be termed positive psychology.[74] Rather than look for family pathologies, Langdon studied what kinds of family dynamics worked well. She interviewed parents and children about a wide variety of topics and used anecdotal evidence to support her points. In seven well-reviewed books and a nationally syndicated newspaper column, Langdon embraced a grandmotherly persona to discuss issues ranging from discipline to homework.[75] Flying under the radar screen by emphasizing domesticity, she nonetheless encouraged all children to "think for themselves" during the McCarthy era.[76]

Others had a harder time escaping hostility. Nominated to the new Subversive Activities Control Board in late 1950, Kathryn McHale, AAUW national president and former advisor to Langdon's program, was attacked for defending a colleague against charges of communism.[77] When newly passed Public Law 733 deemed homosexuals a security risk, the FBI began to investigate McHale on suspicion of lesbianism.[78] Susan B. Anthony II, wartime advocate for Langdon's program, was red-baited for her leadership in the Congress of American Women, whose participants argued "ten women anywhere can organize anything" and who had three key goals: peace, defeating discrimination against women "in all fields of human enterprise," and making Lanham centers permanent. Also under FBI surveillance, Anthony fled the country, returning only after she named potential communists in HUAC hearings.[79] Later, she said she had been red-baited largely due to her embrace of childcare.[80]

Buried Treasure 141

Academia joined politics in attacking early childhood education as social scientific studies questioned the value of early childhood education itself. John Bowlby's highly influential work from that era asserts that mother-child attachment is both "primal and essential" for ensuring healthy development.[81] But even there, political values crept in when Bowlby dismissed those who questioned his findings as being either communists or professional women.[82] His rebuttal appeared effective, as the early criticism he received from Margaret Mead was ignored.[83] Bowlby's research helped support an "American" way of life that limited the possibilities for working mothers and early childhood education for all.[84]

Cold War Legacy

After turning to other issues for fifteen years, Langdon re-engaged with the world of early childhood education in 1963.[85] She played no visible role in helping her program survive McCarthyism.[86] But in a more open political climate, the seventy-four-year-old Langdon involved herself with the administration of the new US president, Lyndon B. Johnson (LBJ). LBJ, who had worked in the NYA under Aubrey Williams, and who, after World War II, had close ties to Helen Gahagan Douglas, was interested in making President Kennedy's ideas about the value of community action a reality. LBJ decided to wage the War on Poverty, in part, by providing federal funds directly to local people. Grace Langdon, now a colleague of Irving Stout at Arizona State University (ASU), helped the Papago, a First Nation in Arizona, become one of the first communities in the United States to apply for a community action program (CAP) grant under the new Office of Economic Opportunity (OEO).

Aware that the OEO wanted to promote schooling, Langdon and Stout convinced Papago leader Josiah Moore to conduct an education survey.[87] Once CAP funds arrived in early 1965, the three of them began interviewing those living on the reservation.[88] In March 1965, they submitted a proposal that incorporated community feedback and called for, among a wide array of concerns, preschools and parent-child centers.[89] Testimony recognized Langdon's contribution.[90] When months went by with no word, Josiah Moore went to Washington, where the OEO Indian desk told him that the decision had been delayed because the application did not mention "integrating minority groups in the Papago program."[91] It is also clear that Langdon's proposal did not mesh with the model of Head Start then being conceptualized.

Langdon's proposal called for year-round schools staffed by well-trained, experienced teachers able to work with small groups of infants, young children, and families. The projected cost of $43,837 amounted to a little over $1,000 per child per year. By contrast, Head Start staff envisioned a summer-school program to help poor children prepare for kindergarten or first grade. Well aware of the political benefits of implementing "maximum

142 Buried Treasure

feasible participation" from local communities but hamstrung by the lack of funding when expenditures grew for the escalation of the Vietnam War, Sargent Shriver had staff play around with numbers and publicized the program's cost as $180 per child.[92] In summer 1965, Head Start opened its doors to approximately 500,000 children it described as "culturally deprived"—including those on the Papago reservation.

Unlike Langdon, Shriver did not emphasize the need for well-trained teachers with experience in early childhood education because Head Start could not pay enough to attract them. Instead, he focused on Head Start's potential to help American children fight poverty through active parental involvement and community engagement. Shriver celebrated efforts to find program staff in local communities.[93] Emphasizing Head Start's popularity as a community action measure, the OEO framed it as a comprehensive child development program and not early childhood education.[94]

Head Start met with mixed reactions from the Papago that first summer of operation. Interviewed in May 1966, the Papago thought of Head Start as a babysitting service at best:

> They came last summer and started a Head Start here. It lasted one summer, then went away. We haven't had anything else. I don't know where the Head Start came from. I don't think it was BIA [Bureau of Indian Affairs]. We were never asked anything about it, it just came. They didn't ask us if we wanted it, they just came with it.[95]

When the Papago CAP project was finally given a green light in late August 1965, it included the contributions of Josiah Moore and Tom Segundo (a former tribal chair who returned to the reservation to ensure the success of all Papago-initiated CAP projects) and Langdon's good friend, WPA and UN nursery school teacher Lea C. Masters (formerly Lea Cowles).[96] Moore and Segundo engaged in community outreach, and Masters prepared class-rooms and hired teachers. Langdon trained them all at ASU. In December, two Papago "preschool and parent-child centers" opened their doors.[97]

Unlike Head Start, Langdon's centers drew praise from the larger Papago community, which soon called for their expansion. The parents appreciated that children learned English through play with toys, and they celebrated parent-child specialist Masters because she made frequent visits to families in the area and made an effort to learn about Papago culture.[98] They also liked Langdon's concept of a parent-child center that helped both children and adults. As one woman remarked, "I'm learning to sew and my daughter is beginning to speak and understand English. I think this program is very educational for both of us."[99]

Langdon's success attracted the attention of Washington policymakers. In early 1967, LBJ's task force on early child development issued a "Bill of Rights for Young Children" in which parent-child centers earned top billing.[100] In response, the OEO placed them under the Head Start umbrella,

Buried Treasure 143

and the Papago "parent-child centers and preschools" began to operate as Head Start centers. Langdon also collaborated with LBJ's task force to create a parent-child center template in 1968, hoping to see it built nearby as a public community school for infants, young children, and families. National consultants included former WPA nursery school participants.[101]

But 1968 was not the year for expanding access to early childhood education. When LBJ decided not to run for a second term, people inside the administration worried how the OEO would fare, especially if a Republican should win. No new projects were funded, and Johnson took no executive action to protect programs like Head Start because he wanted to give maximum latitude to the incoming administration. Almost immediately upon taking office, President Nixon began to dismantle the OEO by putting Representative Donald Rumsfeld (R-IL) in charge.

Although he saved Head Start from the clutches of Rumsfeld, Nixon's decision to place it in the CB's newly created Office of Child Development had devastating consequences when some began to consider making Head Start universal.[102] Both Nixon and the CB had opposed Langdon's earlier efforts on behalf of outstanding early childhood education for all young children. Nixon rose to political prominence as a Cold Warrior by calling into question the loyalty of New Dealers. Hostile to group care for young children, the CB sabotaged Langdon's program during World War II and pushed foster care long after working mothers clamored for other alternatives.[103] Yet the CB and Nixon had come to be seen as enlightened supporters of childcare, and few remembered Grace Langdon.[104] In June 1970, when she died in a nursing home, The *Arizona Republic*'s obituary buried her under her married name and barely listed her achievements.[105]

Edward Zigler accepted Nixon's appointment to become both the Office of Child Development director and CB chief in April 1970, apparently knowing little of the historical context.[106] He created a plan to coordinate the provision of federally supported childcare, operating from the premise that "quality child care can contribute as much to school readiness as good preschool programming."[107] But Zigler got caught between Nixon's budget advisors, who wanted a bare-bones custodial model, and specialists like Marian Wright Edelman, who wanted Head Start to become universal. Accordingly, he crafted a compromise that became the House version of the Comprehensive Child Development Act of 1971 (CCDA).

The CCDA enjoyed broad bipartisan support, especially after Zigler publicized Mary Dublin Keyserling's findings that showed the acute need for childcare.[108] But support splintered over federal funding. Just as Langdon's opponents in World War II wanted the states to operate Lanham children's centers through block grants, the Nixon administration wanted only states to sponsors CCDA schools. By contrast, Edelman—the lead author of Senator Walter Mondale's (D-MN) version of the CCDA—wanted smaller entities to be eligible to sponsor schools. Given her experience dealing with racism while implementing Head Start in Mississippi, she thought it best

144   Buried Treasure

for federal funding to flow directly to local institutions. As had Langdon and her World War II advisory committee, she saw that as the way to avoid segregationist state bureaucracies.[109] Edelman explained that those "concerned about civil rights and equal opportunity must and will oppose any effort to place principal authority for child development in the hands of the states."[110]

Zigler, however, saw tragedy in Edelman's refusal to come around. Had she been willing to compromise, he believed, the bill would have passed, and the United States would have been fast on its way to achieving universal preschool.[111] Likewise, Zigler rejected the argument of feminists like Bella Abzug and Shirley Chisholm, who were unwilling to settle for a Head Start that provided compensatory education only for the poor. More than Zigler, these women wanted to help all working mothers, provide a first-rate education to all children, and ensure high wages for all early childhood educators.[112] As Chisolm put it:

> If we limit day care only to those at the lower end of the economic scale, this bill is going to be labeled a poverty or welfare bill and will be a much more difficult task to secure the appropriations which are necessary. You will recall that this Congress was able to override a Presidential veto of education appropriations. This was because everybody had a stake in those education programs. Day care legislation has a similar constituency. Every woman, almost without exceptions, will support universal day care.[113]

Most problematic for childcare advocates, Zigler let Nixon off the political hook. He blamed Pat Buchanan for feeding Nixon right-wing propaganda—John Birch material and conservative religious tracts on why childcare was un-American.[114] Yet Nixon's anti-communist fear of group care can be traced directly to how Langdon and her program had been buried. Shortly after Langdon died in obscurity, Nixon vetoed the "most radical piece of legislation to emerge" from the 92nd Congress:

> For the Federal Government to plunge headlong financially into supporting child development would commit the vast moral authority of the National Government to the side of communal approaches to child-rearing over against the family-centered approach.[115]

These words, penned by Pat Buchanan, incorporated language from *Human Events*, the same far-right journal Nixon had used to silence Helen Gahagan Douglas in 1950.[116] Although some around him objected, Nixon fought to keep anti-communist language in his veto speech.[117] Having used such words before, Nixon turned to them again to destroy the CCDA.

Langdon's federal childcare program became buried treasure because the extreme right wing targeted those most active in promoting universal

Buried Treasure 145

Figure 5.1 Smear Campaigns[118]

preschool through either WPA nursery schools or Lanham children's centers. This pattern of anti-communism rendered group care for young children suspect through congressional hearings aimed at weakening the New Deal.[119] Anti-communists also destroyed women's organizations that called for federally sponsored nursery schools, including the Congress of American Women.[120] They crippled CIO support for publically subsidized childcare, sidelining working mothers like Eleanor Fowler. Most insidiously,

146 Buried Treasure

anti-communists hobbled the professions of progressive education and child development, undercutting the potential of both to transform society.[121]

The postwar Red Scare buried Langdon and her program's successes. Later, Nixon and the CB played another turn, limiting efforts to universalize Head Start. Margaret Mead's insight—that childcare provoked controversy due to the politicization of federal funding, working mothers, and professional rivalries—became a live issue again in the early 1970s CCDA battle. Her longtime friend and colleague Lea C. Masters recollected that Langdon often began a new project by proclaiming "the greatest thing in the world is just about to happen."[122] She died still waiting.

Notes

1. Margaret Mead, "Note on the Question of Day Care" (January 8, 1945) ENW. Mead concluded, "The intensity with which controversy over the question of day care for young children has been waged indicates that it has tapped deep and probably inarticulate forces in American culture."

2. Under the FWA, state officials in the education and social welfare department felt left out of the loop. In the "Battle of 1943," they tended to support the Thomas Bill over the FWA's Lanham children's centers because the Thomas Bill called for block grants to states, not local communities. Fritz Lanham (D-TX), original architect of the Lanham Act, called for direct aid to local communities as a means to preserve "local control." CIO Education Leader Victor Reuther (like Mead, an advisor to Langdon's program) reframed this message to emphasize that the program minimized "federal domination" and fought Jim Crow at the grassroots level. The National Advisory Committee to the FWA Day Care Program recommended "inclusion of adequate services to children in economically depressed areas and to minority racial groups, particularly in those areas where it is customary or required by law to provide separate schools." From "Recommendations" (November 15, 1944) 2 pages. ENW.

3. See the discussion of the role of religion in childcare debates in Elizabeth Hawes, *Why Women Cry: Women as Wenches* (1943). Hawes, a modernist fashion designer, became a Rosie the Riveter in New Jersey and then a UAW-CIO union organizer in Detroit. She was a member of the Committee for the Care of Young Children in Wartime and a staunch supporter of Langdon's program. Edna Noble White was also a member of the UAW-CIO in Detroit.

4. Lenroot began her attacks when Lanham funds became available to WPA nursery school schools in 1942. See, for instance, "Plan New Program to Guard Children" *New York Times* (March 17, 1942) and "Boarding Homes Needed: Drive to Enlist 5,000 Families Will Start Tomorrow" *New York Times* (July 27, 1942). Lenroot recommended that children live with foster mothers (rather than attend nursery school) if their own mothers worked.

5. Margaret Mead, "Nursery School vs. Foster Home" *Journal of Home Economics* 34 (November 1942) 669. Mead also visited Great Britain in 1943, and wrote an article upon her return for the *Saturday Evening Post*.

6. After the demise of Langdon's program, the CB softened its claims: "While it seems probable that individual care is preferable to group care for the very young child, clear-cut evidence is lacking." See Katherine Bain, "Dissemination of Info on Child Development by Federal Agencies" *Child Development* 19 (March–June 1948) 64.

Buried Treasure 147

7. Langdon quoted Kerr in her December 27, 1944 letter to White. At Wartime Health and Education Hearings in late 1943, Hayes wrote:

> A national central body with funds and authority to undertake centralized planning and direction on social-welfare problems is urgently needed. . . . It would provide the focal point to which labor, management, social agencies, communities, and governmental agencies could come for a solution to war welfare problems; the point at which they could find authority and solution. (490)

Hayes also recommended the Office of War Mobilization as the agency to house this 'national central body.' As labor feared, the so-called human side of reconversion, such as the training and placement of discharged workers and returning veterans, took a back seat to the interests of the military and big business. See Nelson Lichtenstein, *Labor's War at Home: The CIO in WWII* (2010).

8. Edna Noble White to Claude Pepper, November 1944–January 1945:

> If allocation is made for teacher training and cooperative relationships with the state departments, it covers, it seems to me, all the advantages gained by grants-in-aid, without the disadvantages. . . . Only a new agency, such as is contemplated under this new Children's Commission, could advantageously undertake the development of this newer type of education [nursery school] and we are asking that your group give it careful consideration. (January 5, 1945)

See also "Day Care News: Special Edition—National UAW-CIO Women's Conference" 18 (December 1944) 9 and White's letter to her friend and CIO education leader Victor Reuther (January 3). White encouraged Reuther to mention both union support for Langdon's program and the idea of a children's commission in his upcoming DC visit.

9. "Wartime Health and Education" January 2, 1945. Interim report issued to the Senate Committee on Education and Labor from the Subcommittee on Wartime Health and Education, 22 pages. In December 1943, Pepper himself thought the Office of Civilian Defense might house this centralized agency (Wartime Health and Education testimony: 358–359).

10. It only mentioned children once: "providing child-guidance and mental hygiene clinics on a far wider scale." Colonel Menninger defined these clinics as those for "very young children whose parents are concerned about thumb-sucking, or truancy, or temper tantrums, or disobedience" (1699). The other recommendations included: hospital construction, clean water and sanitation, state health departments, army rehabilitation, draft medical records preserved, scholarships for doctors and dentists, and federal funds "for medical care of all recipients of public assistance." As one observer remarked, "No recommendations are made in the report regarding child welfare services but the matter is to have farther study." Frank Pedley, "Medical Economics: Wartime Health and Education" *Canadian Medical Association Journal* 53 (July 1945) 72. I find little evidence that nursery schools were seriously considered in any other legislative proposals inspired by this report, including Pepper's Maternal and Child Welfare Bill (SB 1318) of 1946, Title III.

11. Employment Act of 1945. Hearings before a subcommittee of the Committee on banking and currency, United States Senate, Seventy-Ninth Congress, First Session, on S. 380 (July 30–September 1, 1945) 226.

12. Full Employment Act of 1945. Hearings before the Committee on expenditures in the executive departments, House of representatives, Seventy-Ninth

148   Buried Treasure

Congress, First Session, on H. R. 2202 (September 25–November 7, 1945) 782 (October 26 testimony).

13. Emilie Stoltzfus in *Citizen, Mother, Worker: Debating Public Responsibility for Child Care After WWII* (2003) 43, writes: "As long as policymakers were unwilling to redistribute social responsibility for child care, providing a social structure that supported mothers' ability to share domestic responsibilities with fathers and others, mothers would not have equal opportunity in the workplace."

14. Arthur Williams and Karl Johnson, "Race, Social Welfare, and the Decline of Postwar Liberalism: A New or Old Key?" *Public Administration Review* 60 (November–December 2000) 560–572.

15. Dorothy Baruch, "When the Need for War-Time Services for Children Is Past—What of the Future?" *Journal of Consulting Psychology* 9 (January–February 1945) 45—57.

16. Like conservative southerners, the ACE may have resisted the FWA's federal funding structure because of Langdon's efforts to combat Jim Crow at the local level. ACE's Mary Leeper refused to hire African American Elizabeth P. Mitcham as a child-development specialist even though she had graduated summa cum laude from Howard University.

17. Testimony of Mary Leeper, Federal Aid for Education: Part 1. Hearings Before the Senate Committee on Education and Labor, 79th Congress, SB 181 (January 29–February 8, 1945) 205. Leeper also corresponded with J. Edgar Hoover in the early 1950s (ACEI archives). Similarly, Amos Fries, so-called "friend of public schools" (with extreme right-wing backing) categorically denounced nursery schools as "un-American"—a mother's place was in the home. Ibid: 380. Fries

> urged that every possible thing be done to develop the home and to keep mothers of children under 14 (at least), at home to take care of their children and that, where necessary, funds be raised to aid those mothers in taking care of their children at home instead of turning them over to nurseries or other institutions.

Another right-wing zealot, Margaret Hopkins Worrell, denied that nursery school was even education. Friends with white supremacist, Gerald L. K. Smith, Worrell remained staunchly opposed to public school programs that promoted integration.

18. In April 1945, the Child Welfare Information Service called for the establishment of a department of health, education, and welfare, an idea that came to fruition in 1953. See also Leonard Mayo, "A Cabinet Post for the Home Front" *Survey Graphic* (August 1945) 201–205. By contrast, African American and union leaders spoke at length about the need for federal funding to achieve equality of opportunity and to relieve racial tension. Referring to her own difficulties in funding African American education in Mississippi through the NYA, Mary McLeod Bethune declared, "Passage of this bill would greatly aid the States in raising their educational standards by providing every child with adequate educational opportunities as regards both facilities and instruction" (293). CIO women's auxiliary leader Eleanor Fowler remarked, "we feel that better education for all American children is a very important step in building a lasting peace" (422). Fowler, a long-time supporter of Grace Langdon, had just made headlines by formally requesting Attorney General Biddle to investigate new fascist-like mothers' groups who were arguing for "Kinder, Küche, Kirche" for American women. See "CIO Auxiliaries Ask Resumption of Trial" *Palm Beach Post* (February 12, 1945)

Buried Treasure 149

3. See also Glen Jeansonne, *Women of the Far Right: The Mothers' Movement and World War II* (1996).
19. Federal Aid for Education: Part 2. Hearings before the Senate Committee on Education and Labor, 79th Congress, SB 717 & 181 (April 11–May 4, 1945).
20. The AFT in Chicago resisted such assertions. Their understanding of SB 717: "Appropriations for nonpublic schools are limited to such items as have already been provided for in the NYA & Lanham Emergency Act" (Ibid: 598). See also the CIO's Kermit Eby's testimony (422).
21. As CIO spokesperson, Leo Goodman stated,

> Wartime experience has brought forward the value of nursery and play schools, kindergartens, and such preprimary school services. Not a substitute for care of children in the home, they are a valuable supplement thereto, and are an essential part of the education system.
> (Ibid: 705–706)

22. See Eleanor Roosevelt's "My Day" column (September 8, 1945). Days later, a "Conference of Nine" (the AHEA, NEA, PTA, AAUW, General Federation of Women's Clubs, ACE, NANE, Child Welfare League, and the American Association for Health, PE, & Recreation) met with Harry Truman to call for Lanham's continuation. All nine stated they wanted the CB (not the FWA) to be in charge of nursery schools, with funding channeled through block grants to states, not directly to local communities. Of Langdon's original sponsors, only the Progressive Education Association (PEA) remained loyal. According to the *Journal of Home Economics* (November 1945) 546, Congressman Clyde Doyle of Long Beach (D-CA) withdrew his "Emergency Child Care Bill of 1945" on October 19, 1945, after gaining assurances from both FWA's Fleming and President Truman that Lanham centers would continue with FWA funding until March 1, 1946. Doyle's bill would have funded centers until June 1946.
23. See letters written by Mrs. John A. Howard and Dorothy Ganssle Briggs at "Child Welfare Centers: Extension of Remarks of Hon. Helen Gahagan Douglas" in *Congressional Record* 91 (September 24, 1945) A3998–A4002.
24. Hawes emphasized that:

> All progressive educators and modern psychologists agree it is best for children, with very minor exceptions, to start school at the age of two: to learn early in life to cooperate with other human beings; and, under the guidance of well-trained professionals in child care to be trained painlessly in all those habits which make some people so easy and pleasant to have around.

See her *Why Women Cry: Women as Wenches* (1943).
25. Elizabeth Hawes, "How Every Man May Have a Good Wife—and Stop Crying" *Detroit Free Press* (April 2, 1944) 31. Weeks before, Hawes' fellow CIO leaders—Susan B. Anthony II and Eleanor Fowler—toured Lanham centers with FWA's Florence Kerr in Allentown, PA. See "Prominent Speakers Secured by US Locals to Address Bethlehem Child Care Conference Next Tuesday Night" *The Morning Call* (March 2, 1944) 4.
26. Eleanor Roosevelt resigned from the Office of Civilian Defense in February 1942. It remains unclear why Florence Kerr left the federal government in late December 1944. Committees for the Care of Young Children in Wartime were redbaited. See Alice Keliher Papers and the far-right archive of The Church League of America Collection of the Research Files of Counterattack, the Wackenhut Corporation, and Karl Baarslag & American Business Consultants at NYU.
27. See Natalie Fousekis, *Demanding Child Care: Women's Activism and the Politics of Welfare, 1940–1971* (2011); Emilie Stoltzfus, *Citizen, Mother, Worker: Debating Public Responsibility for Child Care After the Second World War*

150   Buried Treasure

(2003); Sonya Michel, *Children's Interests/Mothers' Rights: The Shaping of America's Child Care Policy* (1999); and Elizabeth Rose, *A Mother's Job: The History of Day Care, 1890–1960* (1999).

28. Mary Moon et al., *Final Report of the War Public Services Program: FWA* (June 1946) 129 pages. According to this report, the majority of Lanham children's centers in thirty-three states were still in operation, months after losing their federal subsidy. Centers operated in all states but New Mexico, with a slightly different distribution than WPA program.

29. "Aid Sought for Child Centers" *The Gazette and Daily* [York, Pennsylvania] (November 28, 1945) 2.

30. These attacks were national in scope. Governor Dewey (R-NY) generated headlines because he called women "Communists" when they protested the closure of childcare centers following World War II, but Dewey was not the only one to make the charge against early childhood educators. See Kate Kirkland, "For All Houston's Children: Ima Hogg and the Board of Education, 1943–1949" *Southwestern Historical Quarterly* 101 (1998) 460–495; Mary B. [Beauchamp] Lane, *Our Schools: Frontline for the 21st Century* (1998); Kathleen Weiler, "Playing Ukrainian Farmer: Progressive Pedagogy and the Cold War in LA" *Journal of Curriculum and Supervision* 16 (Fall 2000) 5–27; and HUAC, "Investigation of Communist Activities in the Los Angeles, CA, Area. Part 2," 84th Congress, June 29, 1955: 1689+. These hearings included the testimony of Irene Bowerman, a nursery school teacher. See also: www.slate.com/blogs/better_life_lab/2017/06/14/anti_communism_and_its_role_in_america_s_lack_of_affordable_daycare.html.

31. Helen Gahagan Douglas, "My Democratic Credo" (March 29, 1946).

32. Langdon may have needed money. See Henry Sullivan et al., *History, Development, and Progress of War Public Services, Div. 2, Bureau of Community Facilities, Federal Works Agency: 212 p.* (February 1946). Langdon wrote *Section B: Services to Children of Working Mothers* (100 pages) [FK]. She also published her *Parents* article and book under her married name, the only year in which she did this in nearly 40 years of writing books, 1931–69. See G. L. Ackerman, "How to Handle a Baby" *Parents' Magazine* 21 (September 1946) p. 23+; G. L. Ackerman, "Children Aren't Like That! Neatness and Promptness in Relation to Wholesome Child Development" *Parents' Magazine* 21 (October 1946) p. 2e–23+; and Grace L. Ackerman, *Home Guidance for Young Children* (John Day, 1946, 2nd ed.). She also continued to receive royalties from her promotion of junket in *Good Housekeeping*. See www.nytimes.com/1991/01/02/garden/elegant-and-loathing-memories-of-childhood-and-junket.html.

33. While Langdon was in California, Eleanor Fowler, among Langdon's staunchest supporters, was named a communist in an article on the CIO in her hometown newspaper, *Delaware County Daily Times* (Chester, PA, June 13, 1946) 6. Langdon focused on finding work. To White she confided, "We shall be very grateful for any business you may be able to send our way" (September 9, 1946) ENW. This is the last of Langdon's personal letters available.

34. "Dr. Grace Langdon's Steps in Education of America" *The New York Age* [New York] (September 2, 1944) 2.

35. As director of the WPA nursery school program, Langdon was still sometimes referred to as Education Advisory Service consultant. See, for instance, articles in the *New York Times* (April 12, 1935) and *Los Angeles Times* (November 15, 1935). The address at 200 Fifth Ave. also housed the American Toy Institute after 1947.

36. Kay Sherwood, "Dr. Advises: Store Surplus Christmas Toys" *Freeport-Journal Standard* [IL] (December 31, 1946) 6. Langdon had initially envisioned her new position as doing community organizing on behalf of children and parents,

Buried Treasure 151

teacher training, disseminating child development research, and helping companies provide goods and services to children. Brochure attached to September 9, 1946 letter to Edna Noble White, ENW.

37. This first UN Nursery School was located at Lake Success, the temporary Long Island headquarters of the UN from 1947–1952. See especially "Child Care Specialists to Gather" *The Oneonta Star* [Oneonta, NY] (October 15, 1948) 5 and Lea Cowles Masters, *Ready to Roll* (1982) Chapter 4: An Educational United Nations, 53–63. Not only did Langdon visit the school regularly, but in her capacity as UN advisor, she met with Edna Noble White and other international early childhood specialists at the estate of Alice Throckmorton McLean (founder of American Women's Voluntary Services) to draw up plans for an International Children's Village for European refugees. See "Mrs. McLean Turns Over Up-State Mansion to World Artists and Europe's DP Children" *New York Times* (July 20, 1948) and "International Valley Maps Plans for Children's Village" [w/photo: Langdon & Edna Noble White] *Oneonta Star* (October 18, 1948) 2.

38. See Eleanor Roosevelt, "My Day" (April 17, 1958) and Stuart Mudd, *Conflict Resolution and World Education* (2013) 197.

39. Christopher Byrne, *They Came to Play: 100 Years of the Toy Industry Association* (2016) 9. Langdon argued that toys were both fun and essential for children's healthy development and worked with the American Red Cross to provide toys for children in need and with the World Education Service Council to deliver toys to refugee children. See Grace Langdon, "Toys Must Be Fun" *Journal of Home Economics* 39 (December 1947) 631–632 and Sara Fieldston, *Raising the World: Child Welfare in the American Century* (2015) 74.

40. Edith Sonn, "Santa's Toy Sack Is Full This Year" *New York Times* (November 27, 1947). As Langdon reminded her audience, "Do remember that every child needs a well-balanced supply of playthings to fit his age level just as he needs a varied supply of food for good nutrition." Grace Langdon, "Tips to Assistant Santas" *The Evening Sun* [Hanover, Pennsylvania] (December 16, 1947) 10. See also "Toys That Please" *Detroit Free Press* (December 7, 1947) 87. For the next fifteen years, Langdon called for children to engage in active, creative, dramatic, and social play through a diversified toy collection. Echoing Patty Smith Hill, she declared "toys are the tools of play." See also Mary and Lawrence Frank, "Dads, Juniors and Toys" *New York Times* (December 4, 1949); "Junior's Love for War Toys Due to 'Times,' Says Expert" *Detroit Free Press* (November 1, 1950) 20; "The Child's Interest Is Point to Consider" *Clarion-Ledger* [Jackson, Miss] (December 12, 1952) 18; "Specialist Urges 'Get Toys that Fit'" *New York Times* (December 13, 1954); Betty Leonard, "Specialists Give Pointers for Choosing Child's Toys" *Star Tribune* [Minneapolis, MN] (February 13, 1956) 26; "Shop with Care for Toys" *Arizona Republic* (November 29, December 6, 1959) 125–126; and Grace Langdon, *Children Need Toys*, University of Nebraska Extension (1962). Langdon also donated toys to Lawrence Frank and Ruth [Horowitz] Hartley for their award-winning *Understanding Children's Play* (1952). In 1959, she made explicit the gender differences she had noted since 1947 for children older than infant, preschool, or kindergarten age: "Boys and girls begin to have different play interests when they reach the 6–8 age group, though they still play together much of the time."

41. Arnold Gesell, "Status of the Preschool Child" *Progressive Education* (February 1946) 132–133+. That Gesell may have come under investigation for support of federal daycare is suggested by the findings at the far-right archive of The Church League of America Collection of the Research Files of Counterattack, the Wackenhut Corporation, and Karl Baarslag & American Business Consultants at http://dlib.nyu.edu/findingaids/.

152 Buried Treasure

42. Katherine Lenroot (CB) and Bess Goodykoontz (OE), "Nursery School Education Today" *Progressive Education* (February 1946) 134–135. See also Ruth Andrus, "Next Steps in the Public Schools" *Progressive Education* (February 1946) 135–138 and "Postwar Planning for Young Children" *School Life* (February 1946) 9–12.

43. Others followed in the wake of Gesell and Lenroot. See, "Some Principles for Consideration in State and Community Planning for the Needs of Children" *School Life* (May 1946) 30–31; NEA, "Child-Care Centers, Nursery Schools and Kindergartens" (September 1946) 9 pages [RB]; Arthur York, "The Place of the Nursery School in the Public-School Program" *Elementary School Journal* 47 (December 1946) 199–203; and Mary Dabney Davis et al., "Recent History and Present Status of Early Childhood Education" *46th Yearbook for National Society for Study of Education* (1947) 44–49.

44. Volume 1 of the *NANE Bulletin* (1946), for instance, mentioned Langdon in two sentences noting that: (1) Langdon, "formerly with the FWA" was set to teach at San Francisco State in summer 1946, and (2) in December 1946, she was in NYC, a partner in the "Langdon-Cromwell Corporation." In 1951, an editor noted seeing her during the Midcentury White House Conference on Children and Youth. But the silence lingered: only twice more did Langdon (1889–1970) receive public attention, once in 1956 for conducting a workshop on "Toys and A Child's Growing" at the University of Minnesota and once in 1968 for teaching a Saturday morning early childhood education course at Arizona State University.

45. Baruch's being ignored was particularly odd since many *NANE Bulletin* editors were former WPA nursery school teachers, including Rosalie Blau and Mary Alice Mallum, from Southern California. Both had been appreciative of Baruch in the 1930s (see Chapter 2). When Baruch committed suicide in 1962, no mention was made of her passing, her substantial contributions to NANE, or any of her other achievements, even as much notice was given to others.

46. "Memorial to Edna Noble White, 1880–1954" *NANE Bulletin* 9 (Summer 1954) 21. The AHEA, which had parted ways with Langdon's program at the end of World War II, referred in White's obituary only to her pioneering role in creating the National Council of Parent Education. It did not mention her longstanding leadership in the nursery school movement in *Journal of Home Economics* 46 (June 1954) 409. Helen T. Woolley, a fellow pioneer at Merrill-Palmer, was not mentioned when she died in 1947, probably because her daughter, Eleanor Fowler, had just been accused of communist leanings.

47. NANE's silence on Grace Langdon and its avoidance of hot-button issues like race relations and labor unions when discussing Baruch and White resulted in part from still-damaged relationships over the Battle of 1943. NANE's membership fractured over whether to side with Langdon at the FWA or with other leaders who favored the Thomas Bill (which put the CB in charge). Membership declined as a result. NANE leaders who came to power after World War II were those who had earlier favored the 1943 Thomas Bill. They resented that congressional women clearly sided with the FWA—that Mary T. Norton (D-NJ) testified on behalf of Langdon's WPA program in 1942, and that Helen Gahagan Douglas (D-CA) testified on behalf of Langdon's Lanham program in 1945. They resented also that labor unions backed Langdon's program, with the CIO's Eleanor Fowler among Langdon's staunchest supporters.

48. Interested in maintaining power in state and local bureaucracies, leaders resisted challenging the status quo. Although the early childhood profession remained progressive when compared to the K-12 or higher education environments, it no longer pushed the envelope in trying to achieve racial, class, and gender equality, although it had done so earlier (see Chapters 1–3). Enough

Buried Treasure 153

sentiment for egalitarianism remained, however, to attract people like Shirley Chisholm (in 1946) to the field. Chisholm ran for president in 1972. She made Nixon's Enemy List, partly because she called for public preschools. Connections between her nursery school background and her later activism deserve exploration. Chisholm, the first woman to make a serious bid for the American presidency, was also an anti-war, feminist, left-wing African American former nursery school leader educated at "progressive" Columbia University before McCarthyism took firm hold. See her autobiography, *Unbought and Unbossed* (1970), and Barbara Winslow, *Shirley Chisholm: Catalyst for Change* (2013).

49. As Ruby Takanishi notes in *Federal Involvement in Early Childhood Education (1933–1973): The Need for Historical Perspectives* (1974), "NANE focused on disseminating information, producing handbooks and bulletins that became "the basis for local community action for early education." By choosing "this approach, the organization shied away from the rough and tumble of political activity, lobbying, and the creation of organized pressure groups. . . . The effects of this approach, however, are unmistakable. Even moderate activity in support of public early education did not materialize" (27).

50. Asserted Stoddard in "The Tasks Which Await Us" *UNESCO* (August 1949) 12, "Resistance to nursery schools, like war, begins in the minds of men; presently in the mental habits of the male administrative animal."

51. Frederick Redefer, "What Has Happened to Progressive Education?" *School and Society* 67 (May 1948) 349.

52. Elizabeth Dilling's *The Red Network* (1934) first labeled the PEA a communist front. See also the Progressive Education Association Records, 1924–1961 at the University of Illinois.

53. Its first list had been in December 1947.

54. See *Final report on the WPA program, 1935–43* (1947) which Dell did not acknowledge writing [FD]. In his 1971 biography of Dell, the historian John Hart argues that his subject personally considered his WPA writing among his finest.

55. For thoughtful overviews, see Robert Justin Goldstein, "Prelude to McCarthyism: The Making of a Blacklist" *Prologue* 38 (Fall 2006) www.archives. gov/publications/prologue/2006/fall/agloso.html and the Truman Library's presentation, www.trumanlibrary.org/dbq/loyaltyprogram.php. According to the Truman Library, screenings resulting in an estimated 2,700 dismissals and 12,000 resignations during the peak years of 1947–1956. The program quieted far more employees than it dismissed.

56. See Landon Storrs, *The Second Red Scare and the Unmaking of the New Deal Left* (2013), which also makes clear that federal loyalty investigations began under FDR.

57. Testimony of Florence Kerr, August 15, 1974. Published in "The Reminiscences of Florence Kerr" *Columbia University Oral History Collection* (1976) 112 pages. For forgotten New Deal women, see especially Robyn Muncy, *Relentless Reformer: Josephine Roche and Progressivism in 20th Century America* (2015) and Kirstin Downey, *The Woman Behind the New Deal: The Life and Legacy of Frances Perkin* (2009). Kerr still awaits a full-length biography, but she is mentioned in two 1982 histories, Alice Kessler-Harris, *Out to Work* and Rosalind Rosenberg, *Beyond Separate Spheres*, as well as in Matthew Dallek, *Defenseless Under the Night: Roosevelt Years and the Origins of Homeland Security* (2016).

58. In *The Second Red Scare and the Unmaking of the New Deal Left* (2013), Landon Storrs uses left feminists to describe women and men who pursued a vision of women's emancipation that also insisted on class and racial justice. In *Feminism Unfinished* (2014), Dorothy Sue Cobble uses the term *social justice feminism* to describe the views of leftist women who wanted to keep protective legislation for

154 Buried Treasure

women in place and so did not support the Equal Rights amendment after World War I. Both descriptions apply to WPA program leaders and supporters.

59. Shortly after passage of the Taft-Hartley Act, the federal government sued the CIO to stop its political activism. While the US Supreme Court ruled in the CIO's favor in June 1948, the CIO PAC stopped calling for public nursery schools. Instead, it emphasized: (1) strong rent control and low-cost housing, (2) action by Congress to stop inflation, (3) taxation according to ability to pay, (4) guaranteed full and fair employment, (5) no wage less than 75 cents an hour for all workers, (6) higher pay for teachers and better schools, (7) adequate health and medical care for all, (8) increased and extended social security, (9) equal pay for equal work, regardless of race, creed, religion, or sex, (10) fair prices to the farmer for his products, (11) adequate protection of the small businessman against monopoly, (12) protection of civil rights, anti-poll tax, anti-lynching legislation, and (13) maintenance of peace through the UN. University of Pittsburgh archives.

60. Information on the Fowlers' economic livelihood inferred from their daughter's website, www.communitycenterforteachingexcellence.org/dr-jane-fowler-morse/. As footnoted in Chapter 1, Cedric Fowler referenced nursery school movement leaders like Grace Langdon in "They Train the Young" *New Outlook* 165 (February 1935) 32–38. His mother-in-law, Helen Thompson Woolley, pioneered the nursery school at Detroit's Merrill-Palmer School in the early 1920s, and his wife, Eleanor Fowler, supported WPA nursery schools as a leader of the WILPF and the CIO women's auxiliary. Cedric Fowler fell victim to red-baiting as a union activist, called to name names by HUAC in 1957.

61. For more on the CIO women's auxiliary, see Dorothy Sue Cobble, *The Other Women's Movement: Workplace Justice and Social Rights in Modern America* (2011). For information on Eleanor Fowler and Dorothy Hayes's peace activism, see Amy Schneihorst, *Building a Just and Secure World: Popular Front Women's Struggles for Peace* (2011); Joyce Blackwell, *No Peace Without Freedom: Race and the WILPF* (2004); and Jacqueline Castledine, *Cold War Progressives: Women's Interracial Organizing for Peace and Freedom* (2012). See also Dorothy Hayes' courageous 1965 HUAC testimony. That her friend Dr. Jeremiah Stamler refused to testify helped lead to HUAC's demise. Helen Gahagan Douglas, Edna Noble White, and Rebecca Hourwich Reyher also participated in the WILPF.

62. See especially Giuliana Lonigro, "Women's History Month: Elizabeth Hawes" (March 30, 2012) http://geeloblog.com/whm-elizabeth-hawes-435/; Alice Gregory, "The Most Brilliant American Fashion Designer" https://tmagazine. blogs.nytimes.com/2014/06/12/elizabeth-hawes-the-most-brilliant-american-fashion-designer/; and Bettina Berch, *Radical by Design: The Life and Styles of Elizabeth Hawes* (1988).

63. HUAC, "Report on the Congress of American Women" (October 23, 1949) 16 (available online; 120 pages).

64. Amy Swerdlow, "Congress of American Women: Left-Feminist Peace Politics in the Cold War" in Linda Kerber et al., eds., *US History as Women's History* (1995) 296–312; Bill Bence, "Elinor S. Gimbel and the Popular Front" http://nyapril1946.blogspot.com/2012/04/elinor-s-gimbel-and-progressive-front.html; and Kate Wiegand, *Red Feminism: US Communism and the Making of Women's Liberation* (2002).

65. Christopher Byrne, *They Came to Play: 100 Years of the Toy Industry Association* (2016) 9.

66. In *Life Magazine*'s November 23, 1953 spread, the first two toys listed were "Happy Harry," a musical pull toy, and Playskool's Wagon of Blocks. Langdon listed more general recommendations at other times of the year. This

Buried Treasure   155

advertisement mentioned Langdon by name. In addition to the Buy American emphasis, it concluded with these words:

> How to Choose Toys, a leaflet by Dr. Grace Langdon, well-known child-development advisor, has been prepared to help you choose the toys which will best fit the interest and essential play needs of the children on your Christmas list. For a free copy of this educational leaflet, write to The American Toy Institute, 200 Fifth Ave, NY, enclosing a stamped and self-addressed envelope.

It is worth noting that Howard Chudacoff, in *Children at Play: An American History* (2007), argues that free-play disappeared after 1950.

67. As Landon Storrs states in her introduction to *The Second Red Scare and the Unmaking of the New Deal Left* (2013):

> The Keyserlings are remembered as Cold War liberals who supported the Vietnam War and celebrated capitalism's ability to eliminate poverty through growth, rather than redistribution. But in the 1930s, as Chapter 5 reveals, both had been leftists. Under the pressure of recurring investigations, both of them moderated their goals and language, and they elided radicalism from their autobiographical narratives.
>
> (11)

See especially Chapter 4, "The Loyalty Investigations of Mary Dublin Keyserling and Leon Keyserling" and Chapter 5, "Secrets and Self-Reinvention: The Making of Cold War Liberalism."

68. Thomasina Walker Johnson Norford served as the Legislative Representative for the Alpha Kappa Alpha Sorority. No doubt she wished to avoid the fate of Mary McLeod Bethune, who as an NYA director, enthusiastically embraced the WPA nursery school program. According to historian Landon Storrs, Bethune was mercilessly targeted by the FBI even after her death in 1954.

69. See Grace Langdon, "Laying Sound Foundations for Family Sharing of Good Reading & Good Fun" *Christian Science Monitor* (November 12, 1949) 11; "Summer's the Time for Fun" *Parents' Magazine* 25 (June 1950) 42–43 and "New Playthings Reviewed" *Parents' Magazine* 25 (September 1950) 188. In 1948, Langdon conducted research on how hospitals could and should include toys for sick children—see her "A Study of the Use of Toys in a Hospital" *Child Development* 19 (December 1948) 197–211.

70. See *NANE Bulletin* (Summer 1950) and Greg Mitchell, *Tricky Dick and the Pink Lady: Sexual Politics and the Red Scare, 1950* (1998).

71. John Farrell, *Richard Nixon: The Life* (2017) 150. Nixon would then distribute this information on pink paper at Douglas rallies—hence the moniker, Pink Lady. In response, Douglas labeled him Tricky Dick, which opponents used for the rest of his life and after.

72. Ibid: 147. See also Ingrid W. Scobie, *Center Stage: Helen Gahagan Douglas— A Life* (1992).

73. *The Tennessean* (August 28, 1949) 47. Archives of far-right groups show that Hymes and George Stoddard were investigated in the late 1940s. See also C. J. Anderson, "Child Champion" in *Hidden History of Early Childhood Ed* (2013) Chapter 10.

74. In full retreat, Langdon did not take part in exploratory discussions regarding a childcare program for the Korean War (although Katherine Lenroot did). See, for example, "Child Care Plans in Crisis Studied" *New York Times* (January 16, 1951) and I. Evelyn Smith, "While Mothers Work at Defense Jobs" *The Child* 15 (March 1951) 125–126+. See also Martha Eliot, "A 20 Year Perspective on Services to Children" *Children* (July–August 1955) 123–126+.

156 Buried Treasure

75. G. Langdon and I. W. Stout, *Those Well-Adjusted Children* (John Day, 1951); G. Langdon and I. W. Stout, *Discipline of Well-Adjusted Children* (John Day, 1952); G. Langdon and I. W. Stout, *Teacher-Parent Interviews* (Prentice-Hall, 1954); G. Langdon and I. W. Stout, *Helping Parents Understand Their Children's Schools* (Prentice Hall, 1957); G. Langdon and I. W. Stout, *Bringing Up Children* (John Day, 1960); G. Langdon and I. W. Stout, *Teaching Moral and Spiritual Values* (John Day, 1962); G. Langdon and I. W. Stout, *Homework* (John Day, 1969). In addition, they created a nationally syndicated column, "Today's Children" from 1959–1965, which often was featured on the same page as the Ann Landers column.
76. See especially Harry and Bonaro Overstreet, "What Do We Want for Our Children? A Review of Langdon and Stout's *The Discipline of Well-Adjusted Children* (1952)" *Detroit Free Press* (April 1, 1956) 20.
77. See descriptions of both Kathryn McHale and Esther Brunauer in Susan Levine, *Degrees of Equality: The American Association of University Women and the Challenge of 20th-Century Feminism* (1995).
78. Landon Storrs, *The Second Red Scare and the Unmaking of the New Deal Left* (2013) 278, 288.
79. See especially Anthony's autobiography, *The Ghost in My Life* (1971).
80. Studs Terkel Radio Archive, *Susan Brownell Anthony discusses her book, "The Ghost in My Life"* (October 29, 1971: 54:28 minutes) https://studsterkel.wfmt.com/programs/susan-brownell-anthony-discusses-her-book-ghost-my-life. Discussion of childcare occurs roughly ten minutes into the interview.
81. John Bowlby, *Maternal Care and Mental Health* (World Health Organization, 1951).
82. Bowlby stated:

> I find two groups with a vested interest in shooting down the [attachment] theory. The Communists are one, for the obvious reason that they need their women at work and thus their children must be cared for by others. The professional women are the second group. They have, in fact, neglected their families. But it's the last thing they want to admit.

> See Evelyn Ringold, "Bringing Up Baby in Britain" *New York Times Magazine* (June 13, 1965) 59. In 1989, Bowlby said:

> This whole business of women going to work is so bitterly controversial, but I do not think it's a good idea. I mean women go out to work and make some fiddly little bit of gadgetry, which has no particular social value, and children are looked after in indifferent nurseries. Looking after your own children is hard work. But you get some rewards in that. Looking after other people's children is very hard work, and you don't get many rewards for it. www.nytimes.com/1998/05/24/magazine/the-disconnected-attachment-theory-the-ultimate-experiment.html

83. Margaret Mead, "Some Theoretical Considerations on the Problem of Mother-Child Separation" *American Journal of Orthopsychiatry* 24 (July 1954) 471–483. See also Margo Vicedo, "Cold War Emotions: Mother Love and the War Over Human Nature" in M. Solovey and H. Cravens, eds., *Cold War Social Science* (2012).
84. Bowlby used government funds to make the case for why parents (especially mothers) should be with their young children. George Stoddard's 1930s research on IQ gains for children in preschool did not regain academic credibility until the 1960s. Social psychologist Lois Barclay Murphy, a staunch supporter of the

Buried Treasure 157

WPA nursery school program, was investigated by the FBI in the 1940s because of her support for integration. In *Eleanor Roosevelt: The War Years and After, 1939–1962* (2016), Blanche Wiesen Cook asserts, "By 1954 all white integrationists were accused of being Communists" (565). See also George Stoddard and Beth Wellman, *The Intelligence of Preschool Children* (1938); Lois B. Murphy, "Effects of Child-Rearing Patterns on Mental Health" (1956); and oral histories of child development pioneers like Murphy in the *Society for Research in Child Development* at www.srcd.org/about-us/oral-history-project.

85. Grace Langdon, "Quality in Nursery Schools" *PTA Magazine* 57 (January 1963) 18–20.

86. Curricula from WPA nursery schools and Lanham children's centers remained in use at private schools like Bank Street, university nursery programs, parent cooperatives, and California's children's centers. See especially, Joyce Antler, *Lucy Sprague Mitchell: The Making of a Modern Woman* (1987); Mary B. Lane, *Our Schools—Frontline for the 21st Century* (1998); Robyn Muncy, "Cooperative Motherhood and Democratic Civic Culture in Postwar Suburbia, 1940–1965" *Journal of Social History* 38 (Winter 2004) 285–310; and Natalie Fousekis, *Demanding Child Care: Women's Activism and the Politics of Welfare, 1940–1971* (2013).

87. Economic Opportunity Act Amendments of 1967 (Part 5, Appendix), House Committee on Education and Labor, 90th Congress (1967) 4139 pages [esp. 3875–3887]. Papago leaders at first assumed they could seek funding for any program that would be of value to the tribe because ASU's Robert Roessel (member of LBJ's task force on Indians) asserted, "It is the intent of Congress that the Papago people develop the program and that it be the kind of program that they want." In September 1964, Papago leaders, including Josiah Moore, suggested road and fence repairs, soil conservation, windmills, wells, and a library, museum, and history books to preserve Papago culture. According to congressional testimony, the Papago CAP proved reluctant to invest in infrastructure improvements which might have required collaboration with the Bureau of Indian Affairs (BIA). This disassociation of the OEO from the BIA was "in line with a sense of growing Papago nationalism." In December 1964, Stout, Moore, and four Papago assistants signed a contract to conduct an educational survey (it received funding of $29,500).

88. Survey conducted February through May 1965. Upon completion, it was published as G. Langdon, J. Moore, and I. W. Stout, *Report of a Survey to Determine the Educational Needs of Papago Children and Adults* (Tempe: ASU, 1965).

89. Moore, an ASU graduate and education consultant, eventually became the Tribal Chair. According to Stephanie Innes in the *Arizona Daily Star* (June 28, 2003), "Moore, a soft-spoken leader, died of cancer in 1993 at the age of 58 while still serving as chairman. He is credited with guiding the tribe into its modern form of government and luring commerce and building schools." He also effected the renaming of his people as the Tohono O'odham Nation.

90. Economic Opportunity Act Amendments of 1967 (Part 5, Appendix) 3885.

91. Ibid: 3884.

92. Historian Maris Vinovskis mentions that the advisory group was "cowed" into silence after recommending a pilot program with well-trained teachers and small class sizes. See Maris Vinovskis, *Birth of Head Start: Preschool Education Polices in the Kennedy and Johnson Administrations* (2005) 74–77 and Elizabeth Rose, *The Promise of Preschool: From Head Start to Universal Pre-Kindergarten* (2010) 19.

93. See especially, Kay Mills, *Something Better for My Children: The History and People of Head Start* (1998) and Barbara Beatty, *Preschool Education in America: The Culture of Young Children from the Colonial Era to the Present* (1995).

158 Buried Treasure

94. In late 1965, LBJ succeeded in getting an education bill passed. It provided for compensatory preschool funding at the discretion of local districts. According to Vinovskis, the OE director pushed to have Head Start moved to his department as a way to efficiently manage federal funds having to do with young children. Shriver resisted the move, and Head Start stayed at the OEO until Nixon became president. Langdon regularly used the child development moniker as WPA nursery school director, Lanham director, and postwar toy consultant.

95. Economic Opportunity Act Amendments of 1967 (Part 5, Appendix) 3894.

96. In early September 1965, Tom Segundo became CAP director.

97. Housed in two local churches in Sells and Santa Rosa, one school had twenty-five children, the other seventeen. Lea C. Masters hired at least one African American woman as a teacher, and all children received free medical and dental exams.

98. In her memoir, *Ready to Roll* (1982), Masters mentioned visiting Langdon in summer 1963. They talked about possibly starting a nursery school on the local Papago reservation near Tempe, Arizona. Masters worked closely with Segundo in community outreach, and the Papago gave her a traditional basket in thanks for her service.

99. Economic Opportunity Act Amendments of 1967 (Part 5, Appendix) 3891. Other comments about parent-child centers include: Voice 1: "The two Centers have become popular among Papago women as places to cut and sew clothing for their families and are known as 'the sewing centers' to all Papago women interviewed" (3885). Voice 2: "I enjoy myself learning to sew clothes" (3891). Voice 3: "The pre-school, parent-child center, which now has a counselor, is doing very well. The parent and children come into the center on the bus and the child goes to pre-school while the parent goes to sewing or cooking class. The biggest problem that we have is in getting personnel to come out here because there is not housing" (3895). In short, "The preschools . . . have achieved popular acceptance, and continuance and expansion of the preschools component would be well received in all areas" (3885).

100. J. McVicker Hunt et al., "A Bill of Rights for Children: The Report of the Presidents' Task Force on Early Child Development" (January 1967) 164 pages.

101. Irving Stout et al., "A Plan of Action for Parent-Child Educational Centers" (1968) 31 pages and "A Source Report for Developing Parent-Child Education Centers" National Institution of Mental Health: DHEW (June 1968) 340 pages. Langdon is named as local consultant. Others included Lois B. Murphy, Mary B. Lane, and Urie Bronfenbrenner.

102. Nixon, "Statement Announcing the Establishment of the Office of Child Development" (April 9, 1969) www.presidency.ucsb.edu/ws/?pid=1991. According to Vinovskis, Head Start insiders in D.C., especially Jule Sugarman, also pushed for housing Head Start in the CB. See also Comprehensive Preschool Education and Child Day-Care Act of 1969, Hearings before the House Committee on Education and Labor, 91st Congress: HR 13520 (November 1969–March 1970).

103. Conveniently, the CB did not own up to its historic lack of support for child-care outside of the home. See for instance, Kathryn Close, "Day Care as a Service for All Who Need It" *The Children* (July–August 1965) 157–160.

104. Even at hearings on the "Comprehensive Preschool Education and Child Day-Care Act of 1969," Langdon's federal childcare program went largely unmentioned.

105. "Obituary for Grace L. Ackerman, 90, author, teacher at ASU" *Arizona Republic* (June 18, 1970). Although recently featured in Doris Weatherford's *American Women during WWII* (2009) 260, Grace Langdon remains largely forgotten in the world of early childhood education. Educator Bernard Spodek spoke of her 1933 dissertation findings as still relevant but did not appear to know who she was. See his "Early Childhood Education: A Synoptic View"

Buried Treasure 159

(January 1980) 13 pages and his 2009 oral history, http://ecrp.uiuc.edu/v11n1/interview-spodek.html.

106. Instead, Zigler regarded the CB as a sweet "apolitical" organization when he joined. See his *The Hidden History of Head Start* (2010) 80–82.

107. Edward Zigler, *The Tragedy of Child Care in America* (2009) xiv. See also Edward Zigler and J. Valentine, eds., *Project Head Start: A Legacy of the War on Poverty* (1997, 2nd ed.).

108. According to Zigler, he was responsible for finding a publisher for Keyserling's *Windows on Day Care* (1972).

109. Bypassing state channels was also the explicit reason OEO used a federal-to-local funding model, which is in part why CAP proved so controversial, as well as why Nixon destroyed the OEO.

110. Quoted in Elizabeth Rose, *The Promise of Preschool: From Head Start to Universal Pre-Kindergarten* (2010) 58. Original source: Statement from Marion Wright Edelman, US House Committee on Education and Labor, Comprehensive Child Development Act of 1971, 404. Many Head Start participants at the local level also resisted closer cooperation with education officials, whom they believed worked in bureaucracies catering to the status quo, especially as it related to segregation. See especially Polly Greenberg's account of Head Start in Mississippi, *The Devil Has Slippery Shoes* (1969). According to Ed Zigler, Shriver used two entities to create prototypes for Head Start, an advisory group with physicians at the helm, and a CAP group, which included Polly Greenberg. These two groups were at loggerheads over the role state and local education departments should play.

111. Based on conversations he had with Elliot Richardson (Nixon's HEW Secretary), Zigler thought a suitable compromise was any entity that represented 500,000 people, and Representative John Brademas (D-IN) was amenable. Mondale and Edelman resisted, and eventually the 1971 compromise bill ended up with 5,000 people as the minimum number. Senator Carl Perkins (D-KY) joined Mondale and Edelman in this call for more local control after he realized his own home county in Kentucky did not have enough people to warrant a sponsor under the House version of the bill. According to Zigler, this low number was a key reason that Nixon vetoed the bill. May 1971 congressional hearings also showed that former Head Start Director Jules Sugarman thought that sponsors at populations of 100,000 or more would have been logistically possible.

112. Elizabeth Rose, *The Promise of Preschool* (2010), serves as an important corrective because it shows the influence of second-wave feminists in the CCDA.

113. Testimony of Shirley Chisholm, US House Committee on Education and Labor, CCDA, 75.

114. Zigler now agrees with historian Kimberly Morgan's final assessment, "In sum, the passions of both the left and the right jointly defeated an attempt to form a national unified day-care policy." See his *The Hidden History of Head Start* (2010) 174 and *The Tragedy of Child Care in America* (2009) 38.

115. Kimberly Morgan, "A Child of the Sixties: The Great Society, the New Right, and the Politics of Federal Child Care" *The Journal of Policy History* 13 (2) (2001) 238.

116. See *Human Events* articles, including "Big Brother Wants Your Children" (September 1971) and "Report on Proposed Child Development Program: Radical Federal Plan" (October 1971). See also James Kilpatrick, "Child Development Act—To Sovietize Our Youth." Buchanan wanted to prevent any expansion of entitlement programs, whereas Mondale believed Nixon used anti-communist rhetoric to pacify right-wingers before his upcoming trip to Red China. See the excellent www.npr.org/2016/10/13/497850292/how-politics-killed-universal-childcare-in-the-1970s and California Newsreel, "Once Upon a Time: When Childcare for All Wasn't Just a Fairytale" (2015) http://www.raisingofamerica.org.

160   Buried Treasure

117. Elizabeth Rose, *The Promise of Preschool: From Head Start to Universal Pre-Kindergarten* (2010) 63.
118. Herblock, *Down in Front*. September 14, 1950. A 1950 Herblock Cartoon, © The Herb Block Foundation. Used with permission. Alice Keliher saved this cartoon from the Washington Post. It is now in those of her papers at NYU that discuss the red-baiting she endured. Keliher attended graduate school with Langdon and helped found the WWII Child Care Committee in New York City. She was also a postwar neighbor and friend of Eleanor Roosevelt.
119. Attacks began with the Dies Committee investigation of the WPA in 1938 and escalated during World War II with attacks of daycare for working mothers. After World War II, anti-communists renewed attacks against WPA-NYA officials (especially those with pro–civil rights records), questioned the loyalty of all New Dealers by implementing the Loyalty Review Board, and smeared liberal Democrats in Congress who supported public nursery schools. FBI investigations weakened Eleanor Roosevelt's political capital (along with that of other childcare proponents from the short-lived Office of Civilian Defense).
120. They targeted suspected communists like Susan B. Anthony II. They blacklisted selected individuals like Elizabeth Hawes and also kept liberal women who had supported Langdon's program (e.g., AAUW's Kathryn McHale) under FBI surveillance. They harassed wealthy progressive supporters of childcare like Elinor Gimbel and accused left-feminist groups like the WILPF of subversion, especially when members (Dorothy Hayes and others) called for public nursery schools, peace-making, and integration.
121. Anti-communists kept tabs on progressive educators calling for federal aid to education or equal opportunity, including many of Langdon's former colleagues at Columbia University. George Stoddard and James Hymes, the two most active men in NANE, were investigated.
122. Lea Cowles Masters, *Ready to Roll* (1982) v. Masters dedicated her memoir to Langdon, "a true inspiration."

Index

Abzug, Bella 144
African Americans 5, 25, 28–29, 81–84, 87, 115, 116, 136, 139
Alexander, Will 106, 107, 120
Alpha Kappa Alpha Sorority 28, 115, 155
Alschuler, Rose 12, 35, 36, 37, 40, 43, 68, 71, 109, 115, 122, 123, 128, 131
American Association of University Women (AAUW) 28, 100,108, 123, 140, 149, 160
American Federation of Teachers (AFT) 15, 26, 40, 149
American Toy Institute 137, 139, 150, 155
Anderson, John 22, 37, 72, 122
Andrus, Ruth 37, 38, 50, 70, 72, 73, 115, 131, 152
Anthony, Susan B., II 16, 104, 116, 130, 139, 140, 149, 156, 160
Arthurdale Nursery School 70, 84–85, 90, 97, 98
Association for Childhood Education (ACE) 12, 21–22, 36, 38, 88, 106, 108, 119, 120, 128, 133, 135

Bain, Winifred 39, 44, 67, 75, 97
Baker, Jacob 24, 57–58
Baruch, Dorothy 40, 43, 56, 70, 75, 99, 116, 130, 137, 148, 149, 152
Bean, Minnie 17
Beatty, Barbara 3, 4, 12, 14
Blau, Rosalie 11, 42, 69, 70, 71, 73, 152
block play 62–65
Bowlby, John 141, 156
Brown v. Board of Education 8, 84, 97
Brunot, James 114, 127

Buchanan, Pat 144, 159
Burtin, Will 66, 78

Cahan, Emily 4, 13
Carmody, John 104, 108, 119, 122, 125
childcare 115–116, 134, 144–146
Children's Bureau (CB) 2, 4, 8, 11, 14, 31, 47, 69, 107–109, 112, 115, 117, 133, 143, 146, 158
Children's Charter 21–22, 23
Chisholm, Shirley 3, 144, 153, 159
Civilian Conservation Corps (CCC) 61, 91, 124, 127
Civil Works Administration 79
Clapp, Elsie 84, 97
Clark, Kenneth 83, 96, 102
Clark, Mamie 83, 84, 96, 102
Close, Katherine 117, 126, 132
Committees for the Care of Young Children in Wartime 136, 146, 149
community activism 88–93
Community Facilities Act 110–115
community schools 80–87
Comprehensive Child Development Act (CCDA) 3, 9, 16,143, 144, 146, 159
congressional hearings 133–141
Congress of American Women 138, 139–140, 145, 154
Congress of Industrial Organizations (CIO) 1, 28, 115–117, 131, 134–135, 137–138, 145–149, 152, 154
Council of National Defense 106, 120
Counts, George 6, 15, 26, 33, 44, 102, 103
Cravens, Hamilton 4, 36
Cremin, Lawrence 6, 15, 34
Cuban, Larry 6, 15

162   *Index*

Davis, Mary Dabney 24, 28, 39, 43, 47, 115, 121, 152
Dell, Floyd 2, 12, 45–46, 68, 69, 70, 104, 120, 138, 153
Dewey, John 12, 18, 20, 22, 34, 37, 56, 90
Dies Committee 1, 79, 90–91, 108, 160
Douglas, Helen Gahagan 12, 16, 71, 135, 138, 140, 141, 144, 150, 152, 154, 155
Douglas, Paul 43, 45, 67
Douglas, Susan 5, 14

Edelman, Marian Wright 143–144, 159
Eliot, Abigail 15, 20, 35, 36, 38, 39, 41

Family Security Committee 110, 124
Farm Security Administration (FSA/OWI) 46, 71, 73, 74, 76, 77, 81, 94, 98, 120, 122, 126
Fass, Paula 3, 12, 99, 127
Federal Emergency Relief Agency (FERA) 10, 24
Federal Security Agency (FSA) 2, 105, 106, 108, 109, 110, 112, 113, 116, 120, 125, 127
Federal Works Agency (FWA) 105, 106, 108, 110, 113, 114, 125, 131, 133, 135, 136, 146, 150, 152
Fleming, Philip 113, 119, 126
Fowler, Cedric 11, 33, 103, 138, 154
Fowler, Eleanor 10, 15, 115, 139, 145, 148, 149, 150, 152
Frank, Lawrence 39, 56, 73
Friedrich, Carl 31
Froebel, Friedrich 20, 22, 56, 63, 77
Full Employment Act 134, 147

Gesell, Arnold 7, 20, 21, 22, 35, 36, 112, 121, 126, 131, 137, 151
Gimbel, Elinor 128, 139, 154, 160
Givens, Willard 13, 17
Glass Hall of Prejudice (Baruch) 137
Greenwood, Barbara 11, 20, 22, 33, 35, 36, 72
Gruenberg, Sidonie 19, 34, 59

Hall, G. Stanley 56
Haskell, Douglas 50, 70, 71, 98
Hawes, Elizabeth 135–136, 139, 146, 149, 154, 160
Hayes, Dorothy 134, 139, 147, 154, 160
Head Start 3, 9, 13, 141–144, 146, 157, 158, 159, 160

Heinig, Christine 25, 33, 35, 39, 69, 76, 98
Hill, Patty Smith 2, 6, 15, 19–20, 22, 23–24, 30, 33, 35, 36, 43, 63, 70, 76, 89, 102, 151
Hilltop Nursery School 89–90, 102, 103
Hine, Lewis 46, 76, 77
Hiss, Alger 138
Hoover, J. Edgar 116, 129, 148
Hopkins, Harry 11, 24, 26, 42, 46, 48, 57, 79, 86, 98
Horowitz, Ruth 82–83, 84, 95, 96, 102, 151
Hostler, Amy 20, 38
House Un-American Activities Committee (HUAC) 93, 102, 103, 138–140, 150, 154
Human Events (journal) 140, 144, 159
Hunter, Howard 105, 119, 120
Hymes, James 3, 6, 13, 15, 103, 131, 138, 140, 155, 160

"infant schools" 19

Johnson, Harriet 15, 19, 34, 36, 77
Johnson, Lyndon B. (LBJ) 141, 142, 143
Johnson, Thomasina 139, 155
Julius Rosenwald Fund 96, 106, 158

Kaiser Child Care Centers 72, 103, 104,117, 131
Keliher, Alice 12, 122, 128, 149, 160
Kerr, Florence 5, 12, 29, 42, 69, 81, 91–93, 105–113, 115–116, 134, 138, 149, 153
Kessler-Harris, Alice 4, 13
Keyserling, Mary Dublin 139, 143, 155, 159
Kilpatrick, William Heard 18, 34, 44, 71
King, Martin Luther, Jr. 82, 95
Kiplinger, Walter 94, 106, 120
Klein, Philip 31, 44

LaGuardia, Fiorello 107, 125
Langdon, Grace: calls for WPA nursery schools permanence 28–30; child development advisor for the American Toy Institute 137, 139–140; collaboration with Irving Stout 140–141; collaboration with LBJ's task force 142–143; congressional hearings

Index 163

133–141; efforts impeded by Children's Bureau 5, 8; efforts on behalf of low-income families 28; fear of WPA nursery school future 105–109; forced to dismiss well-trained teachers 80; inter-agency squabbling 112; Lanham daycare program 111–112; leadership of WPA nursery schools 1, 4; "A Nation-Wide Project for the Daytime Care of Children during the National Emergency" 107; on necessity of community involvement 90; Nixon's veto of federal childcare program 144–146; as nursery school pioneer 22–25; Papago CAP project 141–142; political vulnerability 138; postwar career 9; promotion of WPA nursery schools 46; rendered invisible in scholarship 6; undermining of authority 109

Lange, Dorothea 46, 71

Lanham daycare program 4–5, 112, 117, 135

Lanham funds 110, 113–114

Laura Spelman Rockefeller Memorial fund (LSRM) 22, 24–25, 36, 64

Lenroot, Katherine 8, 69, 106, 107, 110, 114, 115, 117–119, 133, 137, 146, 152, 155

Lindenmeyer, Kriste 4, 11, 14, 44

Lonigan, Edna 140

Loyalty Review Board 138, 160

MacCarteney, Laura Pendleton 58, 76

Manasco, Carter 134

Masters, Lea Cowles 137, 142, 146, 151, 158, 160

McCarran, Pat 11, 113, 126

McHale, Kathryn 38, 140, 156, 160

McMillan, Margaret 15, 20, 35

McNutt, Paul 106, 109–113, 116–117, 120, 124, 125, 128, 130

Mead, Margaret 16, 54, 72, 131, 133, 134, 136, 141, 146, 156

Michaels, Meredith 5, 14

Michel, Sonya 5, 14, 121

Mitchell, Lucy Sprague 15, 19, 34

Mondale, Walter 143, 159

Montessori, Maria 19, 20, 35

Moore, Josiah 141, 142, 157

Murphy, Lois Barclay 37, 73, 74, 99, 156–157, 158

Murray, Philip 134

National Association of Nursery Educators (NANE) 20–23, 29, 36, 38, 44, 56, 108, 114–115, 131, 137–138, 140, 152

National Educational Association (NEA) 15, 17, 149, 152

National Youth Administration (NYA) 25, 39, 43, 61, 69, 91, 95, 104, 122, 124, 127, 141, 148, 149, 155, 160

"Nation-Wide Project for the Daytime Care of Children during the National Emergency, A" (Langdon) 107

New Deal 1, 3, 8, 26, 79

New York World's Fair 66–67, 78

Nixon, Richard M. 3, 9, 138, 140, 143–144, 146, 153, 155, 158, 159

Norton Amendment 109

Norton, Mary 16, 100, 101, 109, 111, 123, 124, 131, 152

nursery school pioneers 18–23

nursery schools: benefits of 17–18; as child development laboratories 22; establishment of 19–20; see also WPA nursery schools

Office of Civilian Defense 29, 42, 105, 107, 110–111, 115, 119, 122, 125, 129, 136, 139, 147, 160

Office of Defense Health and Welfare Services (ODHWS) 109, 111, 112, 114, 115, 129

Office of Economic Opportunity (OEO) 141–143, 157, 158, 159

Office of Education (OE) 106–108, 110–116, 127, 128, 129

Owen, Grace 15, 17, 20, 33, 35

Owen, Robert 15, 19, 35

Papago CAP project 141–142

parent cooperatives 19, 87, 89

parent education 86–88

Pepper, Claude 134, 136, 138, 140, 147

Piaget, Jean 56

play 56–67

Pratt, Caroline 6, 19, 34, 63

Progressive Education Association (PEA) 23, 70, 108, 138, 149, 153

racial attitudes 82–83

Redefer, Frederick 122, 153

Reorganization Act 91, 104, 105, 119

Revolt of the Beavers (play) 90–91, 103

Reyher, Rebecca 24, 38, 68, 154

164 Index

Roosevelt, Eleanor 10, 12, 26–27, 40, 84, 91, 105, 110, 119, 123, 125, 135–136, 149, 160
Roosevelt, Franklin D. (FDR) 23, 28, 79, 109–110, 112, 113, 116
Rumsfeld, Donald 143
Rydell, Robert 7, 16, 67, 78

Schottland, Charles 110, 111, 112, 121, 126, 127
Sealander, Judith 5, 14
segregation 25, 84
Segundo, Tom 142, 158
Shriver, Sargent 142, 158, 159
Snyder, Agnes 15, 89, 102
Social Security Act 13, 69, 107, 121
Songs for the Nursery School (MacCarteney) 58
Spock, Benjamin 7
Stearns, Peter 3, 12
Stoddard, George 4, 9, 15, 20, 21, 26, 33, 35, 36, 40, 41, 46, 47, 81, 122, 138, 140, 155, 156, 160
Stolz, Lois Meek 6, 18, 20, 21–22, 24, 33, 38, 43, 45, 58, 67, 73, 74, 86, 90–91, 93, 99, 103, 117
Storrs, Landon 11, 13, 39, 122, 153, 155
Stout, Irving 140, 141, 156, 158
Studebaker, John 106, 107, 113, 115, 117, 127

Taft, Charles 110, 112, 113–114, 115, 116, 117, 125, 126, 128, 129, 130
Taft-Hartley Act 138, 154
Taft, Robert 110, 128
teachers 47–50
Thomas, Bill 2, 9, 16, 114–117, 128, 129, 131, 146, 152
Thomas, D. Parnell 91
Toy Manufacturers of the United States 137
toys 58–67, 84
Transformation of the School (Cremin) 6
Truman, Harry 126, 138, 149, 153
Tuttle, William 3, 4, 12, 13, 130

Vygotsky, Lev 56

War Manpower Commission 111, 116
Watson, John 7, 73
Weiner, Lynn 4, 13

well-baby clinics 84–85
Weltfish, Gene 103, 139
White, Edna Noble 12, 20–22, 24, 35, 37, 47, 100, 106, 108, 116, 119, 134, 137, 146, 147, 151, 152, 154
White House Conference on Child Health and Protection 21
White House Conference on Children in a Democracy 31, 44
Williams, Aubrey 69, 141
Women's International League for Peace and Freedom (WILPF) 10, 139, 154, 160
Woodward, Ellen 12, 24, 90, 103
Woolley, Helen T. 15, 20, 35, 38, 98–99, 152
Works Progress Administration (WPA) 1–2, 13, 66, 79, 90–91, 41, 106–108, 113, 114
WPA Bulletins: #1: Administration and Program 47; *#5: Suggestions, Drawings and Specifications for Nursery School Equipment* 61
WPA nursery schools: alternative funding sources 89; attempts at creating a permanent program 26–33; benefits of 91–93; as buried treasure 119; class and racial integration 25, 84; community activism 88–93; community involvement 79–93; community schools 80–87; congressional recognition of 111; curriculum 47–50, 61; efforts to serve minority communities 81–82; exhibit at 1939 New York World's Fair 66–67; funding cuts 79–80; growth of 81; introduction to arts and literature 57–58; learning through play 56–67; mandatory closure 114–115; music lessons 58; nationwide distribution of 80–81; negative publicity 90–91; Norton's defense of 109; parent education 86–88; parent participation 87; pioneers 18–23; program foundations 23–25; purpose of 46–47; scholarship on 3–6; teachers 47–50

Zigler, Edward 143–144, 159
Zilversmit, Arthur 6, 18
Zook, George 23, 37